AMERICANS AND THE EXPERIENCE OF DELPHI

Paul Lorenz
David Roessel
Editors

SOMERSET HALL PRESS
Boston, Massachusetts

© Copyright 2013 Paul Lorenz & David Roessel, *Editors*
Published by Somerset Hall Press
416 Commonwealth Avenue, Suite 612
Boston, Massachusetts 02215
www.somersethallpress.com

SCHOOL OF
ARTS & HUMANITIES
THE RICHARD STOCKTON COLLEGE OF NEW JERSEY

All rights reserved. No part of this publication may be reproduced, stored in a retrieval system, or transmitted in any form or by any means—electronic, mechanical, photocopy, recording, or any other—without the prior written permission of the publisher. The only exception is brief quotations in printed reviews.

Cover Photo: Nancy Messina.

ISBN 978-1-935244-11-0

LIBRARY OF CONGRESS CATALOGING-IN-PUBLICATION DATA

Americans and the Experience of Delphi / Paul Lorenz and David Roessel, editors.
  pages cm
  Includes bibliographical references and index.
  ISBN 978-1-935244-11-0
  1. American literature--20th century--History and criticism. 2. Delphi (Extinct city)--In literature. 3. Delphi (Extinct city)--Influence. 4. Greece--Civilization--To 146 B.C.--Influence. I. Lorenz, Paul H, editor of compilation. II. Roessel, David E. (David Ernest), 1954- editor of compilation.
  PS228.D45A44 2013
  810.9'35838--dc23   2013022116

CONTENTS

Foreword — vii
Tom Papademetriou

Introduction — ix
David Roessel

Acknowledgments — xiii

Stones that once were [a] temple — xv
Susan Glaspell

Eva Palmer Sikelianos Before Delphi — 1
Artemis Leontis

Myth, Mystique, Nietzsche, and the "Cultic Milieu" of the Delphic Festivals, 1927 and 1930 — 51
Gonda Van Steen

George Cram Cook's *Road to the Temple* — 89
Linda Ben-Zvi

The Value of Home: Susan Glaspell's *Fugitive's Return* as a Response to F. Scott Fitzgerald's *The Great Gatsby* — 119
Barbara Ozieblo

The Influence of George Cram Cook's Delphic Spirit on Eugene O'Neill — 145
Mike Solomonson

Susan Glaspell's Delphi and the Legacy of Jane Ellen Harrison — 157
Martha C. Carpentier

Female Charioteers in Susan Glaspell's Plays: 181
Re-visiting the Spirit of Delphi and Aristotle's
Poetics in *Inheritors*, *The Verge*, and *The Comic Artist*
Noelia Hernando-Real

The Noble Peasant: Primitivism, Classicism, 201
and the Epistemological Pivot in Susan Glaspell's Career
Michael Winetsky

"For you know that Greece is the chord I thrill to!": 219
The Philhellenic Friendship of George Cram Cook
and John Alden
Steven Wertzberger and Victoria Conover

Introduction to Essay by Neith Boyce 231
Stephanie Allen and David Roussel

Iowa to Delphi 237
Neith Boyce

A Journey toward Gnosis: 243
The Place of Delphi in H.D.'s *Majic Ring*,
Demetres Tryphonopoulos

H.D.'s *Ion*: The Door Swings Both Ways 263
Matte Robinson

The Road from Delphi: Henry Miller and Greece 281
Ian S. MacNiven

The Omphalos and the Pythia in Lawrence Durrell 293
Paul H. Lorenz

Contributors 307

Index 315

Foreword

Tom Papademetriou

On the day prior to the symposium from which this volume originates, I had the opportunity to climb Mount Parnassus with David Roessel leading the way. The hike was not a terribly difficult one, as there were clearly marked trails and a steady but manageable incline. It did take time and effort, and considering that it was June, it was surprisingly cold and blustery. Yet, because the challenge of the hike was not great, I did not expect much as I ascended.

When our small group arrived at the summit, however, it became clear what David had wanted us to see. It was not the height of the mountain that was significant, though it was important that we climbed high, but its location. From its summit, one can see that Mount Parnassus towers above Delphi, which according to ancient tradition is the center of the world. The view from its summit allowed us to look upon the world with clarity, objectivity, and true vision.

In the subsequent days of the symposium we experienced this same clarity, objectivity, and true vision during the important and meaningful presentations, in the recitations of poetry and the performance of drama, and in the ensuing conversations that continued beyond the symposium. The privilege of having had this experience, achieved only by traveling great distances and seeking great heights in a special place like Delphi, made its mark on the participants of this symposium, on the scholars, faculty, and students who participated.

The journey to Delphi also made a deep impression on Hellenic Studies at Stockton College. For Stockton College's fledgling Hellenic Studies program, ambitiously traversing the heights of Parnassus and looking upon Delphi and the world opened a creative way to explore and investigate Hellenism in its many varieties and experiences, from antiquity to the present day. With David Roessel as a guide for this symposium, volume, and many other meaningful endeavors, this journey is exceedingly rich.

While only few may physically climb the summit of Mount Parnassus, the present volume, we hope, will allow readers to share in the exhilarating experience of achieving the summit, and clearly seeing Delphi and the world from the heights.

Introduction

David Roessel

    Every other year, I lead a group of K-12 teachers on a study tour of Greece. In the evening that we are in Delphi, I take them to the Orthodox cemetery just above the temple of Apollo to see the graves of Eva Palmer Sikelianos and George Cram Cook lying side by side in a far corner. There is an American presence at Delphi, one that is unique for an archaeological site in Greece—Palmer Sikelianos and Cook are buried here among the people of Delphi because they left their mark on this place which both inspired them and was in turn inspired by them. The idea of this place, and what it meant, brought them and others across the ocean. Eva Palmer Sikelianos is celebrated for her role in the Delphic Festivals of 1927 and 1930. Cook, one of the founders of the famed Provincetown Players and its guiding spirit, is remembered for wearing a *foustanella* (Greek kilt) and talking about creating a village theatre.

    Ever since I first saw those two graves in the cemetery, I wanted to have a symposium at Delphi to explore the experience of Americans who stood on the stones of Apollo's shrine and drank water from the Castalian spring. And I wanted to hold it at the European Cultural Center of Delphi. One reason for this desire was that, by being physically in Delphi, the centrality of Eva Palmer Sikelianos, George Cram Cook, and Susan Glaspell, Cook's wife, would predominate in a discussion of the importance of Delphi in American literature. For, during breaks between the sessions, we could visit the graves, the ancient site that so inspired these Americans, the Sikelianos Museum that houses a collection dedicated to the festivals that Eva Palmer Sikelianos helped to organize, and the street that Cook and Glaspell had lived on. In short, we could attempt to feel what they felt as we discussed what Delphi meant to them. The opportunity for this symposium came in 2008 with the support of the Interdisciplinary Center for Hellenic Studies and the School of Arts and Humanities of the Richard Stockton College of New Jersey. More than a dozen scholars came to discuss the topic of Americans and Delphi. In addition to the papers, there was a production of Eugene O'Neill's *Desire Under the Elms* directed by Pam Hendrick of the Stockton College Theatre Program, a reading of Cook and Susan Glaspell's *Suppressed Desires* by students of the Theatrical Studies Program of Athens University, and a reading of translations of the poetry of Angelos Sikelianos and commentary from Edmund Keeley. I am grateful for both the funding and fellowship that made those days so remarkable.

This volume includes some of the papers given at the symposium and two that were not. The time period of interest is that between World War I and World War II, and the main focus is unapologetically on Palmer Sikelianos, Cook, and Glaspell. We have the good fortune of having Artemis Leontis, one of the leading scholars of Eva Palmer Sikelianos, lead off the volume. Gonda Van Steen discusses the political background of the Delphic Festivals after the success in 1927. Linda Ben-Zvi investigates the subject of George Cram Cook

David Roessel - Introduction

and Delphi, and Peter Solomonson investigates the influence of Greece on Cook's theatre. Barbara Ozieblo, Martha Carpentier, Noelia Hernando Real, and Michael Winetsky delve into Glaspell's deep and complicated association with Delphi and its ancient site.

While we were able to maintain the centrality of Eva Palmer Sikelianos, George Cram Cook, and Susan Glaspell, we would have been remiss not to include investigations on Delphi in the works of other key writers. The poet H.D. (Hilda Doolittle) had almost an obsession with Apollo and his temple, in part perhaps because in 1920 she reached the port below Delphi where she could see it but, because of bandits in the area, was not allowed to go any further. She finally made it up the mountain to the site in 1932. Demetres Tryphonopoulos and Matte Robinson examine the role of Delphi in H.D.'s work. Finally, Ian MacNiven and Paul Lorenz look at how the idea of Delphi changed in the work of Henry Miller and his friend and companion in Greece, Lawrence Durrell, and examine how they engaged with the site as the world once again slipped into war. In a volume this size, the coverage could not be comprehensive, and, as in all such works, these last essays reflect some of the passions of the editors.

Almost at the last minute, the opportunity appeared to include "Iowa to Delphi," the writer Neith Boyce's previously unpublished review of Susan Glaspell's *The Road to the Temple*, her biography of George Cram Cook. I am very grateful to David Hapgood and David Walsimer for allowing that

The symposium at Delphi was the first ever by the Interdisciplinary Center for Hellenic Studies at Stockton College (there have since been two others). This volume is the first of what will be a series of Stockton Papers in

Hellenic Studies. Tom Papademetriou and I have been able to create an incredibly active, vibrant, and ambitious agenda for Hellenic Studies at Stockton because of the support of a tireless group of supporters—the Friends of Hellenic Studies of Stockton. Founded by Distinguished Professor Emeritus Demetrios Constantelos, it still astonishes me what the Friends have made possible for intellectual life at the college.

But I want to conclude where I began—in the corner of the Orthodox cemetery across the street from what is now the Sikelianos Museum, where Eva Palmer Sikelianos worked so hard to create ancient Greek theatre. This is not simply a little piece of America in Greece, but a piece of America that has been fused into both the ancient site and the modern village. It is that symbiotic relationship we are after with all the cultural figures discussed here, as well as to encourage analysis of the subject for those figures which we don't cover. It was a privilege to be able to go to Delphi and try to understand its remarkable influence with everyone who attended the symposium.

Acknowledgments

We would like to start by expressing our thanks to all of our colleagues who took part in the first Stockton Hellenic Studies symposium in 2008. The symposium, sponsored by the Richard Stockton College of New Jersey, was held in Delphi, Greece. With your help, we did something special.

We are very grateful to Valentina Cook and the Estate of Susan Glaspell, and Isaac Gewirtz and the Berg Collection at New York Public Library for permission to publish Glaspell's poem "Stones that were once [a] temple." That we could include her poem in this volume means a great deal to all of those involved in its production. We are also grateful to David Hapgood, William Dalsimer, and the Estate of Neith Boyce for permission to publish Boyce's essay "Iowa to Delphi." We would also like to thank the Beinecke Library at Yale University and its helpful staff.

Everything started, as it always starts, with the Friends of Hellenic Studies at Stockton. They are truly amazing. Peter Yiannos was a Friend, and also the leader of the Tri-State American Foundation for Greek Language and Culture. The AFGLC and the Friends have created Hellenic Studies at Stockton, led by the vision of Demetrios Constantelos. It was a great pleasure that he could join us at Delphi. Further support for the symposium and its events came from Dean Robert

Gregg of the School of Arts and Humanities at Stockton and Herman Saatkamp, President of Stockton.

Pam Hendrick and Mark Mallett created a production of Eugene O'Neill's "Desire Under the Elms" that we could take to Delphi and Athens, and Iosif Vivilakis arranged for a staged reading of Glaspell and Cook's "Suppressed Desires." It was wonderful, and important, to have theatre at a gathering where performance was central. Edmund Keeley provided translation of the works of Angelos Sikelianos, and the municipality of Delphi opened the Sikelianos Museum so that we could visit. The European Cultural Center at Delphi was a marvelous host.

We are especially grateful to those from Stockton who helped make all of this possible, Assistant Dean Nancy Messina (whose photograph is on the cover), Tom Papademetriou and Katherine Panagakos of Hellenic Studies, Rodger Jackson, Marieann Bannan, Deanna Tumas, Sarah Messina, Christa Fratantoro, and all of the students.

On a more personal note, I would like to thank everyone for their patience as I dealt with a retinal detachment; Paul Lorenz for doing more than his fair share of the work; James Pomar for his editorial assistance; and Tom and Dean Papademetrou for seeing this volume through to completion. It is a nice finish to what was, for Stockton, our own little Delphic Festival.

Stones that once were [a] temple

Susan Glaspell

I stood in what had been a temple,
My hand upon a broken column;
It rested there and I forgot that it was there
As I stood alone in what had been a temple
On what is still a mountain,
Following sails on the sea
And clouds on mountains
Pleased too by little nearer things,
Pansies and poppies in the grass,
And cypress tree
Loving that living moment of many things that moved
    a little–just a little–just enough.
It was my hand–my hand upon the broken column–
    first felt another moment,
Felt the moving in a moment farther than the
    farthest mountain
Felt living beauty across the centuries of flowers in grass
And sails on sea
And cypress tree
What did they feel–those Greek of long ago–the day
    rising column stood at what now is the break?
Perhaps a hand lay where mine lies forgot- it too
    was resting there,
Loving the living moment of flowers in grass and
    sails on sea;

And cypress tree
And because that hand was still and was forgotten,
And mine was still and was forgotten,
I live again in what lived then,
And what lived then moves now in me.

Printed with permission of Valentina Cook.
Transcribed by Steven R. Wertzberger (source: typescript of poem, with the author's manuscript corrections, unsigned and undated, Berg Collection, NYPL).

Susan Glaspell's "Stones that were once [a] temple," courtesy of The Henry W. and Albert A. Berg Collection of English and American Literature, The New York Public Library, 283 Astor, Lenox and Tilden Foundations. Copyright 2013 by the Estate of Susan Glaspell. Transcription published by permission of the Estate of Susan Glaspell.

This previously unpublished work by Susan Glaspell describes an experience the author had while visiting the Sanctuary of Apollo in Delphi, Greece. Glaspell travelled to Greece in March of 1922 with her husband George Cram Cook, who planned to revive the Delphic festival. Glaspell left Greece after his death in 1924.

Eva Palmer Sikelianos Before Delphi

Artemis Leontis

After centuries of silence, on May 9, 1927, the fourth-century BCE open-air amphitheatre at Delphi resounded with a performance of Aeschylus's *Prometheus Bound*. Three decades earlier, the theatre was underground, until archaeological excavations carried out by the French School between 1891 and 1901 unearthed it. Restored as a ruin with broken benches, cracked dancing floor, and despoiled scene building, the theatre felt like it had been standing forever. Likewise the performance of *Prometheus Bound* in the theatre signified a surviving antiquity, even though nothing quite like it had ever been done before. The staging used Modern Greek forms to convey ancient drama: actors recited the play's lines in Yannis Gryparis's vernacular Greek translation;[1] the chorus of young Athenian women sang melodies in the modes of Greek Orthodox Church chanting; the chorus followed the steps, rhythms, and sinuous lines of Greek folk dancing to mobilize poses drawn from archaic Greek vases of the sixth and early-fifth centuries BC; and the entire cast wore costumes woven according to techniques learned from peasant women by the play's director, Eva Palmer Sikelianos (b. New York 1874-d. Athens 1952), an American expatriate living in Greece since 1906. The costumes, the actors' masks, the singing, the dancing, the naturalistic scenery resting on the slopes of Mt. Parnassus in its springtime revival—all these things gave the "feeling" that Greek drama had never died: the Greeks were alive and still on earth.[2]

Many artists, intellectuals, and dignitaries in attendance raved about the living presence of Greek tradition.[3] Yet the configuration of elements brought together in that modern revival was untested, even unimagined in Greece before Eva Palmer staged the play at Delphi. Koula Pratsika, the chorus leader, who took part in the arduous, two-year process of learning to sing and dance her parts in unison with 15 young Athenian women, recognized Palmer's leading role in her own discovery of "an unknown Greece": "We followed Eva's lead to discover an unknown Greece, the existence of which we hadn't imagined, a Greece of our own and for ourselves" (Pratsika 127).[4] If, prior to following Palmer's lead, Greeks had not yet discovered a "Greece of [their] own and for [themselves]" as Palmer imagined it, what resources did Palmer draw on to bring that tradition into being? Where did this "unknown Greece" come from?

The question of the Delphic revival's sources becomes an interesting puzzle as it intersects with Palmer's life. In her old age, Palmer recalled in her autobiography, *Upward Panic*, that she had "left everything behind" when she moved to Greece in 1906 (Palmer-Sikelianos 51). She was referring specifically to her belongings; but her account of the journey to Delphi seems to erase all her prior learning in America and France. It fills in the ensuing "blank" (45) with "an enlightenment" (107) that grows from Palmer's experiences in Greece. As for artistic debt, her autobiography reiterates the contribution of Greeks alone and of two Greeks in particular: Penelope Sikelianos Duncan (1882-1917), whose singing of Greek music wiped away Palmer's ear for Western music, and poet Angelos Sikelianos (1884-1951), Penelope's brother and Palmer's husband from 1907 to 1939. Thus Palmer posited a complete break from her non-Greek past as the condition for her encounter with the living Greek tradition she projected at Delphi. Yet if we push against Palmer's myth of her rebirth in Greece, we find that Palmer's direction of the *Prometheus Bound* in the theatre at Delphi drew on a lifetime of learning. Long before Delphi, before she had even encountered Penelope in Paris in April 1906 or traveled to Greece to meet Angelos Sikelianos that same year in August, Palmer was already searching for ways to revive the Greeks. As I will argue here, those earlier experiments, the many contexts where she performed some version of Hellenism, have a direct bearing on her work at Delphi. The media Palmer pursued at Delphi—Greek dress, poses drawn from art, music, dance, and poetry—came to her long before Delphi.

Palmer standing physically before Delphi is a familiar image, and almost every study of her contribution to Greek drama turns on her worshipful embrace of Sikelianos's Delphic Idea as the principle of the Delphic revival. In contrast, her work in the performing arts temporally before Delphi—including, rather significantly, her conversations with fellow American George Cram Cook (1873-1924) in 1923, which inspired the turn to Delphi, as we will presently see—remains unexplored. In what follows, I revisit the question of Palmer's contribution to the Delphic revival through a careful study of her work "before" Delphi. Scouring newspaper articles, unpublished archives, correspondence, and other sources that touch on her life from

1900 to 1927,[5] I sketch a series of performance scenes from her earlier period. As I move through these scenes, I navigate the complex of currents that later converged in her work at Delphi to produce the sense of a Greek tradition that was both ancient and alive. By drawing connections between the dramatic performances at the Delphic Festivals and the many lesser-known contexts in which Palmer performed versions of Greekness, I rethink the question of the relationship between living traditions and lived lives, revival and biography.

Posing as Sappho in a "Charming Tableau"

A tableau of "Sappho" was Eva Palmer's first publicized theatrical role. A listing of events in Bar Harbor, Maine published in the *New York Times* on 26 August 1900 included a piece of theatrical entertainment to benefit the village hospital in the island upscale resort where Palmer and her family spent their summers. Alice Pike Barney, mother of Natalie Clifford Barney (1876-1972), Palmer's lover of that summer and for the next six years, was hosting the amateur theatrical, much of it written by Natalie. The evening's entertainment closed with four "charming tableaus: Sappho, Miss Eva Palmer; Helen of Troy and Sarah Bernhardt, Miss May Palmer; Cleopatra, Miss Alice Clifford Barney."[6] The *New York Times* assumed the announcement would carry social weight for its readers, as "the list of characters and workers in the enterprise includes the names of the most well-known people here." Yet Palmer's pose as Sappho in this theatrical event holds something more than social interest for anyone wishing to understand her artistic development within the cultural politics of the era. Dressed *"à la grecque"* (Rodriguez 57) and reciting Sappho's verse in ancient Greek to bring the spirit of the dead letter to life, Palmer took several steps in a direction she would later pursue and revise at Delphi.

"Tableau," short for "tableau vivant" or living picture, names an individual or group of participants who perform a picture. Tableaux are pictures come to life through costumes, gestures, and props. They create drama through artistic imitation, turning the stage into a living performance of a painting, sculpture, or bas-relief, which may itself be an imitation of a literary or dramatic scene. In Palmer's day, tableaux were frequently used in college performances of Greek drama and even epic verse,[7] where they illustrated scenes that were narrated rather than played. The dramatic effect of a performance that "looked like a picture"[8] lay in both the animation of the dead letter and the affirmation of antiquity's passing through the mimesis of inanimate scenes.

Palmer's Sappho tableau indicates her awareness of the connection between tableaux and modern performances of the Greeks. That Sappho was Palmer's subject adds another layer of consideration. It connects this performance to Palmer's participation in an emergent "Ladies' Greek,"[9] the institutional context of women's entry into Greek learning in British and American women's colleges, where "women imagined Greece on their own terms and within a female homosocial context" (Prins, "Greek Maenads, Victorian Spinsters" 46), at an angle to male-centered scholarly learning. At the time when Palmer was learning Greek as a student of literature at Bryn Mawr College (Palmer entered Bryn Mawr in 1896 and kept a room there through the fall of 1900, though she did not graduate), women scholars in Classics such as Jane Harrison were developing feminist approaches to the Greeks that emphasized the role of transgressive sexual figures, for example, the maenads, who held orgiastic rites honoring Dionysus on Mt. Parnassos (Harrison 390). Greek learning in this women's context attached itself to a range of desires, from the longing for intellectual status to same-sex eros to grounds for the creation of utopic female communities. Sappho stood at the crossroads of all those desires.

At Bryn Mawr, Palmer would have encountered Sappho on multiple fronts. In her Greek courses she read Sappho's poetry and very likely learned of current archaeological discoveries, for example, the unearthing of papyrus scraps with Sappho's poetic fragments in the Egyptian sands of Oxyrhynchus beginning in 1895. In Latin she probably studied the reworking of Sappho's life and verse in Ovid's *Heroides*, and in a course she took on British Victorian criticism offered by Mamie Gwinn (Palmer-Sikelianou 25),[10] she may have read Swinburne's "Notes on Poems and Reviews" with his defense of "the very words of Sappho" (Swinburne 10). From the mouth of M. Carey Thomas, President of Bryn Mawr, who set the school's serious tone and high-minded direction, Palmer would have heard Sappho named "'the greatest lyric poet in the world'" (Horowitz 395), a sign of women's as yet untapped genius and the importance of same-sex solidarity (Blankley 11).[11] By August 1900, Palmer had gained enough classical learning to introduce "Sappho's poetry and...an appreciation of Greek culture" (Benstock 277) to Natalie Clifford Barney and Pauline Tarn (a.k.a. Renée Vivien),[12] another intimate friend in Bar Harbor that summer,[13] and to perform Sappho's verse in ancient Greek.

In addition, Palmer's travels to Europe would have further exposed her to artistic depictions of Sappho found in the museums Palmer made a practice of visiting all her life. During her year-long stay in Italy from 1898 to1899 (Palmer-Sikelianos 27), she may have seen firsthand the Roman fresco at Pompeii depicting a learned woman with writing tablet in her left hand and stylus in her right pressed thoughtfully against her lips. People identified that portrait with Sappho from the time of its discovery in the late eighteenth century.[14] Palmer may also have observed the image of Sappho holding a scroll inscribed with her name in Raphael's "Mount Parnassus," a fresco painted on an interior wall of the Stanza della Segnatura in the Vatican Palace. And she would have been acquainted with at least a few of the astounding number of artistic renderings from the late eighteenth century to Palmer's own day representing Sappho the singing, teaching, fantasizing, leaping, dying, loving, classical poetess. Even if we cannot confirm the exact sources of her pose, it is nonetheless evident that Palmer was tapping into an image of enormous popularity, complex significance, and powerfully personal effect.[15] Palmer's personal interest in embodying that image is suggested by several undated photographs of herself as a young woman, for example, where she casts a downward, transgressive look of "jouissance," while her knee-length hair falls in pre-Raphaelite abundance over her flowing, Greek-style gown.[16]

Palmer may have imitated any one of these works of art or produced a creative patchwork for her Bar Harbor performance. Whatever the template, she endowed her Sappho with a classical look in the manner of so many nineteenth-century paintings: a Greek-style costume, sandals, a lyre-like instrument, and "faux Greek columns" (Rodriguez 57). The visual effect was certainly artistic. It was probably also quite arresting. Palmer had striking features, none more impressive than her nearly floor-length red hair, and she used them to cultivate a pre-Raphaelite look. Barney saw her as a "medieval virgin" (Rodriguez 56), and Pauline Tarn, quite significantly, as a radiant marble statue: "Looking at her, I felt that divine and terrible trembling that a perfect statue inspires, a dazzle of radiant marble, a long-loved picture of infinite harmony" (from *A Woman Appeared to Me*, quoted in Rodriguez 116). While playing on the powerfully artistic effects of her own looks, Palmer would have also keyed into the overdetermined ambiguity of Sappho's image to produce a coded message. To the broader audience of Bar Harbor's village hospital entertainment, Sappho, alongside Helen of Troy, Sarah Bernhardt, and Cleopatra, signified an unconventional female figure of great prodigy, concentrated emotions, and uncertain proclivities. A few spectators may have caught the sequence's erotic undertones and anti-bourgeois message, but only Palmer's small circle of initiates, including Barney and Tarn—who knew what the ancient Greek verses meant and who attributed to both their author and their performer homoerotic feelings—would have seen and heard in Palmer's Sappho performance inspiration for what Barney called their own "inverse" passion.[17] In Barney's later recollection, Palmer's performance of the Sappho tableau marked the beginning of her affair with Barney (Rodriguez 157).

Whatever the precise personal circumstances, beneath the still, Apollonian harmony of Palmer's classical tableau, an ecstatic mode was churning. At this stage in Palmer's thinking, the Greeks stood for reason and beauty, while passions represented another human side tugging her in another direction. She wrote to Barney in 1901, "Could we be reasonable and wholly Greek and beautiful, or would we throw reason to the winds and make our lives as a flash of lightening across the sky? Yes that tonight if I had you near me." (Palmer-Sikelianou and Papadaki 101). Over time she would find "wholly Greek" grounds for fusing beauty and that "flash of lighting across the sky" to infuse her direction of the rather immobile, archaic *Prometheus Bound* with a Dionysian spirit. Also anticipating her direction of the *Prometheus Bound* was her attachment to visual images as sources for embodying the missing figure of Greek poetry. In the Sappho tableau, we see the seeds of the method she developed for copying poses from Greek statuary and vase-painting and aligning each pose with an emotion expressed in the chorus's words. Likewise at Delphi, Palmer concentrated her passion for the missing figures of drama in gestures she drew from still art in order to deliver a performance aimed to draw in an audience of initiates.

Singing Wagner's "Liebestod"
    An important element of Palmer's Greek tableau was her performance of poetry through song. Indeed, finding the music at the root of poetry adequate to convey the dramatic effect of the words occupied her throughout her adult life. From 1901 to 1902 her interest in the musical performance of words took a particular form. She studied classical voice in New York City with the difficult goal of singing "Liebestod" from Richard Wagner's *Tristan and Isolde*. Later in Greece from 1915 to 1920, Palmer resumed her voice studies, this time to

master the very different musical system of Byzantine chanting. In both instances Palmer's underlying motive for taking on two huge musical challenges was to push language "into the realm of music" (Palmer Sikelianos 105) so as to move an audience in a special way. In her later work, her musical interests would become bound up with giving an "adequate music" to Greek tragedy (172). At this earlier stage, her very systematic voice studies attended to her desire to perform—and revive—*höchste Lust* (German, "highest bliss").

The attention Palmer gave to music throughout her life began at home. Palmer came from a musical family with many acquaintances in the musical world. Her mother, a gifted pianist, entertained world-class musicians frequently (Palmer-Sikelianos 32), and Palmer emulated this practice as an adult—for example, by hosting Dimitri Mitropoulos in her villa on the Corinthian gulf in 1924 and Richard Strauss at Delphi in 1926 (Konstantinidis 7-12). Palmer also studied music. Violin was her instrument in her youth, but she was much too interested in performing poetry and drama to ignore her voice. As early as 15, she experimented with ways to set to music the verses of Algernon Charles Swinburne and Edgar Allen Poe. Since classical opera, choral music, and art song were the forms she knew from her earliest years, it makes sense that she turned to studying that tradition when she first tried to cultivate her voice's dramatic potential. Palmer mentions her lessons in classical voice in her correspondence with Barney in 1901 and 1902.

In studying Wagner, Palmer had a very personal objective. Members of the Palmer family were all enthusiasts of the great German Romantic composer. When Eva planned a pilgrimage to the Beyreuth Festival in

August 1904, her mother and sister May both wrote letters anticipating her journey, and Courtlandt, Eva's brother who became a professional pianist and composer, wrote after the fact to inquire about the festival.[18] Eva later recalled the powerful effect Wagner's "strange" harmonies had on Courtlandt in his early childhood (Palmer-Sikelianos 13). But Courtlandt, with whom she was extremely close in her youth, had cooled toward Eva in 1900 after she returned from Rome and became involved with Barney.[19] Eva's correspondence bears witness to the souring of Courtlandt's feelings, his disapproval of her choices, and his harsh recriminations throughout her life.[20] In March 1902 she determined that, after two years' separation, "Music is the only thing that could bring us back together."[21] She wrote to Barney that she might win over Courtlandt if she could ever learn to sing an aria by Wagner. So Eva imagined progressing far enough in her voice studies to perform "Liebestod" (German, "Love death") from the sepulchral last scene of *Tristan and Isolde*. She thought that her singing this particular piece of music—with its trochaic feet recalling Greek lyric poetry—would bring her closer to him. As she wrote to Barney, "If I could sing the Liebestod for him I should be near him in a way that you are surely imaginative enough to see," (Palmer-Sikelianou and Papadaki 134). And later she wrote Barney of her wish to be ready to sing the piece for Courtlandt by June 1902. The provisional plans Palmer laid out in her letters suggest both how far she had gone in her voice studies[22] and how keenly she attended to musical drama's emotional effects.

Thematically "Liebestod" is a strange choice of music for winning back an estranged brother, for the nearly seven-minute song is one of the most sustained musical expressions of erotic love. Kneeling before the dead Tristan, Isolde sings phrase after phrase without harmonic resolution until she reaches *höchste Lust* with Tristan in her embrace. At this moment of musical climax, she imagines Tristan risen from the dead. Tristan remains lifeless, however, and as the orchestra plays the resolving notes, Isolde dies of grief. Neither the song's erotic content nor the scene's failed resurrection was lost on Palmer. In her odd suggestion that Barney was "certainly imaginative enough to see" the effect the song might have on Courtlandt (Palmer-Sikelianou and Papadaki 134)—that Barney could draw on her experience of the effects of Palmer's singing on herself to imagine "Liebestod's" potential effect on Courtlandt's brotherly love—Palmer recognizes the seductive power of musical drama. Sung well, a song of love in death could ignite many forms of *Lust*.

Indeed Palmer's lust for singing Liebestod was complex, perhaps as rich as the semantic field of the German word *Lust*. It was equally a means to reignite the old *Lust*, the pleasure and joy, in her relationship with Courtlandt, and to pursue her *Lust*, her lustful longing for Barney. Palmer used song to give Barney pleasure, balancing the pleasure Barney gave with her verse. Both saw their erotic union as one combining song and verse. "I will write, you will sing, and better than all we will live,"[23] Barney wrote to Palmer. For Barney in her moments of amorous rapture, Palmer was not just a singer. Her life was itself a song: "I am so glad that I have never carved a statue or painted a picture or produced anything as beautiful as yourself. Life has been your art—you have set yourself to music, your days are your sonnets."[24] Palmer anxiously kept raising her own expectations of what she had to do to please Barney. At first it was enough for her to recite or sing choral passages from literature (Palmer-Sikelianou and Papadaki 42). The next step was to master the art of song, to become for Barney an artist: "Ah dearest I shall be happy if I can ever sing to you if I can ever give you the kind of spontaneous yet lasting delight that your lines give me, I would be an artist for you as well as a lover, a beloved, a friend I would lift that side of me up to the line of my capacity for loving you" (Palmer-Sikelianou and Papadaki 89).

Over time Palmer came to feel she had to share with Barney the feeling of an entire chorus. She especially wanted Barney to experience music's seductive power on the grander scale offered by choral music sung for a large audience. In vocal ensembles, Palmer sensed an "invisible force" capable of lifting "the masses." Late in 1901 she described for Barney a Christmas Oratorio Society concert she attended at Carnegie Hall, where her father's friend Andrew Carnegie had invited all the city's popular choruses to fill the hall.

> I wish you were with me yesterday, to see how great and beautiful that invisible force is on the masses, the small pawns, which you despise...The performance of the oratorio was magnificent, all the people received it with enthusiasm, and in the end everyone stood and sang the "Halleluiah Chorus," a great choral piece by someone, Händel, I think. I assure you it was grand to hear all those people on stage, in the hall, and the orchestra and organ playing, and playing so well. It gave me a feeling I wanted to share with you. (Palmer-Sikelianou and Papadaki 98[25])

Despite her best efforts, Palmer was not able to use her study of operatic song for her intended effects. By March 1902, as she was preparing to sing "Liebestod"

13

to reconcile with Courtlandt, Palmer perceived that her attempts to achieve solo perfection, supported by hard, disciplined work to attain its mastery, contained the seeds of the death of Barney's love. It occupied a dividing line between herself and Barney, becoming a source of other differences between them. While Palmer saw in music something "so beautiful, so disembodied and universal that I feel for it as the man did for his country who said he was sorry he only had one life to give for it" (Palmer-Sikelianou and Papadaki 144-45), Barney did not think Wagner's music, or at least the expectations of perfection Palmer's performance of it raised, were worth the effort, preferring instead "inspiration independent of technique" (142).[26] Quoting Victorian poet George Meredith's "The Promise in Disturbance" (1862), Palmer noted a "jangled strain" that made a "mess where fruitfulness was meant" and precipitated her own "black descent" from hope that she could make herself "perfect" for Barney to a realization that "before you I have failed and broken faith, and been in all ways a poor miserable thing" (Palmer-Sikelianou and Papadaki 152). In June 1902 Palmer's *Lust* for Barney won out over her *Lust* for Courtlandt. She ended her voice lessons without singing for Courtlandt in order to follow Barney to Paris. She spent the next four years between Paris and the East Coast anxiously trying to please Barney as she pursued her ambitions to "go on the stage."[27]

Striking Outwards with a Passion for Swinburnean Choruses
Palmer's failure to seduce through solo operatic song did not bring an end, however, to her musical-dramatic pursuits. Instead it initiated a search for a new form of expression: something choral and dramat-

ic involving the "great and beautiful...invisible force" that Palmer herself experienced in the audience's "enthusiastic" response to the Carnegie Hall "Halleluiah" chorus. And Palmer did not ignore the lessons she learned by studying Wagner's music or the writings of Wagner's onetime protégé, Friedrich Nietzsche[28] She began looking for new ways to synthesize poetry and music in the wake of Wagner's grand fusion of dialogue and chorus, image, music, and dance. She would strive to create such a dramatic synthesis throughout her life, most famously in the Delphic productions of *Prometheus Bound* and *The Suppliants* in 1927 and 1930, but first in the summer of 1905—just a few years after she found Wagner's music inadequate to deliver her own drama—when she directed a performance of Swinburne's *Atalanta of Caldyron* in the open air at Bar Harbor.

It is no accident that Swinburne's *Atalanta* was the work that brought Palmer closest to producing Greek tragedy before she actually directed a Greek tragedy. Here was a modern recreation of a Greek tragedy by the premier English poet of the late Victorian period, a writer whose "mind and memory were more deeply immersed in the poetry of the ancients than that of any other English poet" (Gosse 110). Even more to the point, Swinburne is a poet of strong affinities with both Wagner[29] and Sappho,[30] two figures of intense interest to Palmer and her two points of entry to the Greeks, as we have seen.

Palmer knew all the choruses of *Atalanta* by heart by the time she was fifteen. She would privately perform "impassioned recitation[s]" for her "spellbound" classmates (Palmer-Sikelianos 105) in her room at Miss Porter's School in Farmington, Connecticut. When "Mrs.

Dowe," headmistress of the school, put a stop to those occasions because she found them "too exciting" (105), she was probably showing good sense. Swinburne's hunt narrative is a wild exploration of women's burning desires. In fact Palmer's recitations of Swinburne became a regular piece of her lovemaking to Barney (Palmer-Sikelianou and Papadaki 42). Palmer's autobiography suppresses this rather personal fact from an important piece of her life that she kept hidden. But Palmer also remains silent about Swinburne's part in a crucial moment of her artistic development. Palmer writes that Mrs. Dowe's "interruption" of her Swinburne recitations when she was 15 "was for me in a way, an end. My passion for Swinburnean choruses, for melody in words, from that time struck inward instead of outwards. As far as personal performance was concerned, it never came to the surface again, even in the few amateur plays which I directed, or in all the work I did in Paris for the stage" (Palmer-Sikelianos 105-106). Yet from a letter Palmer sent to Barney in 1905 (Palmer-Sikelianou and Papadaki 234-35), we learn that Palmer's "passion for Swinburnean choruses" *did* strike outwards again in a plan to stage *Atalanta* with amateur actors in an open-air, Mediterranean-like setting in Bar Harbor.[31]

Palmer described for Barney each step she took to produce *Atalanta* that summer of 1905. Several details show that her work on *Atalanta* anticipated her production of *Prometheus Bound* at Delphi. First there was the stage. After returning to Bar Harbor from Paris in late July,[32] she approached the European-educated Anne Mills Archbold, who granted her access to the terrace of "Archbold Cottage," as her grand summer home was called, for her rehearsals and performance.

Designed by architect Fred L. Savage in 1903-1904, the cottage drew its inspiration from Tuscan villas. The terrace was its most unique feature, with its fountain at the center, "trailing vines and blossoms," and twelve supporting stucco arches overlooking a panorama of mountain, forest, and ocean (Bryan et al. 210, quoting from the *Bar Harbor Record*).[33] Palmer's decision to work in this Mediterranean-inspired, open-air structure, presaging her work in the open-air theatre at Delphi, was not at all out of character. The scene of women playing out their desires among "marvelous ruins of temples...[and] strange old gardens in warm flowering fields"[34]—in many ways an imaginary recreation of Sappho's Mytilene as it was depicted in nineteenth-century art—was both a fantasy she and Barney shared and something they tried to reproduce in Barney's garden theatricals at Neuilly. According to Rodriguez (155), in June 1905, a month before her arrival at Bar Harbor, Palmer was participating in one of Barney's first theatricals in Barney's garden in Neuilly. The experience of that open-air event, and the ideal she and Barney generally held of replicating Sappho's garden, would have suggested to her to seek out the open-air space of Archbold Cottage for *Atalanta*.

Then there was the choreography. Palmer planned to give movement to Swinburne's chorus. For assistance she invited "Mrs. Barker" from Boston, "a woman about forty-five, full of enthusiasm, and sincere love of good things.... She has spent most of her life making a study of dances, rhythm, balance, movement in general, and knows a great deal about the very sort of dancing that I wanted the chorus to do" (Palmer-Sikelianou and Papadaki 234). While it is hard to pin down just who Mrs. Barker was or what she actually did "know" about "the very sort of dancing" Palmer "wanted the chorus to do," we surmise that their minds met on ground prepared by contemporary performances of Greek drama. On one end, amateur and professional experiments in staging a large Greek chorus before 1902 did little to animate the chorus (Pluggé 97-99), and only gradually began to add movement after 1902, some of it modeled on "the choral dances of modern Greek peasants (99). The tendency was to mass the chorus's members in still, harmonious, tableau-like groupings—like figures on a bas relief—and then to have the limbs and bodies sway.[35] On another end, there was Isadora Duncan, dancing alone, suturing the Apollonian classicism of a motionless statue with "menacing Furies and frenzied Bacchantes" (Dils and Albright 290). Palmer and Barker would have found common ground somewhere between these two points in their combined effort to endow Swinburne's chorus with some kind of "Greek" movements to convey the driving force of the verse.

Of course there were costumes, and one can justifiably imagine them as "Greek," since the play's mythological subject calls for Greek dress and anyway recreating the "Greek clothes we see on statues, bas-reliefs and vases" was Palmer's obsession all her adult life (Palmer-Sikelianos 47). More astonishing, there was original "Greek music" in *Atalanta*. To fill out the marriage of verse and movement, we learn that Palmer was "getting the Greek music" (Palmer-Sikelianou and Papadaki 234). Thus Palmer was setting tragedy to music as early as August 1905, twenty-two years before she taught the chorus to sing the words of *Prometheus Bound* using the Byzantine compositions she commissioned from Konstantinos Psachos.[36] Indeed Palmer was arranging music all her life, whether in improvised recitations, or as melodies for the poetry of friends, or as pieces she wrote out in Byzantine notation for performances of tragedy and dance in the 1930s. Palmer's assertion that she was getting *Greek* music is especially startling. Palmer later claimed that before coming to Greece she had not been able to solve the "old platonic problem" of Greek music (Palmer-Sikelianos 93), or to find music that was "truly adequate" (172) to Greek tragedy as Nietzsche imagined Wagner's lessons for tragedy in his *Birth of Tragedy*. Here we see that Palmer was not just wrestling with the idea of Greek music in theory. In 1905 she actually attempted to produce "Greek" pitch, tone, and rhythm to match Swinburne's Greek tragedy in English verse. Her direction of *Atalanta* was both a continuation of the "Ladies' Greek" she learned at Bryn Mawr College and cultivated through her relationship with Barney, and her first Wagnerian fusion of dialogue and chorus, image, music, and dance.

Amateurs in the Garden, from Bar Harbor to Delphi

As much as Palmer later denigrated her theatrical activities in the U.S. and Paris as the work of "a rich dilettante, amateur smatterer on the outside fringe of the theatre" (Palmer-Sikelianou 44), throughout her life she remained committed to that "amateur… fringe," through which theatre was a piece of community building. On a grander scale in the Delphic Festivals, she enlisted amateurs for the choruses of the *Prometheus Bound* and *Suppliants*, Pyrrhic dances, athletic competitions, folk art and handcraft exhibitions, and performances of *kleftika* and folk songs. This was a continuation of Palmer's work in amateur productions in Bar Harbor in 1900 and 1905 and indeed in all of her work in theatre. The use of amateur performers allowed her to experiment freely, without consideration for social conventions or business profits. And it gave her opportunity to use singing and dancing to build a "Eutopia," as she once called the artistic union of "free" people who "are both generous enough, beautiful enough, to make a clear sustained poem of our two lives" (Palmer-Sikelianou and Papadaki 85). Thus amateur theatre was a condition of theatre: not an inferior creation but a higher ideal uniting a group of like-minded individuals and raising them up to a higher creative, communal end. This was as true of her creations in Bar Harbor and Paris as it was at Delphi and, in the 1930s in the United States, at Smith and Bryn Mawr Colleges and with the Federal Theatre Project in New York City.

At Bar Harbor in 1905, Palmer counted on the good will of wealthy friends and acquaintances to volunteer their time and spaces, while she covered the expense of costumes and props with her own resources and dealt with the uncertainty of it all. Her *Atalanta*, for example, was not a professional actor, but Mildred Barnes, a fellow New York heiress, who years later, as Mildred Barnes Bliss, donated her vast Georgetown property of Dumbarton Oaks and its Byzantine and Pre-Columbian collections to Harvard. When Barnes dropped out of rehearsals, Bar Harbor's *Atalanta* fell through, and Palmer had to turn elsewhere to try to stage the play. Palmer's commitment to amateur actors was in part a risky necessity, since she did have an unlimited flow of cash to pay professional actors.[37] Yet it was also an artistic choice.

Palmer remained in the United States for a few months after she attempted to stage *Atalanta*, sustaining a hope that Sarah Bernhardt would invite her to perform in New York City in Maeterlinck's "Pelleas and Melisande"[38] and also quite possibly in G. Constant Lounsbery's three act play, "Delilah."[39] The performance with Bernhardt never took place. In the meantime she met with some success on stage, even as Barney was trying to woo her back. Responding rather possessively to Palmer's other invitations—including one from "several New York women" who wanted Palmer to act in an "ideal theatre" they were planning[40]— Barney made this counteroffer in a letter written in the fall of 1905[41]:

> come back and help in a new plan I have for starting a *theatre d'amateurs*—so many are talented that it seems a shame not to do something with them. My plan is to take a small theatre once a month and give just once or twice something exceptionally good...

A principle of Barney's proposed theatre was its "amateur" status, something that aligned itself closely with Palmer's interests. Barney also insisted on an all-female cast, "*avec ... des femmes vraiment comme* Colette, Ilse, ... *toi*, [Lilian] Russell, Isadora Duncan." In terms of repertoire, Barney patterned the theatre on Palmer's experiments: it would concentrate on reviving classical subjects and classicizing authors, "sometimes little Greek plays with music and dancing...sometimes we might have an act of Swinburne or Shelly—(the French care about good English verse more than the English) and an Idylle of Theocrites, Oscar Wilde"s Salomé.... In time there is success in reviving really beautiful things and doing this well, and in the meantime there is the pleasure of it."

Much has been made of the garden performance in June 1906 of Barney's dramatic poem, *Equivoque*

(Ambiguity), a theatrical adaptation of Sappho's poetry produced entirely in the spirit of Barney's unpublished letter to Palmer. The play revisits the legend of Sappho's suicide. Critical attention has centered on the play's revisionist narrative. With its extensive scholarship and quotations from Sappho's poems in Greek, the play was a "scholarly tour de force" (Wickes 94). Palmer's role in the play as Timas, "the bride who leaves Sappho to marry" (Benstock 291) and so provokes Sappho's suicide, has given critics reason to draw parallels between Timas's role as the soon-to-be-bride in Sappho's legend and Palmer's biography, specifically her incumbent abandonment of "Barney's circle": "Eva Palmer herself was to leave Barney's circle for marriage: she wed the Greek brother-in-law of Raymond Duncan and dedicated her life to the rediscovery of Greek arts" (Benstock 291). Scholarly discussion of this theatrical event has for the most part concentrated on these parallels at the expense of careful attention to other things. For one thing, Timas in Barney's play does not abandon Sappho in the end. Instead, when she makes the discovery that she is still the object of Sappho's love, she leaves the marriage altar to pursue Sappho, discovering her as she makes her suicidal leap. Timas joins Sappho in the sea's sensual waters.

The fixation on Palmer's/Timas's imminent marriage is the reason for another critical oversight. Palmer was not just an actor in the play. The sequence of letters between Palmer and Barney in 1905 and 1906 (KMS Dossiers I and II) suggests that Palmer's work on *Atalanta* pushed Barney to propose her *"theatre d'amateurs."* It also shows that Palmer was involved in this production at every step. Palmer surely "gathered costumes and props" (Rodriguez 156), as others have suggested and

Barney's notes to Palmer confirm. But the footnotes and Greek sources that made *Equivoque* "scholarly" were also most likely Palmer's contribution rather than the work of the impatient Barney, whose education was a "hit-or-miss-mélange" (Rodriguez 62). Palmer knew Greek better than Barney. The "Aeolean harp music and traditional songs performed by Raymond Duncan and his Greek wife, Penelope" Sikelianos (Rodriguez 154) would have been Palmer's inspiration too. The Duncans were Palmer's new-found friends. She had met them in Paris in the spring of 1906,[42] and in April invited them to stay for a time in her house. It was Palmer who discovered Penelope Sikelianos's art of singing Greek folk music, and it was she who identified this as the alternative musical sound she felt she had been yearning for. Thus a great deal about the performance of *Equivoque* has Palmer's signature on it.

Once we recognize the broader role Palmer was playing in Barney's circle, from her Sappho tableau in Bar Harbor to her staging of *Equivoque* in Paris, we observe that Palmer's journey to Greece in August 1906 did not precipitate an absolute end or a herald a new beginning. For years before she fled Paris for Greece, Palmer was gathering together the elements of her Greek revival: tableaux inspired by the visual arts, music adequate to Greek tragedy, the dramatic fusion of poetry-music-dance, Greek dress, amateur theatre, open-air performance. Her work combining these elements in a performance such as *Equivoque* left a lingering mark on the famous "Sapphic community of Barney's salon" (Parsons 54) that would evolve from Barney's theatricals at Neuilly. It also gave Palmer the building blocks she would use to direct the *Prometheus Bound* at Delphi in 1927.

What was missing from the director's arsenal that she would later use at Delphi were the modern Greek equivalents of the artistic building blocks she was already cultivating. That retooling began almost immediately after Palmer found herself on Greek soil. As soon as she set foot in the Duncan's "Palace of Agamemnon" in Kopanos at the foot of Mt. Hymettos, all of Greece became her garden, its open air her stage, and performing a living Greekness her daily care. For example, she immediately made an everyday practice of wearing Greek-style tunics, something she previously reserved for theatrical performances in Barney's garden and other private outdoor spaces. To give her dress a native quality, she studied the intricacies of weaving with Greek village women, then wore only things she herself wove. In addition to her "Greek" dress, she attended to gestures, poses, movement, music, poetry, and language. She regularly visited the National Archaeological museum in Athens, filling notebooks with her hand-drawn replicas of the precise angles and accents of the human form found in the museum's enormous collections. Her study of Greek art was itself a continuation of an older practice of studying vase-paintings in the Louvre in Paris, only in Greece she focused on pre-classical renderings of the human figure, relating them to life she found outside the museum. She worked hard to imitate their twisted positions with her body, and she learned to animate them according to the footwork and hand-holding positions of traditional Greek dance. To sustain a "Greek" pitch and tone, she followed the lead of Penelope Duncan, dedicating herself to the challenge of learning folk songs and Greek Orthodox chanting in the old modal style as it was researched and taught by

Penelope's teacher, Konstantinos Psachos, who later composed the music for the choral odes of *Prometheus Bound*. And she gained a full appreciation of the musical and rhythmic range of the Greek language by hearing Angelos Sikelianos, her husband from 1907 to 1939, recite 2500 years of Greek literature, including his own. Finally, she traded in her ecstatic love for the Sapphic Barney for worship of the prophet-poet Sikelianos.

Before Delphi

If we keep in mind the elements of Palmer's earlier efforts to stage the Greeks, we begin to view the "unknown Greece" she made visible at Delphi as a radical makeover of the Ladies' Greek she supposedly left behind in Paris. Or better, we begin to see the affinities of media and forms she cultivated in the "amateur fringe" in the U. S. and Paris with experiments that were being enacted in Greece in the early twentieth century.[43] Still there is one element that was entirely new, and that was the idea of using the archaeological site of Delphi as the stage for a contemporary revival of the human spirit.

The Delphic idea, the zoning of Delphi as an *omphalos*, a divine center for reviving modern spirits worn down by individualism and machines, has been credited to Angelos Sikelianos. He first mentioned his "Delphiko Orama" (Delphic vision) to poet Kostis Palamas in a letter written from Moni Profitou Ilia, a monastery two miles west of Delphi on September 27, 1919 (Bournazakes 103). He began writing his "Delphikos Logos" in June 1921 (111) but only presented it as two talks "on prophetic forerunners, ancient and modern, and the idea of a global freedom and international brotherhood of all the peoples of the Earth" given in Athens in January 1923 (119). He published a different version of the essay in 1927 with a near simultaneous translation into English by Alma Reed.[44] Ever since November 1914, Sikelianos had been making pilgrimages to pagan and Christian sacred sites with his friend, author Nikos Kazantzakis: first to the sacred peninsula of Mt. Athos, then to Dafni, Eleusis, Kaisariani, Delphi, Epidaurus and other sites in the Peloponnese, and finally to Jerusalem in 1921. Together the two writers developed a notion of creating "a religion, everything ripe, to bring out whatever is most holy and deep within us" (Bornazakes 71). During this same period, Sikelianos experienced a series of devastating losses. First his sister Penelope succumbed to tuberculosis at a sanitarium in Davos in 1917. Then his brother Hector died of a heart attack in 1919. And in 1920 Kalypso Katsimbali, a young woman from a prominent, learned Athenian family, who was madly in love with Sikelianos, committed suicide in despair. "*O Sikelianos neochristianizei*" (Sikelianos is neo-Christianizing"), one critic responded to Sikelianos's religious writings, unsure how to reconcile the Christian themes in the current work of the formerly pagan Sikelianos (Bournazakes 99).

The religious thought of Sikelianos was mystical and syncretic. He tended to identify the abused body of Christ with Orpheus and Prometheus. He also drew out metaphorical meanings from the ancient landscapes. At a time when a poem about Greek Pascha was occupying his thinking, Sikelianos was looking to ground his mystic, ecumenical vision. At first it was Jerusalem that drew his attention. Then he thought he would establish a *"kosmiko monasteri"* (cosmic, worldly monastery) with Kazantzakis on the slopes of Mt. Penteli (Bournazakes 113). Gradually Moni Profitou Ilia, a monastery two miles west of Delphi on the southwest slopes of Mt. Parnassos, and Agorgianni on the far side of Mt. Parnassos became his regular haunts, and Delphi appealed to him as a place of renewal.

Yet the vision of Delphi as a region "of mystery and magic, of religious affinities, of hidden, secret storehouses of revelation and inspiration and healing," in the words of poet H.D. (H.D., *Majic Ring* 247), had multiple beginnings, some of them nearly simultaneous with Sikelianos's and all part of a shared intoxication with ancient Greek words, images, and landscape. One that probably had no direct bearing on the Delphic Festivals but came from the "Ladies' Greek" milieu that inspired Palmer was the "Delphic vision" of H.D., a fellow Bryn Mawr student. In a waking dream during her visit to Greece, H.D. saw "a head, a chalice, a lamp resembling the Pythia's tripod, and fluid picture of Nike, Winged Victory, climbing a ladder 'write themselves' on the wall" of a hotel (Sword 164). There followed a "series of hallucinated dance 'tableaux,'" as H.D. called her spontaneous dance performances, including one of "a Greek mountain boy" and another of Lady in a tower with jewels "'full of traditional occult power' and named, like the earth mother, Rhea" (Sword 164, quoting H.D.'s *Majic Ring*"). That was in Corfu in the spring of 1920, not long after Sikelianos wrote of his "Delphiko Orama" to Palamas.

H.D.'s Delphic vision suggests the entangled density of the inter-textual web within which both Sikelianos and Palmer were working when they arrived at the decision to organize the Delphic Festivals in 1924. It also serves to identify a shared feature of H.D.'s and Palmer's performance of the Greeks that was *not* initially part of Sikelianos's Delphic Idea: the performance tableau with a mythic or dramatic subject. In both H.D.'s very spontaneously performed "hallucinated dance" in Corfu and Palmer's much more fully developed revivals of Greek drama in the ancient theatre of Delphi, we find the element of a visually inspired tableau that aspires to animate Greek myth as part of a modern revival. The dramatic performance of myth in the divinely zoned Delphi sanctuary became the anchor of the Delphic Festivals in 1927 and 1930. Indeed, that and the exhibition of handicrafts were the pieces of the Festivals that succeeded, while Sikelianos's broader Delphic Idea of bringing together overseers of a new world peace and culture at Delphi never caught on. But the revival of drama at Delphi was not part of Sikelianos's Delphic Idea from the start. In fact it was missing from Sikelianos's Delphic vision until the American theatre director George Cram "Jig" Cook, dressed in the shepherd's clothes, directed a Cain-Abel passion play with shepherds on Mt. Parnassus near Agorgianni, one of Sikelianos's favored places of retreat, in the summer of 1923 (Glaspell 392) and, in the fall of that same year, formed the Delphic Players (403).

Jig Cook's journey leading him to Greece in 1922 bears an uncanny resemblance to Eva Palmer's. An almost exact contemporary, he studied Greek at Harvard, graduating in 1893, while he also sustained a lifelong interest in music and drama. Although he pursued graduate studies in Germany and became a professor of English at the University of Iowa and then Stanford, his ardent Hellenism stood at an odd angle to the old, male-centered scholarly institutions of learning. In his case it was because of his "democratic, quasi-socialist, political orientation" (Chansky 42). As founder of the Provincetown Players, an amateur theatre troupe with humble beginnings on a makeshift stage in Provincetown, Massachusetts, Cook played out his idea of a communal modern theatre with ancient Greek precedents in an "amateur fringe." He wanted to create a "beloved community of life-givers" (Glaspell 241), but he found himself at a creative standstill in 1922, unable to achieve his end of producing theatre reflecting his social and political interests. So he too dropped everything and traveled to Greece.

Cook met Palmer and Sikelianos in Agorgianni in the summer of 1922. The next spring, Cook, his fourteen-year-old daughter Nilla, and his wife and collaborator, Susan Glaspell, came to stay for a month in Xylokastro near the Sikelianos's house in Sykia on the Gulf of Corinth. Jig's motivation for coming to Xylokastro—according to Nilla, the only direct source who writes about the visit—was "to be near her" (Cook 18), that is to say, to be near Palmer. Nilla explains: she "admired Kyrios Kouk and his poetry, and he admired her and her weaving" (18). Surely the long conversations between Cook and Palmer that month went beyond poetry and weaving to touch on the two expatriates' experiences in Greece, their sense of the antiquity of Greek village life, their visions for a Greek revival. Their many intersecting lines of interest can be traced through a careful comparison of Palmer's writings and *The Road to the Temple*, Glaspell's biography of Cook. A cursory look at these two works gathers together a number of shared themes, though it is impossible to sort out matters of priority. Both Glaspell and Palmer are stubbornly silent about Cook's and Palmer's interaction, treating the event as if it never happened and the ideas they shared about the importance of Greece for modern life as if they existed exclusively in their protagonist's head.[45]

For example, Glaspell writes of Cook's fascination with the Greek loom (349) and his interest in Greek dress (388), particularly the shepherd's clothes (422), which he eventually adopted. And the book is filled with images of Greek village women spinning, signs for him and Glaspell of "something older than ancient Greece" (332). Did Cook develop an interest in Greek dress independently, or was he influenced by Palmer, who had been weaving and wearing her Greek clothes for nearly two decades at the time of their meeting? Cook's investment in "Greek letters" as a foundation for self knowledge (266) betrays ideas circulating as widely in well-established halls of learning such as Harvard University as in women's colleges such as Bryn Mawr and in the society that attended revivals of Greek drama (Hains 25). The same can be said of his desire to reproduce "strange Greek songs, whose scale is not our scale" (261).[46] Cook's long-lasting embrace of "dancing that is like sculpture" (246), borne out by his direction of Louise Bryant's *The Game* with the Provincetown Players in 1916 using the sculpturally inspired dance vocabulary of "Isadora Duncan, Ruth St. Denis, Maud Allen, and Vaslav Nijinsky" (Chansky 26), connects his work and Palmer's at an earlier stage. They would have had much to say about that, and also about the utopian, communal aspect the amateur theatre they supported. Finally, we see that the two expatriates sought an escape in Greece's contemporary reality from a modern world that wore them down. They enthusiastically studied modern Greek as an extension of the ancient language, a key to making nearly three millennia of written Greek a living thing. For both, "the unwritten music in the words we speak" (246) was a source of dramatic interest. Surely the conversation between them on these topics was endless, perhaps even promising of future collaboration.

Instead of collaboration, Palmer's revival of the *Prometheus Bound* in the ancient theatre at Delphi stood in the place of performances of Cook's short-lived Delphic Players. After Cook died unexpectedly at Delphi on 11 January 1924, Angelos Sikelianos announced his plans to produce Greece's first large Delphic Festival with a revival of drama in the ancient theatre as the festival's centerpiece. Initially he publicized the production as a "memor[ial] to George Cram Cook, founder of the Provincetown Players" ("Greek Drama to be Given again at Ancient Delphi"). As the occasion of the festival neared, however, the dedication to Cook's memory disappeared from the publicity, and Sikelianos became the author of the Festival, with the American Palmer his uxorial "assistant" ("Modern Greeks to Evoke Life of Classic Times").

This is where most stories of Palmer's work begin, as the present essay surely did: with Eva Palmer Sikelianos, humble servant of a poetically inspired revival, standing reverently before Delphi, seizing a brief moment's joy at the Festival's conclusion as the audience expresses its powerful verdict: "the drama has been reborn…in the original land of its birth" (Palmer-Sikelianos 118). Palmer physically before Delphi erases Palmer temporally before Delphi. Her artistic journey disappears. The complex set of intertwining academic and socio-cultural discourses she inhabited, the artistic approaches she borrowed, tested, and revised through repeated attempts to stage her Greekness all seem irrelevant before the audience's overwhelming "feeling" that an ancient Greek tradition was alive in that performance at the theatre of Delphi.

Palmer's work temporally before Delphi gave her the tools she needed to render the *Prometheus Bound* as a convincing revival at Delphi. By placing Palmer's Modern Greek lessons alongside her earlier "Ladies' Greek" lessons in reviving the Greeks, we begin to understand how the unknown, unimagined Greece she brought into view at Delphi drew its force from ideas that had been tested in staged revivals in multiple sites. Palmer's cosmopolitanism, her restless efforts to hone her tools for staging the Greeks at every point in her journey from Bar Harbor, Bryn Mawr, and New York to Paris, Athens, Lefkada, Sykia, and the villages of Mt. Parnassos, made her an agent of Greek tradition's "recovery" on multiple fronts. Perhaps we can better appreciate her artistic success at Delphi if we recognize how pervasively her lived life informed her approach to Greece, and how completely she made her biography disappear before the magical, mythical moment of revival in the ancient theatre.

Works Cited

"Bar Harbor." *The New York Times* 26 Aug. 1900; ProQuest Historical Newspapers The New York Times (1851-2) pg. 14. Print.

Barney, Natalie Clifford. *Actes et entr'actes*. Paris: E. Sansot, 1910. Print.

Benstock, Shari. *Women of the Left Bank: Paris, 1900-1940*. Austin: University of Texas Press, 1986. Print.

Ben-Zvi, Linda. *Susan Glaspell: Her Life and Times*. New York: Oxford University Press, 2005. Print.

Blankley, Elyse. "Sappho's Daughters." Review of *The Amazon and the Page: Natalie Clifford Barney and*

Renée Vivien. The Women's Review of Books 5.10-11 / (July 1988): 11. JSTOR. Accessed: 08/01/2009. Web.

BMHA Eva Sikelianou Papers, Benaki Museum Historical Archive. Kifissia, Greece.

Bournazakis, Kostas. *Chronographia Angelou Sikelianou, 1884-1951* (Angelos Sikelianos Chronography). Athens: Ikaros, 2006. Print.

Brantley, Ben. *The New York Times Book of Broadway: On the Aisle for the Unforgettable Plays of the Last Century.* New York, Macmillan, 2001. Print.

Bryan, John Morrill, Fred L. Savage and Richard Cheek. *Maine Cottages: Fred L. Savage and the Architecture of Mount Desert.* New York: Princeton Architectural Press, 2005. Print.

Chansky, Dorothy. *Composing Ourselves: The Little Theatre Movement and the American Audience. Theater in the Americas.* Carbondale, Ill: Southern Illinois University Press, 2005. Print.

Cook, Nilla Cram. *My Road to India.* New York: L. Furman, Inc, 1939. Print.

DeJean, Joan. *Fictions of Sappho, 1546-1937.* Women in Culture and Society. Chicago: University of Chicago Press, 1989. Print.

Dils, Ann, and Ann Cooper Albright. *Moving History / Dancing Cultures: A Dance History Reader.* Middletown, Conn: Wesleyen University Press, 2001. Print.

Dragoumis, M. Ph. "Constantinos A. Psachos (1869-1949): A Contribution to the Study of His Life and Work." *Studies in Eastern Chant* 5. Ed. Egon Wellesz, Dimitri E. Conomos, Milos M. Velimirovic. Crestwood, NY: St. Vladimir's Seminary Press, 1966. 77-88. Print.

"Dumbarton Oaks Park." www.tclf.org/landslide/2006/dumbarton_oaks/site_profile.pdf. Web.

Ehnenn, Jill R. *Women's Literary Collaboration, Queerness, and Late-Victorian Culture*. Hampshire: Ashgate Press, 2008. Print.

Glaspell, Susan. *The Road to the Temple*. New York: Frederick A. Stokes Co, 1941. Print.

Gleason, Clarence W., ed. "Current Events: Smith College." *Classical Journal*, Classical Association of the Middles West and South 8 (1913): 84-86. Print.

Goldhill, Simon. "A Touch of Sappho." *Classics and the Uses of Reception*. Ed. Charles Martindale and Richard F. Thomas. Malden, MA and Oxford: Wiley-Blackwell, 2006. 250-73. Print.

Gosse, Edmund. *The Life of Algernon Charles Swinburne*. New York: Macmillan, 1917. Print.

"Greek Drama to be Given Again at Ancient Delphi." *New York Times (1857-Current file)*; Oct 11, 1925; ProQuest Historical Newspapers The New York Times (1851-2005) pg. X8. Web.

Gregory, Eileen. *H.D. and Hellenism: ClassicLines*. Volume 111 of Cambridge studies in American literature and culture. Cambridge: Cambridge University Press, 1997. Print.

Goujon, Jean-Paul. *Tes Blessures sont Plus Souces que Leurs Caresses: Vie de Renée Vivien*. Paris: R. Deforges, 1986. Print.

H. D. and Demetres P. Tryphonopoulos. *Majic Ring*. Gainesville: University Press of Florida, 2009. Print.

Hains, D. D. "Greek Plays in America." *The Classical Journal* 6.1 (Oct., 1910): 24-39. Print.

Harrison, Jane Ellen. *Prolegomena to the Study of Greek Religion*. Cambridge: University Press, 1903. Print.

Hartigan, Karelisa. *Greek Tragedy on the American Stage:*

Ancient Drama in the Commercial Theater, 1882-1994. Westport CT: Greenwood, 1995. Print.

Hassiotis, Natasha. "Commentary from the Documentary, 'A Century of Contemporary Dance in Greece,' NET (New Hellenic Television) January-February 2001. http://www.sarma.be/text.asp?id=389. Web.

Horowitz, Helen Lefkowitz. *The Power and Passion of M. Carey Thomas*. Champaigne: U-Illinois Press, 1999. Print.

KMS Eva Sikelianou Papers, Octave Merlier Archive, Kentro Mikrasiatikon Spoudon (Centre for Asia Minor Studies). Athens, Greece. Print.

Konstantinidis, Thanos. *O Richard Strauss sto Delfiko Spiti ton Sikelianon* (Richard Strauss in the Sikelianos' House at Delphi). Athens: Agra, 1998. Print.

Leontis, Artemis. "Eva Palmer's Distinctive Greek Journey" *Women Writing Greece: Essays on Hellenism, Orientalism and Travel*. Ed. Vassiliki Kolocotroni and Efterpi Mitsi. Amsterdam: Rodopi, 2008. 159-84. Print.

Lingas, Alexander. "Tradition and Renewal in Contemporary Orthodox Psalmody," in *Psalms in Community: Jewish and Christian Textual, Liturgical, and Artistic traditions*. Issue 25 of Symposium Series "Society of Biblical Literature." Eds. Harold W. Attridge and Margot E. Fassler. Leiden: Brill, 2004: 348-356. Print.

McGann, Jerome. "Wagner, Baudelaire, Swinburne: Poetry in the Condition of Music." *Victorian Poetry* 47:4 (Winter 2009): 610-32. Print.

"Modern Greeks to Evoke Life of Classic Times." *New York Times (1857-Current file);* Jan 16, 1927; ProQuest Historical Newspapers The New York

Times (1851 - 2006): X20. Web.

The New York Times (1857-Current file) ProQuest Historical Newspapers *The New York Times* 1851-2005. Web.

Nietzsche, Friedrich Wilhelm. *The Birth of Tragedy, And the Case of Wagner*. Trans. Walter Kaufmann. New York: Vintage Books, 1967. Print.

Palmer-Sikelianou, Eva and Lia Papadaki. *Grammata tis Evas Palmer Sikelianou sti Natalie Clifford Barney* (Letters of Eva Palmer Sikelianos to Natalie Clifford Barney). Athens: Kastanioti, 1995. Print.

Palmer-Sikelianos, Eva and John Peter Anton. *Upward Panic: The Autobiography of Eva Palmer-Sikelianos*. Choreography and dance studies, v. 4. Chur, Switzerland: Harwood Academic Publishers, 1993. Print.

Parsons, Deborah L. *Djuna Barnes*. Tavistock, Devon, UK: Northcote House in Association with the British Council, 2003. Print.

Porter, James I. "What Is 'Classical' about 'Classical' Antiquity? Eight Propositions." *Arion*_13.1 (Spring/Summer 2005): 27-61. Print.

Pratsika, Koula. "Anamneseis apo tis protes Delfikes Eortes tou 1927" (Recollections from the first Delphic Festivals of 1927), in *Angelos Sikelianos, Eua Palmer-Sikelianu, Delphikes Eortes. Eidikon Aphieroma Tes Epitheoreseos Eos* (Special double issue of *Eos* on Angelos Sikelianos, Eva Palmer-Sikelianou – the Delphic Festivals), [1966-1967]. Athens: Papadema, 1998: 126-129. Print.

Prins, Yopie. "Greek Maenads, Victorian Spinsters." In *Victorian Sexual Dissidence*. Ed. Richard Dellamora. Chicago and London: University of Chicago Press, 1999. 43-81. Print.

_____. *Ladies' Greek. Translations of Tragedy*. Princeton, N.J.: Princeton University Press, forthcoming. Print.

_____. *Victorian Sappho*. Princeton, N.J.: Princeton University Press, 1999. Print.

Reynolds, Margaret. *The Sappho History*. New York: Palgrave Macmillan, 2003. Print.

Robinson, Jacqueline. *Modern Dance in France, an Adventure, 1920-1970*. Choreography and dance studies, v. 12. Amsterdam: Harwood Academic Publishers, 1997. Print.

Rodriguez, Suzanne. *Wild Heart: A Life: Natalie Clifford Barney and the Decadence of Literary Paris*. New York: HarperCollins, 2003. Print.

Sappho and Henry Thornton Wharton. *Sappho: Memoir, Text, Selected Renderings, and a Literal Translation*. London: J. Lane, 1895. Print.

Sikelianos, Angelos. *Delphikos Logos: (arche ton ariston)*. Athens, Estia, 1927. Print.

Sikelianos, Angelos, and Alma M. Reed. The Delphic Word: The Dedication. New York: H. Vinal, 1928. Print.

Snyder, Jane McIntosh. "Sappho in Attic Vase Painting." In *Naked Truths: Women, Sexuality, and Gender in Classical Art and Archaeology*. Ed. Ann Olga Koloski-Ostrow and Claire L. Lyons. New York: Routledge 2000. 108-119. Print.

"State School of Dance." http://en.ksot.gr/index.php?id=171. Web.

Stein, Gertrude, Edward Burns, and Carl Van Vechten. *The Letters of Gertrude Stein and Carl Van Vechten 1913-1935*. New York: Columbia University Press, 1986. Print.

Stratton, Clarence. "Greek Influence upon the Stage."

Art and Archaeology 3-4 (1916): 251-63. Print.

Swinburne, Algernon Charles. *Notes on Poems and Reviews*. London: John Camden Hotten, 1866. Print.

Sword, Helen. *Engendering Inspiration: Visionary Strategies in Rilke, Lawrence, and H.d.* Ann Arbor: University of Michigan Press, 1995. Print.

Sypher, Francis Jacques, "Swinburne and Wagner." *Victorian Poetry* (Vol. 9, No. 1/2, Spring - Summer, 1971): 165-183. JSTOR. Web.

Wickes, George. *The Amazon of Letters: The Life and Loves of Natalie Barney*. New York: Putnam, 1977. Print.

Winterer, Caroline. "Victorian Antigone: Classicism and Women's Education in America, 1840-1900." *American Quarterly* 53.1 (Mar., 2001): 88. JSTOR. Accessed: 10/08/2009. Web.

Van Steen, Gonda. "'The World's a Circular Stage': Aeschylean Tragedy through the Eyes of Eva Palmer-Sikelianou." *International Journal of the Classical Tradition* 8. 3 (Winter 2002): 375-93. Print.

Vicinus, Martha. *Intimate Friends: Women Who Loved Women, 1778-1928*. Chicago: University of Chicago Press, 2004. Print.

Vivien, Renée, Natalie Clifford Barney, Eva Palmer, and Jean-Paul Goujon. *Album Secret*. [Muizon, France]: Editions "A L'Ecart," 1984. Print.

Zanona, Joyce. "Swinburne's Sappho: The Muse as Sister-Goddess." *Victorian Poetry* 28.1 (Spring 1990): 39-50. Print.

Acknowledgments: I have received invaluable assistance from many individuals in preparing this paper. David Roessel guided the writing of the piece. Stavros Th. Anestidis, Director of Kentro Mikriasiatikon Spoudon (Center for Asia Minor Studies, henceforth

KMS) and Researcher Dr. Ioanna Petropoulou gave me access to Palmer's correspondence in the Octave Merlier archive in the KMS, which had been unavailable research until that time. Valentina Tselika and the staff of the Benaki Museum Historical Archives (henceforth BMHA) assisted my work in the Eva Sikelianos archives. Lia Papadaki made available her transcripts of correspondence between Palmer and Natalie Clifford Barney found in the Natalie Clifford Barney Archive of the Bibliothèque littéraire Jacques Doucet, which she edited and translated for Greek publication. I have maintained an ongoing dialogue with her and with Mary Hart, Eleni Sikelianos, Vassilis Lambropoulos, Mrs. Effie Spyropoulou, Eleni Dallas (niece of Konstantinos Psachos), Julian Anderson, and Gonda Van Steen on various aspects of Palmer's life and work. In particular, Yopie Prins has helped orient my research on Palmer as a practitioner of an artistic and scholarly approach to the Greeks representative of broader trends in the United States and Europe, while she, Liz Wingrove, and Peggy McCracken have patiently responded to drafts of this paper. I am deeply indebted to all these people, while I also recognize that my generous interlocutors bear no responsibility for weaknesses in my work.

Notes

1 Ioannis Gryparis (1870-1942) was a poet, translator, teacher, and in the 1930s, director of the National Theatre of Greece.
2 Porter discusses how "feeling" and "sounding classical" (43) are an "instance of [a] kind of inarticulate knowledge," pieces of socially conditioned experiences (40).
3 Van Steen (377) refers to several scathing reviews, reminding us that the Greek reception of the event was not all positive.
4 Pratsika (1899-1984) carried the "revivalist, nostalgic spirit" of the Delphic Festivals through a lifetime of dance (Hassiotis). Her work included the role as "high priestess" in the torch-lighting ceremony at Ancient Olympia in 1936 and decades of teaching dance in the National Theatre of Greece and the Greek Ministry of Culture's "State School of Dance," which she founded and directed. See the homepage of "State School of Dance" for a summary.
5 Palmer's correspondence is concentrated in the Natalie Clifford Barney Papers in La Bibliotheque Litteraire Jacques Doucet, Paris; Eva Sikelianou Papers in the Benaki Museum Historical Archives (BMHA); and Eva Sikelianou Papers in the Octave Merlier Archive in the Centre for Asia Minor Studies (KMS). Only a small selection of Palmer's letters to Barney in the Bibliotheque Doucet has been published, appearing in Papadaki's Greek translation (Palmer-Sikelianou and Papadaki). Wherever I quote passages from those letters, I am relying on Papadaki's transcripts in their original English or French, on which Papadaki based her Greek translations.
6 *New York Times* 26 Aug 1900; ProQuest Historical Newspapers The New York Times (1851-2) pg. 14. "Miss May Palmer" was Eva's sister; "Miss Alice Clifford Barney," was Natalie Clifford Barney's sister, better known as Laura.
7 According to Hains, "Radcliffe College brought out a series of "Homeric Pictures" in 1894 (28).
8 For Montrose Moses, critic of *The Theatre*, *The Trojan Wom-*

an revival performed in the stadium of the City College of New York in 1915 "looked like a picture," and this pictorial effect was exactly what the director Granville Barker wanted (quoted in Hartigan 16).

9 Yopie Prins coins the elegant term "Ladies' Greek" in her forthcoming book, *Ladies' Greek: Translations of Tragedy*, to refer to the turn women give to Greek tragedy following their entry into Greek studies in Victorian England and America. She has developed the very rich idea of a gendered late-Victiorian reception of the Greek tragedy, summarizing it with this phrase.

10 Gwinn was a Swinburne expert. She was at least the collaborator, if not the author, of an unpublished thesis of 1882 attributed to M. Carey Thomas on "Swinburne's Place in the History of English Poetry" (Horowitz 149-51). Her study of Swinburne's work continued all her life, "but she never published a word" (Horowitz 151).

11 According to Winterer (88), "As president of Bryn Mawr College, Thomas looked rather to Sappho to define the educated woman."

12 Palmer probably absorbed Sappho in H. T. Wharton's 1895 third edition of his *Sappho*, with its introductory "memoir" and simultaneous presentation of the Greek text and multiple English translations— just as H.D., another Bryn Mawr College student roughly of Palmer's era, "absorbed Wharton's Sappho (both Greek and English texts)" (Gregory 154). When Renée Vivien, Palmer's guest at Bryn Mawr in the fall of 1900, returned to France with a copy of Wharton, she owed that discovery not just to Barney, as DeJean (279) states, but to the learned Palmer. Goujon correctly argues that Palmer gave Vivien her first lessons in ancient Greek: "De Sapho, dont elle possédait l'oeuvre, Eva Palmer parla longuement à sa nouvelle amie [à qui elle] donna ses premières leçons de grec ancien" (142-43). A careful reading of Palmer and Barney's correspondence shows that Palmer had the upper hand in learning: she guided the more haphazardly-educated Barney by researching topics

and supplying her with Greek verses, names, and historical and mythological figures for her writing. Although Barney valued spontaneity and misunderstood or at least belittled Palmer's attention to learning, she welcomed Palmer's erudition when she needed help. Occasionally she even acknowledged her own ignorance and her debt to Palmer: "the only real learning comes from within, mine has I know, but then that only admirably accounts for my being so ignorant. Come back that I may form myself wise in all things through the one important wisdom: that of loving you" (Barney letter dated 6 October 1900 sent from Bryn Mawr to Palmer in New York City, KMS Dossier II).

13 *The New York Times* article situates the Bar Harbor tableau in 1900. Palmer's letters to Barney, with their references to Tarn and emergent feelings of erotic attachment expressed at about the same time in 1900, suggest that the three events—Palmer's Sappho tableau, Tarn's visit to Bar Harbor, and the beginning of Palmer's and Barneys six-year affair, happened in close sequence. Vivien, et al, *Album Secret* provides visual evidence of the company the three kept that summer. Barney's and Palmer's later correspondence fills out the picture by showing that for several years "their intimacy thrived on voyeurism and shared lovers in addition to the pleasure they found in one another. See for example Palmer-Sikelianou and Papadaki 113-15.

14 At this time, Palmer would not have had access to fifth-century BCE Attic red-figure vase paintings depicting Sappho with an instrument or listening to her competitor Alcaeus. See Snyder (108-119) for descriptions of four such vase paintings.

15 In the nineteenth-century "Sappho craze" (Ehnenn 18), many versions of Sappho were in circulation simultaneously, producing a popular figure of ambiguous meaning: the original lyric poet and "great poetess" (Prins 54); the teacher surrounded by her dedicated pupils; the spurned heterosexual lover whose unrequited love for Phaon sent her over the Leucadian cliff; the ancient courtesan; and the same-sex

lover. The numerous pictorial renditions of Sappho from that era cover this wide range. A sampling includes Angelica Kauffmann's "Sappho Inspired by Love," 1775; Johann Heinrich von Dannecker's statue of Sappho, c. 1800; Antoine-Jean Gros's "Sappho," 1801; Baron Gros's "Sapo," 1801; Jacques Louis David's "Sappho and Phaon," 1809; Charles Nicolas Rafael Lafond's "Sappho Sings for Homer," 1824; Anne-Louis Girodet Trioson, "Sapho Dédaigne les occupations de son sexe," 1827; Honore Daumier's "Death of Sappho," 1842; Soma Orlai Petrich's "Sappho," 1855; Gustav Moreau's "Sappho Leaping from the Leucadian Cliff," 1864 and "The Death of Sappho," 1876; Simeon Solomon's "Sappho and Erinna in a Garden at Mytilene," 1864, and "Erinna Taken from Sappho" 1865; Charles Gleyre's "Le coucher de Sappho," 1867; Charles-August Mengin's "Sappho," 1874; Sir Lawrence Alma Tadema's "Sappho and Alcaeus," 1881; and Gustave Klimt's "Sappho" 1888-90—to name just a few. For an analysis of Tadema's painting and the play of other contemporary images, see Goldhill. Reynolds discusses many of these paintings in her chapter, "Picturing Sappho." She argues that the effect of modern representations of Sappho is to "invite the viewer to place himself or herself alongside.... We feel with, in, or through [Sappho], and thus are permitted a glimpse of the *jouissance* that moves beyond the law, even when the apparent facts of the story told about Sappho seem to maim or confine here" (84).

16 See, for example, Palmer-Sikelianou and Papadaki, Figure 11: "Eva with loose hair" (photo 106 in the Eva Sikelianos Papers, BMHA). The photograph eerily recalls Mengin's obscure painting of "Sappho," which Palmer probably did not know.

17 Barney used the word "inverse" to describe her attraction to women in a letter to Palmer dated 15 February 1902 sent from Paris to New York (KMS Dossier II).

18 May Palmer letter dated 10 August 1904; Catherine Abbé letter dated 18 August 1904; and Courtlandt Palmer letter dated 27 August 1904, all to Palmer at Thonon-les-Bains ho-

tels in Haute-Savoie, France (KMS Dossier I).

19 In 1902 Palmer wrote that Courtlandt's harsh words to her in Bar Harbor two years earlier had damaged their close relationship (Palmer-Sikelianou and Papadaki 134).

20 Courtlandt was equally disapproving of Angelos Sikelianos and of Palmer's decision to stay in Greece. When she returned to the U.S. impoverished, he would not give her the money she needed to return to Greece, as she desired. Paradoxically it was the money he left her after his death in 1951 that allowed her to fulfill her wish.

21 Palmer wrote to Barney about her plan in a letter postmarked 7 March 1902 (Palmer-Sikelianou and Papadaki 134).

22 Palmer once performed in pianist Christine Baker's salon, where, as Palmer informed Barney, her former violin teacher Madame Ludwig Breitner "said with apparent sincerity that my work was beautiful, judged as an artist and not as an amateur, *que j'avais ce quelquechose [à] moi qu'il faut [à] l'artiste, qu'elle entendait chacune de mes paroles, qu'elle aimait enfin la qualit, de ma voix*" ("that I have what it takes to be an artist, that I hear each phrase, and in the end she liked the quality of my voice") (Palmer-Sikelianou and Papadaki 109). Palmer also reported that Baker offered to collaborate with her (Palmer-Sikelianou and Papadaki 149).

23 Barney letter to Palmer, Paris, 1 March 1901 (KMS Dossier II).

24 Barney letter to Palmer, Paris, 1 March 1901 (KMS Dossier II). Barney used a similar line to open her 1906 theatrical, *Equivoque*: "Your life is your most beautiful poem you are your own immortal masterpiece" (quoted in Vicinus 481).

25 This is my translation of the original French: "*J'aurais voulu que tu fus avec moi hier afin de voir combien grand et beau peut-être le "pouvoir informe des masses,...des petits pignes" que tu détestes.... L'oratorio était magnifiquement fait et joliment bien apprecié par tous ce peuple, et [à] la fin quand c' était fini tout ce monde se levait, et tout ça chantait ensemble le "Halluliyah," grand choeur de je ne sais qui, Haendel je crois. Je t'as-*

sure que c'était grandiose d'entendre toutes ces personnes sur la scène, dans la salle, et l'orchestre et l'orgue chanter comme cela ensemble, et bien chanter encore. Celà m'a donné, une émotion que j'aurais voulu que tu partages."

26 According to Rodriguez, Barney developed a love for Wagner's work from the time of her European tour in 1894 (68).

27 *The New York Times* announced "the resolution of Miss Eva Palmer to go on the stage" on 5 April 1903 in its "Current Club Topics." In July 1903 Mrs. Patrick Campbell invited Palmer "to join her company" (Palmer-Sikelianos 43), an invitation Palmer refused because she did not wish to meet Campbell's condition of abandoning "la liberté des jeunes fille Americain" (Palmer letter to Barney, undated, KMS Dossier I). We can date Campbell's ultimatum to Palmer rather precisely through an unpublished letter that appears to be Barney's generous response: "I have no right to stand in the way, now that you have a chance of doing something serious… You, and Mrs. Campbell—I wish you might…. Do come, je t'attends, apporte des roles, accept Mrs. Patrick's offer, and we will discuss details when I see you" (Barney letter to Palmer postmarked 21 July 2003 and sent to 27 Albany Street, Regents Park, London, Angleterre, KMS Dossier II). On 30 December 1905, *Life* reviewed Palmer's performance of "Romeo to Miss Harlan Child's Juliet in an exquisite rendering of several scenes" as performed in A. S. Barney's studio on 28 December. The *Life* article also announced that "Palmer has been asked by Mme Sarah Bernhardt to act with her in Maeterlinck's "Pelleas and Melisande" (Clipping from "Henry Romeike Cutting Service," KMS Dossier II). The performance with Bernhardt never took place.

28 A letter from Palmer's mother, Catherine Abbé, sent from New York to Neuilly, offers evidence that Nietzsche was occupying Palmer's thinking before she came to Greece. Here Abbé states her intention to read Nietzsche in order to "understand you, if I can, at least know your point of view and to ponder over it" (KMS Dossier II). In *Upward Panic*, Palm-

er writes of choosing to reread Nietzsche's *Birth of Tragedy* while convalescing from a prolonged siege of double of pneumonia in 1938, when her doctor allowed her to read just one book that she knew "rather well...just to remember passages that I like" (Palmer-Sikelianos 170).

29 Swinburne's Wagnerian affinities have been the subject of much scholarly elaboration since Sypher published "Swinburne and Wagner" in 1971. McGann's recent essay shows just how systematically Swinburne developed Wagner's ideas on the connections between music and poetry from the point of view of the poet. He traces Swinburne's interest in Wagner from the time Swinburne "received from Baudelaire a gift of *Richard Wagner et Tannhäuser à Paris*" (McGann 611) in 1863 through his writing of "Atalanta" (1865) and the Sapphic "Anactoria," (1866), in which "the structure of movements and modulations...expend themselves through perpetual [Wagnerian] transformation" (630), to his three memorial "tributes to Wagner and his music" ("The Death of Richard Wagner," "Lohengrin," and "Tristan und Isolde") (622). McGann argues that Swinburnean "harmony," the "gravitational center ... that pervades his work" (620), is in fact a working out of a Wagnerian-inspired notion that poetry must "re-present our phenomenal world in a musical form so that the phenomena will be taken for what they are: unique sets of appearances whose very transient passages expose and define the dynamic event that realizes and sustains them" (631).

30 The character of Swinburne's identification with Sappho has been another subject of Swinburne studies since Zonana argued that Swinburne's adoption of Sappho as Muse recovers a suppressed "female creativity and female sexuality" (48).

31 I am not able to confirm that the production of *Atalanta* rehearsed at Bar Harbor reached the stage. Palmer mentions efforts to take her *Atalanta* to "Mrs. Gardner's" theatre (that is to say, the Isabella Stewart Gardner Museum) in Boston in two letters to Barney (Palmer-Sikelianou and Papadaki

235; KMS Dossier II). In a third, dated September 23, 1905, she confesses, "I am a little puffed up by my success this summer" (KMS Dossier I). I have not found independent evidence of a Boston production.

32 "What's Doing in Society" in *The New York Times* reported that "Dr. Robert Abbé, Mrs. Abbé, and the latter's children, Miss Eva Palmer and Cortlandt (sic) Palmer, have arrived at their Bar Harbor cottage, Brookend" (*The New York Times* 22 July 1905: 7. ProQuest Historical Newspaper The New York Times, 1857-Current file).

33 "Archbold Cottage" burned down in Bar Harbor's great fire of 21 October 1927, but surviving pictures (Bryan, et al. 211) confirm this description.

34 Undated letter from Palmer to "Natalie my beloved," KMS Dossier I.

35 In the 1889 Smith College *Electra* (the first revival of a Greek play at a women's college) (Pluggé 14) "[t]he members of the chorus…as a whole seem to have reacted in a more or less formalized manner to the dramatic situations presented on the stage…The movements of the dance were described as slow and solemn, consisting chiefly of body swaying, without much change in position. Gesture and facial expression constitute the important elements of this dance" (97-98).

36 Konstantinos Psachos (1866-1949), Professor and Director of the School of Byzantine Chant in the Athens Conservatory from 1906 to 1919, was a scholar and practitioner of Eastern Orthodox church music dedicated to "preserv[ing] traditional forms of Byzantine psalmody" and "defending the integrity of the received tradition of chanting in the face of Westernization" (Lingas 351).

37 Palmer's correspondence with her stepfather, Dr. Robert Abbé, shows that she was living on a fixed monthly income from her father's family trust, and that she frequently could not make ends meet.

38 On 30 December 1905, *Life* reviewed Palmer's performance of "Romeo to Miss Harlan Child's Juliet in an exqui-

site rendering of several scenes" in A. S. Barney's studio on 28 December, and announced that "Palmer has been asked by Mme Sarah Bernhardt to act with her in Maeterlinck's "Pelleas and Melisande" (Clipping from "Henry Romeike Cutting Service" in KMS Dossier II).

39 Lounsbery, a friend of Palmer, encouraged her to anticipate Bernhardt's invitation. According to Palmer, Lounsbery told her that "Sarah had asked her about me...She said she had told her by all means to have me and had asked for me in the role of Delilah ... in case [the theater manager and actor Edouard] de Max really does the play. I...shall try to get Sarah to hear me again and then I hope she will judge me impartially" (Letter Palmer to Barney, October 12, 1905, KMS Dossier I). Bernhardt performed, without Palmer, in Alexander Dumas's *La Dame aux Camélias* at the Lyric Theatre in New York on Dec. 12, 1905 (Branstley 56).

40 Letter Palmer to Barney, undated (KMS Dossier II).

41 Letter Barney to Palmer, "Tuesday" (KMS Dossier II). Although undated, Barney's reference to Palmer's plans to act with Sarah Bernhardt in North America date the letter in the fall of 1905.

42 John Anton gives April 1905 as the date of the meeting (Palmer-Sikelianos 46). But Palmer remembers that Duncan was nursing Menalkas at the time of their meeting, and Menalkas was born late in 1905. Furthermore, the May-day general strike to which Palmer refers took place in 1906. So the correct date of their meeting is April 1906.

43 I discuss those experiments in "Eva Palmer's Distinctive Greek Journey" (171-78).

44 Palmer's autobiography gives a very different timeline. She locates the moment she first heard Sikelianos speak about the Delphic Idea temporally during their first meeting in August 1906 (Palmer-Sikelianos 63). She says that Sikelianos met her and then, the very next morning, held forth on his Delphic Idea, in which he placed drama as a "bridge" or "causeway" to "spiritual understanding" through the overpowering emotions it produces by way of its unity of

poetry, music, dancing, acting, architecture, painting, and sculpture (65-66). I have not found independent evidence that Sikelianos developed his Delphic Idea before 1920 or aligned it with the performance of theatre as a means to spiritual revival before George Cram Cook inaugurated his "Delphic Players" in the summer of 1923.

45 Glaspell only mentions the visit to Sykia, without naming Angelos or Eva Palmer Sikelianos, to explain how she acquired Theodora, an Asia Minor refugee in the Sikelianos household who "was presented to us as a possible servant" (37). Palmer mentions George Cram Cook as the lost translator of Angelos's poetry (Palmer-Sikelianos 71). Each woman's silence about the other and about the theatre interests that joined them is resounding.

46 Interest in "music composed in imitation of ancient Greek modal scales" became a feature of several American college productions of Greek drama from 1907-1919, beginning the 1907 revival of *Iphigenia a Taurus* at the University of Iowa (where Cook taught from 1895 to 1899), for which original "Greek" modal music was composed (Pluggé 92).

Myth, Mystique, Nietzsche, and the "Cultic Milieu" of the Delphic Festivals, 1927 and 1930

Gonda Van Steen

Nietzsche, "the archetypal cultural modernist" in the words of Roger Griffin (298), had written powerfully about the Apollonian and the Dionysian constituents of ancient Greek drama, which together formed the unifying "community of tragedy."[1] The Sikelianoi[2] applied those constituents not only to their Aeschylean productions but also to the Delphic Festivals as a whole. In the Nietzschean vision, Apollo and Dionysus had shared the site of Delphi in a harmonious arrangement that symbolized the balanced marriage of *logos* and sacred *mania*. The couple therefore arranged for actors to reenact the myth of Apollo's victory over the female serpent Python (as described in the *Homeric Hymn to Apollo*, 356-374), to show the fusion of opposites, such as the Olympian and the chthonic, the celestial and the terrestrial, the male and the female element (Wiles, *Greek Theatre Performance* 183-184). For the Sikelianoi, the resulting unity of the Apollonian and the Dionysian had fostered the spread of knowledge in antiquity through the channels of oracles, a panhellenic religion, and shared institutions, which had transcended the spiritual as well as the territorial boundaries of the classical *poleis* or city-states. In ancient Delphi, the principles of athletic, political, and ideological unification and of harmony between body and mind had expressed themselves in the Pythian Games and in the protection offered by the Amphictyonic League. This alliance guarded and administered Delphi and represented a collective effort of several city-states. In the conviction of the Sikelianoi, the post-World War I era was precisely the time to give new life to those old but very valuable ideals of unity and political dialogue.[3]

Inspired by Nietzsche, Eva's performances were truly pioneering and steered away from the trappings of the commercial star system. This focus on the collective instead of on the individual was in line with what theater scholar David Wiles has termed the "anti-individualist philosophy of the 1920s" ("Use of Masks" 251). He characterized this decade as a "hugely creative period, when radical formal experiments were possible" and "[v]isual artists, dancers, and theatre practitioners were keen to converge" and to rediscover Greek drama, which they deemed "primitive and ritualistic" ("Use of Masks" 262). Such aspects that directly relate to political theater became all the more relevant throughout the 1930s and 1940s, and they may fruitfully be explored through the study of fascist theater and politics, as well as their kinship with the broader cultural context of modernism.

I place the Sikelianoi's work at the Delphic Festivals squarely within the struggle that accompanied Greek society's transformation during the interwar decades and its transition into 1930s modernism. Fissures and fault lines immediately show in the critical reception of the Delphic revival productions and their makers.[4] Many enthusiasts subscribed to the ideal of the sacred high art of ancient drama that had been rediscovered through the male genius of Angelos Sikelianos, whereby they relegated Eva's role to a metaphorical footnote. At both festivals, however, Eva took care of most production aspects—a daunting task to which she took a holistic approach, to effectively "author" a new theatrical experience.[5] Some reporters and critics perceived a threat in Eva, the wealthy aristocrat and female foreigner, who seemed to be leading the way in the search for authentic Greekness, ancient through modern. Others have praised Eva for bringing ancient drama to a theatrical space that has rarely seen revival productions. Many critics and journalists regarded the stagings more as a cultural and political event than as a theatrical achievement, and they saw a way for Greece to become a respected player among the Western nations. They failed to recognize the couple's Delphic Vision and Nietzschean quest for an originary unity and knowledge, identified—and romanticized—as guiding principles of the interwar era.[6]

One of the most vocal critics of the first Delphic Festival was the author who signed with the initial "S." to a two-part article in the communist newspaper *Rizospastis* of mid-May 1927 (also Sideris 356-357). This article, "Social Critique of the Delphic Festivals," appeared on 15 and 16 May, or within mere days of the event. The reporter for the *Rizospastis* hardly discusses the actual stage performances or any other of the activities held at Delphi, but he (she?) offers a possible reaction to the political and cultural discourse of the contemporary Right. The writer supported the Marxist tenet that art should express its social context and should not be perceived or practiced in purely aesthetic terms. In the opinion of the vocal Left, the bourgeoisie's manipulation of art production was yet another act of the superstructure's exploitation of the lower class. The Delphic Festival was therefore a case in point to prove the "mystification" in which the Greek bourgeoisie and its representative Sikelianos had engaged. But the festival was also the bourgeoisie's act of admitting to its debilitating mode of "gloomy pessimism" (15 May 1927): the events constituted the waning elite's nostalgic and failed attempt at reviving a past culture of great achievement, that of Greek antiquity. Sikelianos was, according to the author, prone to obscurantism and mystification, and he "typifie[d] … all the spiritual manifestations of the dominant capitalist establishment of the entire world, but especially of the Greek bourgeois class" (15 May 1927). The elite upheld such retrospective efforts because it lacked creative powers of its own. Its ultimate aim was to artificially extend its own declining life, or to resuscitate itself, by exploiting art. The author's closing paragraphs bring his ambition of history-writing, his perspective on widespread cultural pessimism, and his Marxist justification together:

> The Greek capitalist system finds itself today in this situation: … incapable … of developing an original intellectual culture.
> This weakness then engenders the nostalgia for antiquity and causes the drive toward idealist reenactments of ancient Greece. The utopia, in its Delphic guise or in whichever other form, functions as a balm of consolation for the ruling class. Given that the real world is so disappointing, the world of the illusions constitutes the only way out. (16 May 1927)

Theater of the Right: "the drive toward idealist reenactments"

Much of what S. states strikes us as dated and a tad

paranoid. Also, his underlying assumption seems to be that cultural innovation and spontaneity are the specific provinces of the Left. But instead of disregarding his and others' comments, could we see them as a defense against contemporary trends in conservative dramaturgy or theater in the hands of the Right? Evidently, Greek Marxist writers and critics of the 1920s and 1930s saw art either undermine the ruling capitalist order, when art became a political tool in their own hands, or they saw it bolster the dominant ideology, when the latter made art "subservient" or severed it from its societal context. But when the dominant class came to overlap with a fascist ruling class, as in Italy and Germany, the use of art in the right-wing bourgeois ideology grew far more complex. The question of whether the Sikelianoi subscribed to the growing fascist-bourgeois movement of the 1920s and 1930s is an uncomfortable one, but it still needs to be asked. What would S. have looked for in the couple's theory and practice to convince himself that this international movement drove their Delphic initiative, despite their proclaimed interest in the Greek peasant population and its arts and crafts? Even more important, what would he have found that remains hard to contest? In the late 1920s and early 1930s, many expressions and markers of the Delphic Festivals (such as the public swearing of oaths) may have been received as relevant and contemporary, or even as ideological common ground, but they could be interpreted in a negative light by today's students of that formative and formidable era.

 For S., Sikelianos could not be original: the self-styled visionary was merely creating a dramatic illusion to bolster a social and political illusion. His *Prometheus* performances were mere "idealist reenactments" (S., *Rizospastis*, 16 May 1927), which emerged in many other contemporary forms as well. Was the author thinking of some of the historicizing stage events and the "drive toward ... reenactments" of ancient Rome that Mussolini was mounting? Did he claim that Sikelianos's "histrionics" took after the theatrical and metatheatrical mechanisms of the fascist regimes? At the time of the first Delphic Festival, Mussolini, who identified with Julius Caesar, was busily appropriating imperial Rome.[7] Mussolini took a propagandistic interest also in the productions of classical Greek tragedy staged at the ancient theater of Syracuse in Sicily. After seeing the 1924 open-air performances there, he was so enthused that he prepared to found the National Institute for Ancient Drama (Sideris 356; Garland 170; Van Steen, "Aeschylean Tragedy" 387-388). Some of those who attended the first Delphic Festival and watched the revival tragedy *Prometheus*, had their eyes on fascist Italy's "achievements." Sideris noted that, when the 1927 athletic games were finished, a prominent Greek archaeologist by the name of Alexandros Filadelfeus walked down into the ancient stadium, eulogized the Sikelianoi, and urged that the Delphic Festivals become a national Greek institution: he invoked the exemplum of Mussolini (Sideris 356).

In the 1930s, Nazi Germany notoriously appropriated classical Greek tragedy and culture at large. Among many other mass events, Hitler staged the 1936 Berlin Olympics and exploited the propaganda potential of the modern Games to the full, in his foreign and interior policies alike, to show off and vindicate the fascist ideology. The tell-tale "ancient-style" torch relay was invented for the occasion, to give historical—Greek—depth to the values of the Nazi regime. In the same year, director Lothar Müttel staged a production of Aeschylus's *Oresteia*, which he transformed into an Aryan manifesto, "symbolic of the eventual victory of the Aryan races over the *Untermenschen*" (Garland 171). This propagandistic Nazi staging of the famous trilogy uncritically supported law and order, depicted mankind's progression from darkness to light, and affirmed the eventual triumph of the Aryan race, which was symbolized by the (male) Olympian dynasty.[8] The theater historian Erika Fischer-Lichte agreed that, in the 1930s, the Nazis used and abused concepts of the peoples' theater of Max Reinhardt, whose early twentieth-century mass productions left a deep impact on Greek theater directors and actors as well. Even though the origins of mass events themselves may well lie much further in the past, Fischer-Lichte summed up the German connection: "The idea of theatre as a festival, or peoples' theatre [or Theater of the Five Thousand] to which Reinhardt had given shape and expression through two productions [i.e., Sophocles's *Oedipus the King* and Aeschylus's *Oresteia*] was devalued and perverted into an instrument of Nazi propaganda" ("Invocation of the Dead" 258).[9] She acknowledged also the formative influence of the Wagnerian festival on Baron Pierre de Coubertin, who championed the modern Olympic movement (*Theatre, Sacrifice, Ritual* 74-75). Theater and nationalistic sports, or ritualized performance and political propaganda met closely in the 1936 Olympics but also in Greek sporting events and other mass festivals of the late 1930s.

Events of the late 1920s through mid-1930s made it manifest that mass sport and spectacle were becoming the wave of the future and that the totalitarian politicians were the first to take advantage of a mass stage for themselves and their politics.[10] Competitive sporting spectacles (or disguised exercises in disciplinary and military training) and dramas-made-national were typically designed to bolster the power of regimes, parties, or up-and-coming individuals. Open-air events, from mass rallies to historical reenactments, were used and manipulated also by Ioannis Metaxas, the Greek dictator of the late 1930s and a bounteous admirer of fascist-style public discipline. Greece had sent a delegation of athletes to the 1936 Olympics in Berlin and, as the Games were going on from 1 through 16 August, Metaxas formally established his "Regime of the Fourth of August 1936." All international media attention, however, had turned to Olympia, the Greek point of departure of the torch run. The torch-lighting ceremony that kicked off the relay took place on 20 July 1936 in the ancient stadium of the site of Olympia (Mandell 129-133). In other words, Metaxas consolidated his hold on domestic Greek power in the days leading up to the opening ceremonies of the Berlin Olympics and as the Nazis promised more German funds to advance excavations at the ancient site of Olympia.[11] Moreover, he celebrated the fortieth anniversary of the revival of the Olympic Games in the ("old") Olympic Stadium at Athens with a theatrical display of scenes of Hellenic glory through the ages (Yalouri 39-40).

The dictator thereby left conventions in place for staging such Greek "historical" reenactments in narrativized and mythified forms. As if the rediscovered ancient Greek aura or spectacular Olympic auspices of his rule were not (ominous) enough, Metaxas proclaimed his foundation of the "Third Hellenic Civilization," modeled after Hitler's Third German *Reich*. Like Mussolini and the National Socialists in Germany, Metaxas, too, experimented with new spaces (stadiums and other vast arenas) and with contemporary techniques or quasi-fascist trappings to represent and engage the masses: he orchestrated mass "choruses" marching, speaking, and chanting in unison, and exploited loudspeaker and radio broadcasts. Metaxas's enthusiasm for and exhilaration at the co-optive totality of mass public stagings, especially marked on celebratory occasions and national anniversaries, rings through many of his diaries, published in no less than eight volumes. See, for instance, his entry on 25 March 1938:

> What a dream that was yesterday and today!— Yesterday at the Pedion tou Areos with the National Youth. My work! ... Ceremony. Enthusiasm. Apotheosis. The army's parade splendid. In the afternoon, a parade of ... the National Youth ... – The phalanxes of EON had no end to them! All in uniform! About 12 to 14 thousand! The impression on the people was stunning! (299)[12]

Metaxas craftily transformed theatrical spectacle into a mass culture and hegemonic apparatus. Even though his concerted efforts to develop a power base through a strong Greek youth movement eventually failed, Metaxas sponsored youth theater companies to produce patriotic and moralizing plays, preferably on national holidays and the regime's anniversaries (Vasileiou 59-61). Most of the plays they staged were— well-publicized—versions of a rather limited repertoire of modern Greek works that proffered a 1930s "canon," as it were, of school and amateur plays: typically, the rather mediocre playwrights embraced themes of Greek continuity and some specialized in showing key scenes of Greek history through the ages.[13]

While it may be hazardous to draw inferences from the mass events that characterized primarily the 1930s, it remains true that mass propaganda and the roots of mass spectacle originated in the 1920s and, with Mussolini, well before the first Delphic Festival took place. Not surprisingly, therefore, some participants in the 1927 festival not only recognized but also invoked the potential of institutionalized revival tragedy modeled after Italian-fascist mass spectacle. Did the Sikelianoi inspire, promote, or resent this kind of thinking? Were they themselves swayed by the resonance of the grand open-air productions staged at Syracuse? Did they encourage or discourage this "drive toward ... reenactments"? (S., *Rizospastis*, 16 May 1927). Also, is a connection between the Delphic Festivals and the Aryan ideology of German Nazism premature or too far-fetched? Did Sikelianos give his ideological opponents any ammunition of the kind that radicalized the social critique of the *Rizospastis*? Some of these questions may be answered with a disturbing "yes." The link between the Delphic Idea and Aryanism can also be confirmed. But let us break down these difficult questions and dark answers into smaller parts and pieces of evidence.

Modern scholars have generously bestowed idealism and pacifism on the Sikelianos couple. In her writings, Eva made explicit claims to such idealism, as when she described the slow progress toward Angelos's wish of founding the Delphic University:

> We had hoped to bring from many countries, – and by that time [1930] we knew better who they were, "non-attached," the men-of-good-will, the "Overseers", the *Epoptai*, to form Summer Schools every year (connected with local Greek Games and exhibitions, and

with a Festival every three years) which, little by little, would have formed a permanent Nucleus, a first bulwark against dogmatism and fanaticism all over the world. (*Upward Panic* 136)

Eva made an attempt at determining the role of the military, but did not leave her definition unchanged (see below): "The army is dedicated to the propagation of fear and distrust, to constant practice in the efficacy of destruction" (*Upward Panic* 137). Before long, however, the Sikelianoi embraced the army crowd as a generative force, open to a more profound spiritual intellectualism and also to the more emotional, modernist longing to return to the primordial origins and truths, to nature, and to the body.

David Wiles invoked the Sikelianoi's dismay at various worldwide setbacks, such as the First World War and the false start of the League of Nations, the rise of Italian fascism, and the plight of the Greek refugees from Asia Minor after the Great Catastrophe (*Greek Theatre Performance* 183). Others have seen the couple's efforts inspired by the struggle against capitalism itself, the aggressive commercialization, and industrialization that alienated the masses. But what did contemporaries see and read that has fallen through the cracks of theater history-writing? Is there enough to worry S. and us? Did the Sikelianoi leave their fellow-Greeks convinced that they were not interested in developing theater as a political art, as Mussolini and later Hitler were doing when they created political ritual and involved the masses as actors? Do the Delphic productions constitute a variant of the fascist-style "aestheticization of politics"– in the definition and proposed "politics of art" of Walter Benjamin, the "Frankfurt School," and the contributors to the 1930s mass culture debate (Benjamin 243)? Was S. one of the few who was aware—and alarmed—early on that festivals like the Delphic Festivals could easily be transformed into the choreographed, proto-fascist mass spectacles, which became tools in the hands of the political Right?

Dangerous Nietzsche—Dark Sikelianos?

The cult of creative figures such as Nietzsche, Wagner, Henri Bergson, or the poet-"mystic" Gabriele D'Annunzio became a modernist phenomenon that resulted in products such as Leopold von Schroeder's book, *The Fulfillment of the Aryan Mystery at Bayreuth* (1911). Von Schroeder was among those for whom the act of attending Wagner's operas, key examples of Germanophile Romanticism, at the Bayreuth Festival was an "initiatic experience" induced by the "direct contact with the numinous, transcendental power of myth summoned up through the 'total work of art' [a *Gesamtkunstwerk* characterized by 'eurhythmy']" (Griffin 136, 137 [both quotations]). Griffin characterizes the "spread of Nietzscheanism" somewhat ironically as "just one index of the transformation of the intellectual and artistic climate of turn-of-the-century Europe into a powerful incubator for what Colin Campbell has called the 'cultic milieu,' where groups of like-minded intellectuals collaborated in promoting ideas of change with a fervour that caused their main sources of ideas to be treated as revered prophets" (136). Griffin continues:

> The extreme syncretism that is a feature of such milieux is symptomatic of the modernist ideological process of ludic recombination at work typical of revitalization movements ... Fin-de-siècle Europe hosted countless cells and currents of palingenetic ideo-

> logical activity symptomatic of the West's deepening nomic crisis. Collectively they formed a diffuse counter-cultural environment where personality cults and radical ideas of imminent historical transformations could prosper outside the political process. (136)[14]

Nietzsche has generously been credited as one of the formative philosophical influences on the Sikelianoi, for "elevating" and "purifying" their "homecoming" to Greece's mythic origins. With the occasional Wagnerian swerve, the couple assigned to tragic theater the role of putting modern Greece (back) in touch with the reawakening of myth, and thus to create and feed the need for a revival of a national sense of drama. But did Nietzsche also leave the traces of his political and racial ideology? Sikelianos published a series of seven long-forgotten articles in the newspaper *To Eleftheron Vima* (later known as simply *To Vima*) of December 1927 (reprinted ed. Savvidis 67-118). The critic Alkis Thrilos singled out this series for its "dense cloudiness" ("Mute Pythia" 264) and mentioned its topic almost in passing: according to Sikelianos, mankind, through the achievements of the superior Aryan race, has conquered several "eternal truths." These—unexplained—eternal truths were known in Greek antiquity but have since languished in oblivion. The Delphic initiative, Sikelianos claims, can and must make these truths manifest again. Moreover, these truths stand opposed to the inferior values of the Semitic race (summarized by Thrilos, "Mute Pythia" 264). Sikelianos unabashedly connects the Delphic Idea with all the superior qualities (creativity, courage, altruism, wisdom, intellectual acumen, moral discipline, and so on) derived from the "logic" of Aryanism—and does so at length and on numerous occasions (72, 88-91, 102,

108). He does not shy away from a few blatantly racist and anti-Semitic statements, either, as he welcomes the rise of the Aryan ideology and the expansion of one of its "corner stones": the Delphic Effort (89-90, 102 [quotation]).[15] For those seeking to establish racial links between the valiant Aryans and the ancient Greeks, Hitler and some of his state-sponsored scholars provided plentiful "evidence" that the Aryan or Nordic master race had achieved its full potential only when it reached and founded the ancient Greek world.[16]

Nietzsche left his most formative influence, perhaps, on the choreography of Eva, who consumed his *The Birth of Tragedy*.[17] In fact, Eva may well be called the person most keen on applying Nietzsche's ideas in *The Birth of Tragedy* to the actual execution of modern tragic performances. For Nietzsche, Greek tragedy had emerged out of the creative force of music–an idea he may have taken from Wagner's music theater and theater as a communal, ritualistic festival (Fischer-Lichte, *Theatre, Sacrifice, Ritual* 46-47). Nietzsche rejected language-based theater and argued that the tragic chorus, the embodiment of the primeval Dionysian principle, should be restored to its full force to convey collective, true emotion (Wiles, *Greek Theatre Performance* 184). Gathered in the circular ancient theater, thousands of people at once could become both recipients and channels of this emotion, which would make them one in spirit, according to Nietzsche's concepts of Oneness, or primordial unity (*"das Ur-Eine"*) (Palmer-Sikelianou, *Upward Panic* 222-223, 225). With Nietzsche, Eva found "drama poised between an awareness of chaos and a will to form, between process and structure" (in the words of Vassilis Lambropoulos 81).

Eva's work with the chorus was also imbued, however, by a strained, Nietzschean emphasis on the aesthetics of group movement. She stressed circular and centripetal movements that had to draw the public into the "sacred circle" of the ancient theater at Delphi. On a semi-mystical plan, the Delphic orchestra was, for Eva, part of the ur-form of the dynamic circle that transfers energy and inspiration to its spectators-turned-participants. Admirers of Nietzsche considered the Greek open-air theater to be the ideal, ritual place for all social classes to gather and experience the Dionysiac ecstasy of classical tragedy and to commune with the universal truths (Wiles, "Use of Masks" 262). Eva was seeking theatrical solutions, among others, to the aesthetic and social challenges posed by the masses on stage and in the audience. To later observers and historians, however, Eva's chorus might reflect some of the characteristics of the political culture of the 1930s and, in particular, of the "mass ornament" – to use the famous term minted by Siegfried Kracauer. Author of the famous essay "The Mass Ornament," Kracauer was a cultural historian, critic, and sociologist who fled Germany when the Nazis came to power. He recognized the political force of bodies of gymnasts or actors working in unison to represent the unity of the national community. Thus the stage-management of the masses as represented by a well-trained chorus could hold the promise of a new order and of society's regeneration in body and mind. Sikelianos himself was fascinated by the archetype of the young athletic Greek male, embodied in the ancient ephebe (Papadaki). He had scores of young men participate in the Pythian Games, the athletic component of the Delphic Festivals, which largely emphasized, however, military feats and manly prowess. Many of these young men were Greek army recruits, accustomed to physical training in true military fashion. This arrangement enforced the idea of army service as a performance.

Pacifism with the Assistance of the Greek Army: "love at first sight"

Despite their proclaimed antimilitarism and pacifism, the Sikelianoi accepted the Greek army's help on numerous occasions. Any outside observer who noticed the recruits, the army trucks, the tents, and all the other equipment might have come away with the impression that the Greek army and therefore the state played a very active role in the making of the Delphic Festivals. Eva felt that she was being compromised by the army's generous and consistent support, and she reflected on some such occasions in her autobiography. She recounted how Yiorgos Kontoleon, a gifted architect and friend, selected thirty men to perform the Pyrrhic dance at the first Delphic Festival: they had to practice their steps while wearing heavy, hand-made, ancient-style armor. When these men proved to be unreliable, Eva took the advice to approach the commander of the First Army Corps in Athens. To her surprise, the army embraced her initiatives and was more than willing to help. The commander was "immediate in his response," and needed "[n]o explanations, no persuasions" (*Upward Panic* 111). The Greek army's no-holds participation realized the national potential of the first Delphic Festival. The commitment of the armed forces was reaffirmed at the time of the second festival (Palmer-Sikelianou, *Upward Panic* 112, 133).[18] Eva went ahead, accepted the military's assistance, and disregarded the philosophical dilemma posed by her extensive use of its exceptional resources. The Greek army did not let go of the legacy of the Delphic Festivals even when, after 1930, many others did. Again, Eva reminisced:

> Life was peaceful. One day a knock at the garden gate: it was an officer who had been sent down from Thrace, twenty-five hours journey, by General Vlachos, Commander-in-Chief of the Greek army on the borders of Thrace and Macedonia. Would we come up to Thrace? Would we lend all the equipment of the Delphic Stadium? And would Angelos speak to the officers of the border forces of Greece? The army wished to institute games in our honour.
>
> Again the army! And, as before, with complete spontaneity... . What, for them was this unpredictable, irrelevant attraction of an impetus which seemed, on the surface, contradictory to their very reason for living? Delphi is engaged in an effort to make peoples see each other, cross national borders, with love in their eyes.... Nevertheless, from the very beginning, the army was the only organized unit in Greece which responded with lightning rapidity to the Delphic Idea. (*Upward Panic* 137-138)

Did Eva remain blissfully ignorant of the Greek army's right-wing nationalist mission? She continued to sublimate its interest, involvement, and impact:

> They [Greek military men] instantly recognized the Delphic Effort as being profoundly Greek.... It was as if they had found their own (*Upward Panic* 139).
>
> It was as if it [the Delphic Idea] were already part of their [Greek military men] inner consciousness, it was like love at first sight... . This action [by the Greek army] was so spontaneous, so impersonal, and from so many different quarters, that one is tempted to seek for reasons beyond the phenomenon. (*Upward Panic* 138)

Angelos accepted the invitation to speak to the

Greek military forces stationed in Thrace. His speech of 1931, delivered in Katharevousa, was reprinted in the collection *Pezos logos*, or "Prose" (ed. Savvidis 286-308). He opened with praise for the army's participation in the Pythian Games of the Delphic Festival of the year before. Displays by military recruits, many dressed as ancient Athenian hoplites, had "enhanced" the second festival not only with an entire third day's worth of activities, but also with overtones of Greek national pride (Frangou-Kikilia 25-26). Angelos then pointed up the discrepancy that many perceived between his pacifist aims and his use of the army (286). He, too, sublimated a–rather strained–rationale: he argued that the presence of the young male recruits fitted his ideals in that they embodied his vision for regeneration (286). He then placed the "sacred" Greek army at the service of the Orphic ideal: the army's location in Thrace, land of the mythic Orpheus, was to support the spiritual connection (287, 308). Angelos explained the terms of Greek superiority, derived from classical times, through Aryanism. He credited his country's military with protecting the ancient Greek heritage, but also with behaving as a proper heir to that rich tradition.

Eva's memory of Angelos's speaking engagement before the army divisions of Thrace led her to make her own claims to exceptionalism for the Greek character:

[T]he Greek people have a few subconscious Apollonian characteristics ...
This ... leads one to feel that Greece, today, comes nearer than any other country to being something more than itself. That is to say, that to be a nationalist in Greece binds one, almost irrevocably, to being also a super-nationalist. It was this super-nationalism

of the Delphic Effort which made the officers of the
Greek Army immediately feel at home ... . They [the
Greek military men] did not know that super-nation-
ality is a profoundly Greek characteristic which once
had been consciously developed, and might be again
(and this was the subject of Angelos' speech to all of
the officers of Thrace and Macedonia ...) and that this
is today one of the things which makes Greece worth
fighting for, and worth dying for. (*Upward Panic* 139-
140)

In the above passage, the reader may want to try replacing "super" with "*über*," or "Apollonian" with "Aryan." The result is startling and transforms the passage into a transparent gloss on the – Greek-grown – Aryanism that her husband practiced. Within the same context, Eva seemed to believe that the "religion of Apollo," which she explained as the "history of the Delphic Sanctuary" was a sufficient safeguard against any tendencies toward aggression or militarism. This "religion," she asserted, was the only one in Europe's history to remain "completely innocent of military aggression, and also of domineering priest-craft" (*Upward Panic* 138). She posited the "fundamental lack of fanaticism of the Greek people," her master race, as a superior asset, as a viable object of study and emulation, and also as another safeguard of pacifism and world unity (*Upward Panic* 138-139). Needless to say, when claims to ethnic exceptionalism become claims to racial supremacy, it is rather naïve to deny that militant or militaristic nationalism is not far behind.

The International Drive toward Mass Spectacle

The journalist for the *Rizospastis* may have had reservations about the right-wing turn that he saw mass spectacle take in the leading countries in Western Europe and about the mounting pressures on the Delphic Festivals to follow suit. The act of orchestrating military men and the masses came easy to Sikelianos, who publicly espoused the Aryan ideology and the prominent role of the military. But did any of the attendees who came from Western Europe make the explicit connection or help to solidify it? Let me single out one foreign visitor for his long-standing, external perspective. Gabriel Boissy, a French writer and theater critic, attended both the 1927 and the 1930 festivals at Delphi.[19] His main praise of the festivals was that their "mystagogy" filled the spiritual void of the times (as in his—translated—article in *To Eleftheron Vima* of 20 May 1930, titled "The *Mystagogia* of Delphi"). Eva welcomed the responses of critics such as Boissy, who themselves embraced the festivals' potential for orchestrated mass spectacle:

> Gabriel Boissy, with most of our old friends, had arrived. And what is one to say about these critics? They really were not critics in the usual sense. They told us our faults, but they did it in a spirit which was not critical at all. It was almost as if they had forgotten their function, and had become visionaries like ourselves. And one wonders: Was this extraordinary response, this almost apostolic mission of the Press, in regard to Delphi, due to the fact that we ourselves were ultimately concerned with the play? It was not an end in itself, but an instrument, used consciously, to reach a goal infinitely beyond. (*Upward Panic* 135)

Boissy's repeatedly quoted suggestion that the Delphic Festivals be moved to the ancient theater of Epidaurus was not a criticism of the setting at Delphi. It was, rather, his expectation that the mass potential of the stage productions might be better realized in a much larger outdoor theater (translated in *Ethnos*, 3 and 4 May 1930; also Sideris 404, 408). Boissy also urged that the Delphic Festivals be held "at least every two years" (*Ethnos*, 3 May 1930), in other words, that they become a national Greek institution. In the mid-1930s, Boissy advocated again for mass spectacles to be staged in vast outdoor ancient theaters, but by then his comments served the French Right. In his capacity of cultural correspondent for the right-wing weekly *Le Flambeau*, he envisioned a stage for an idealized France that would find form and content in the massive theaters preserved from classical times (Irons 283-284; also Boissy, "Mounet-Sully"). The open-air mass spectacle, defined as the theater of the future, was to revive the stage practice of the ancients. This "restoration of the theater" to the heart of the community would "unite the people in common celebration of past heroism" (Irons 284).

Boissy and the Sikelianoi shared a vision, but the French ideal was unabashedly serving right-wing politics through the 1930s. To the Sikelianoi's credit, however, they saw the revival of classical theater as a medium, not as a purpose per se, and they did not let themselves be swept up in the maelstrom of excitement about mass spectacle. This singular position hampered and curtailed the couple's fundraising efforts after the second Delphic Festival (*Upward Panic* 136-137). Paradoxically, because the Delphic Festivals did *not* continue, the Sikelianoi could remain true to the Delphic Idea as a comprehensive spiritual program, whose political implications seemed to fade over the years. At a crucial historical turning-point, they steered clear of the typical 1930s institutionalized drama festival or orchestrated mass spectacle that, both in Greece and in Western Europe, was subjected to growing state interference of the Right (Van Steen, "Aeschylean Tragedy" 388). In Nazi Germany and in fascist Italy, mass spectacle soon led to mass integration on a totalitarian model. The Delphic Festivals at most made for the discovery of "nationalist capital" in ancient drama—in terms derived from Pierre Bourdieu. International interest in this Greek national capital was duly noted in the Greek press, with *To Eleftheron Vima* in the lead, throughout the 1930s and especially under Metaxas (Vasileiou 59-61, 62-63, 294-295).

In 1937, for instance, Yiorgos Vlahos, president of the Board of the Royal Theater and a long-time advocate for the nationalistic mission and make-over of Greek revival productions of ancient drama, publicly called for the creation of a standing cast of actors and a state-sponsored classical chorus, which was to undertake the lead roles and the choral parts of productions staged at future festivals (Van Steen, "When to Stop Performing?" 31). Vlahos thus proposed an essentialist treatment for revival tragedy, which resonated well, however, not only with the agendas of contemporary Greek and international politics and established theater practice—but also with the tenets of the racial as well as cultural superiority of the Greeks based on the strong-as-ever continuity argument (Vasileiou 296). Angelos, however, who had dabbled in the long-lived, more abstract concepts of the Aryan philosophy, specifically refused to compromise the autonomy of his chorus and stagings (Vasileiou 294 n. 8; the various opinions are reflected in the articles by N. Yiokarinis in *To Elefteron Vima* of 19 and 21 July 1937). Eva, who had followed her husband on the path of proclaiming Greek racial supremacy, soon felt the pressure of political and ideological ramifications, as authoritarian patterns began to encroach more and more on the field of cultural production. Under the circumstances, the Sikelianoi made the right decision to stop when it was still possible to forge a purer legacy for the festivals. Years later, Eva reflected on the difficult months following the second Delphic Festival, which had started to suffer under the weight of its own success:

> We were struggling again ... for the completion of the Delphic Plan. The performance of great drama had done its work ... it had set moving the spirit of Upward Panic. But the artistic success of the second Festival ... made the next Delphic step more than ever important. The very insistence of the Greek Government, and of our patrons in Athens, that we continue the play for its own sake showed clearly enough that the Means was in danger of becoming an End. The time had come when the Delphic work had either to stop, or be debased. (*Upward Panic* 137)

Although the Delphic Festivals have often been criticized for being elitist and aristocratic, they nonetheless gave the impetus to a theatrical revolution in the modern Greek reception of ancient drama. Some detractors went on a Marxist-leftist attack less against the actual stage productions than against the bourgeois establishment and its firm hold on Greek political, social, cultural, and intellectual life. Studies of Hitler's Germany and Mussolini's Italy in the 1930s have stressed the importance of mass theater as a response to the anxieties brought on by modernity (Irons 293). The critical reception of the Delphic Festivals may provide insights that advance the analysis of how Greek theater of the late 1920s and 1930s interfaced with the challenges of the mass age. The right-wing vision of mass theater espoused by Boissy, for one, and the Aryan strand in Sikelianos's Delphic Idea reveal important and perhaps unsettling areas of ideological common ground. However, the case of the Delphic Festivals and of the Sikelianoi also reveals how easily ideological uses of the classical past could be condemned as abuses when, with the benefit of hindsight, they could be seen to prepare an evil like militarism or fascism—only considered evils well into the 1930s and 1940s, if not even later. Thus, our closer look at the phenomenon of the Delphic movement and also at its negatives may contribute to the further study of the modernist fault lines of Greek cultural and political history of the interwar era and of the relative value of various traditions of reception at large.

Works Cited

Benjamin, Walter. "The Work of Art in the Age of Mechanical Reproduction." In *Illuminations*, edited by H. Arendt, tr. Harry Zohn, 219-253. New York: Harcourt, Brace and World, 1968. Print.

Bernal, Martin. *Black Athena: The Afroasiatic Roots of Classical Civilization*. 3 vols. New Brunswick, New Jersey: Rutgers University Press, 1987-2006. Print.

Boissy, Gabriel. "Boissy about the *Suppliants*" (in Greek). *Ethnos*, 3 May 1930. Print.

_____. "About the Delphic Festivals" (in Greek). *Ethnos*, 4 May 1930. Print.

_____. "Mounet-Sully, Isadora Duncan, Angelos et Eva Sikelianos: Bergers de la Nouvelle Alliance hellénique." *Le Voyage en Grèce: Cahiers périodiques* (ed. H. Joannidès) 7 (1937): 11. Print.

Campbell, Colin. "The Cult, the Cultic Milieu and Secularization." In *A Sociological Yearbook of Religion in Britain* 5, edited by Michael Hill, 119-136. London: SCM Press, 1972. Print.

Carpentier, Martha C. *Ritual, Myth, and the Modernist Text: The Influence of Jane Ellen Harrison on Joyce, Eliot, and Woolf.* Amsterdam: The Netherlands: Gordon and Breach, 1998. Print.

Cartledge, Paul. "What Have the Spartans Done for Us? Sparta's Contribution to Western Civilization." *Greece and Rome* 51.2 (2004): 164-179. Print.

Falasca-Zamponi, Simonetta. *Fascist Spectacle: The Aesthetics of Power in Mussolini's Italy*. Berkeley: University of California Press, 1997. Print.

Fischer-Lichte, Erika. "Invocation of the Dead, Festival of Peoples' Theatre or Sacrificial Ritual? Some Remarks on Staging Greek Classics." In *(Dis)Placing Classical Greek Theatre,* edited by S. Patsalidis and E. Sakellaridou, 252-263. Thessaloniki: University Studio Press, 1999. Print.

_____. *Theatre, Sacrifice, Ritual: Exploring Forms of Political Theatre*. London and New York: Routledge, 2005. Print.

_____. "Resurrecting Ancient Greece in Nazi Germany—the *Oresteia* as Part of the Olympic Games in 1936." In *Performance, Iconography, Reception: Studies in Honour of Oliver Taplin,* edited by Martin Revermann and Peter Wilson, 481-498. Oxford: Oxford University Press, 2008. Print.

Flashar, Hellmut. *Inszenierung der Antike: Das griechische Drama auf der Bühne der Neuzeit, 1585-1990*. Munich: Beck, 1991. Print.

Fleming, Katie. "The Use and Abuse of Antiquity: The Politics and Morality of Appropriation." In *Classics and the Uses of Reception,* edited by C. Martindale and R. F. Thomas, 127-137. Malden, Massa-

chusetts and Oxford: Blackwell, 2006. Print.
Foss, Clive. "Augustus and the Poets in Mussolini's Rome." In *Style and Tradition: Studies in Honor of Wendell Clausen*, edited by P. Knox and C. Foss, 306-325. Stuttgart and Leipzig: Teubner, 1998. Print.
Frangou-Kikilia, Ritsa. *Five Studies on Angelos Sikelianos* (in Greek). Athens: Theoria, 1984. Print.
Garland, Robert. *Surviving Greek Tragedy*. London: Duckworth, 2004. Print.
Glitzouris, Andonis. "The Delphic Festivals (1927, 1930): The Revival of the Ancient Greek Chorus in the *Prometheus Bound* and in the *Suppliants* of Aeschylus" (in Greek). *Ta Historika* 15.28-29 (1998): 147-170. Print.
_____. *The Stage Director's Art in Greece: The Emergence and the Establishment of the Art of the Stage Director in Modern Greek Theater*(in Greek). 2 vols. Athens: Ellinika Grammata, 2001. Print.
_____. " 'Resurrecting' Ancient Bodies: The Tragic Chorus in *Prometheus Bound* and *Suppliant Women* at the Delphic Festivals in 1927 and 1930." *The International Journal of the History of Sport* 27.12 (2010): 2090-2120. Special issue "Sport, Bodily Culture and Classical Antiquity in Modern Greece" [Reprinted in *Sport, Bodily Culture and Classical Antiquity in Modern Greece*, edited by E. Fournaraki and Z. Papakonstantinou (London and New York: Routledge, 2011)]. Print.
Gori, Gigliola. "Supermanism and Culture of the Body in Italy: The Case of Futurism." *International Journal of the History of Sport* 16.1 (1999): 159-165. Print.
Griffin, Roger. *Modernism and Fascism: The Sense of a Beginning under Mussolini and Hitler*. Houndmills,

Hampshire, UK and New York: Palgrave MacMillan, 2007. Print.

Heilke, Thomas W. *Nietzsche's Tragic Regime: Culture, Aesthetics, and Political Education*. DeKalb, Illinois: Northern Illinois University Press, 1998. Print.

Irons, Jessica. "Staging Reconciliation: Popular Theatre and Political Utopia in France in 1937." *Contemporary European History* 14.3 (2005): 279-294. Print.

Karyotakis, Kostas Y. "The Delphic Production of the *Prometheus Desmotes*" (in Greek). In *Chronography of K. Y. Karyotakis (1896-1928)*, edited by Y. P. Savvidis, N. M. Hatzidaki, and M. Mitsou, 185-186. Athens: Morfotiko Idrima Ethnikis Trapezis, 1989 [originally published as a review titled "The Delphic Festivals" in *Alexandrini Tehni* 1.9 (August 1927): 11]. Print.

———. *The Poems (1913-1928)* (in Greek), edited by Y. P. Savvidis. Athens: Nefeli, 1992. Print.

———. *Kostas Karyotakis: Battered Guitars, Poems and Prose*. Trans. William W. Reader and Keith Taylor. University of Birmingham: Centre for Byzantine, Ottoman and Modern Greek Studies, 2006. Print.

Kitroeff, Alexander. *Wrestling with the Ancients: Modern Greek Identity and the Olympics*. New York: greekworks.com, 2004. Print.

Kracauer, Siegfried. "The Mass Ornament." In *The Mass Ornament: Weimar Essays*. Trans., ed., and with an introduction by T. Y. Levin, 75-86. Cambridge, Massachusetts and London: Harvard University Press, 1995. Print.

Krüger, Arnd. "Germany: The Propaganda Machine." In *The Nazi Olympics: Sport, Politics, and Appeasement in the 1930s*, edited by A. Krüger and W.

Murray, 17-43. Urbana and Chicago: University of Illinois Press, 2003. Print.

Krüger, Arnd, and William Murray, eds. *The Nazi Olympics: Sport, Politics, and Appeasement in the 1930s.* Urbana and Chicago: University of Illinois Press, 2003. Print.

Lambropoulos, Vassilis. *The Tragic Idea.* London: Duckworth, 2006. Print.

Lasansky, D. Medina. *The Renaissance Perfected: Architecture, Spectacle, and Tourism in Fascist Italy.* University Park, PA: The Pennsylvania State University Press, 2004. Print.

Leontis, Artemis. "Mediterranean *Theoria*: A View from Delphi." *Thesis Eleven* 67 (2001): 101-117. Print.

——. "An American in Paris, a Parsi in Athens." In *A Singular Antiquity: Archaeology and Hellenic Identity in Twentieth-Century Greece*, edited by D. Damaskos and D. Plantzos, 359-370. Athens: Benaki Museum, 2008. Print.

——. "Eva Palmer's Distinctive Greek Journey." In *Women Writing Greece: Essays on Hellenism, Orientalism and Travel*, edited by V. Kolocotroni and E. Mitsi, 159-184. Amsterdam and New York: Rodopi, 2008. Print.

Mandell, Richard D. *The Nazi Olympics.* Urbana and Chicago: University of Illinois Press, 1987 [1st ed. 1971]. Print.

Metaxas, Ioannis. *Metaxas, His Personal Diary, 1933-1941: The Fourth of August, the War of 1940-1941* (in Greek). Ed. F. Vranas. Athens: Gkovostis, 1987. Print.

Nietzsche, Friedrich Wilhelm. *The Birth of Tragedy and Other Writings.* Ed. R. Geuss and R. Speirs. Trans. R. Speirs. Cambridge: Cambridge University

Press, 1999. Print.

———. *The Birth of Tragedy*. Trans. D. Smith. Oxford: Oxford University Press, 2000. Print.

Palmer-Sikelianou, Eva. *Upward Panic. The Autobiography of Eva Palmer-Sikelianos*. Edited by J. P. Anton. Philadelphia: Harwood Academic Publishers, 1993. Print.

———. *Letters of Eva Palmer-Sikelianou to Natalie Clifford Barney* (in Greek). Ed. and trans. L. Papadaki. Athens: Kastaniotis, 1995. Print.

Papadaki, Lia. *The Archetype of the Ephebe and the Delphic Movement of Angelos Sikelianos* (in Greek). Athens: Kendro Neoellinikon Erevnon, 1995. Print.

Petrakis, Marina. *The Metaxas Myth: Dictatorship and Propaganda in Greece*. London: Tauris, 2006. Print.

Politis, Fotos. *Fotos Politis: Selection from His Work. Twenty Years of Critiques* (in Greek). 2 vols. Athens: Estia-Kollaros, 1938. Print.

Pringle, Heather. *The Master Plan: Himmler's Scholars and the Holocaust*. London: Fourth Estate (Harper Collins), 2006. Print.

Roilou, Ioanna. *Performances of Ancient Greek Tragedy and Hellenikotita: The Making of a Greek Aesthetic Style of Performance, 1919-1967*. Saarbrücken, Germany: VDM Verlag Dr. Müller, 2009. Print.

Rotas, Vasilis. "Aeschylus's *Prometheus* in the Theater of Delphi" (in Greek). *Vradini*, 16 April 1927. Print.

———. "The Content of the Delphic Festivals: After the Delirium, Facing Reality" (in Greek). *Ellinika Grammata* 1.4 (4 August 1927): 127-134. Print.

———. *Theater and Language (1925-1977)* (in Greek). 2 vols. Athens: Epikairotita, 1986 [1:33-52 reprint of article in *Ellinika Grammata*]. Print.

S. "Social Critique of the Delphic Festivals" (in Greek).

Rizospastis, 15 May 1927, and continued 16 May 1927. Print.

Schroeder, Leopold von. *Die Vollendung des arischen Mysteriums in Bayreuth*. Munich: J. F. Lehmann, 1911. Print.

Sideris, Ioannis. *The Ancient Theater on the Modern Greek Stage, 1817-1932* (in Greek). Athens: Ikaros, 1976. Print.

Sikelianos, Angelos. *Prose*. Vol. 2, *Delphic Writings (1921-1951)* (in Greek). Edited by Y. P. Savvidis. Athens: Ikaros, 1980. Print.

Spotts, Frederic. *Hitler and the Power of Aesthetics*. London: Hutchinson, 2002. Print.

Stone, Marla. "A Flexible Rome: Fascism and the Cult of *Romanità*." In *Roman Presences: Receptions of Rome in European Culture, 1789-1945*, edited by C. Edwards, 205-220. Cambridge: Cambridge University Press, 1999. Print.

Thrilos, Alkis [Eleni Ourani]. "The Mute Pythia: About the Meaning of the Delphic Festivals" (in Greek). *Anayennisi* 2.5 (1928): 216-223 and 2.6 (1928): 255-265. Print.

———. "The *Prometheus Desmotes* at Delphi" (in Greek). In *Greek Theater* 1 (1927-1933) (in Greek), 43-52. Athens: Akadimia Athinon, 1977 [originally published in *Nea Estia*, 1 June 1927]. Print.

———. "The Delphic Performances and the 'Mother Ideas' of Mother Earth" (in Greek). In *Greek Theater* (in Greek) 1 (1927-1933), 298-308. Athens: Akadimia Athinon, 1977 [originally published in *Nea Estia*, 1 June 1930]. Print.

Van Steen, Gonda A. H. "'The World's a Circular Stage': Aeschylean Tragedy through the Eyes of Eva Palmer-Sikelianou." *International Journal of the Classical Tradition* 8.3 (2002): 375-393. Print.

———. "When to Stop Performing? The Delphic Festivals, Nietzsche, and Mounting Militarism of the Late 1920s and 1930s." *Dialogues* 2 (2008): 1-46. Print.

———. *Theatre of the Condemned: Classical Tragedy on Greek Prison Islands*. Oxford: Oxford University Press, 2011. Print.

Vasileiou, Areti. *Modernization or Tradition? Prose Theater in Interwar Athens* (in Greek). Athens: Metaihmio, 2004. Print.

Wiedmann, August K. *The German Quest for Primal Origins in Art, Culture, and Politics 1900-1933*. Lewiston, NY, 1995. Print.

Wiles, David. *Greek Theatre Performance: An Introduction*. Cambridge: Cambridge University Press, 2000. Print.

———. "The Use of Masks in Modern Performances of Greek Drama." In *Dionysus since 69: Greek Tragedy at the Dawn of the Third Millennium*, edited by E. Hall, F. Macintosh, and A. Wrigley, 245-263. Oxford: Oxford University Press, 2004. Print.

Witt, Mary A. F. *The Search for Modern Tragedy: Aesthetic Fascism in Italy and France*. Ithaca, NY and London: Cornell University Press, 2001. Print.

Wyke, Maria. "Sawdust Caesar: Mussolini, Julius Caesar, and the Drama of Dictatorship." In *The Uses and Abuses of Antiquity*, edited by M. Wyke and M. Biddiss, 167-186. Bern: Lang, 1999. Print.

Yalouri, Eleana. *The Acropolis: Global Fame, Local Claim*. Oxford and New York: Berg, 2001. Print.

Ziolkowski, Theodore. *The Sin of Knowledge: Ancient Themes and Modern Variations*. Princeton and Oxford: Princeton University Press, 2000. Print.

Acknowledgments: David Roessel and Tom Papademetriou kindly extended an invitation to the members of our research team on Eva Palmer-Sikelianou to join in the Hellenic Studies Symposium, "Americans and the Experience of Delphi," held by the Richard Stockton College of New Jersey at the European Cultural Centre of Delphi on 24-26 June 2008. I thank all of those who participated in those stimulating sessions and who contributed papers, comments, and questions on previous occasions. I am indebted to the organizers and to Paul Lorenz for assuming the arduous task of editing the conference papers. All translations from modern Greek are my own, unless otherwise noted. The quotation in my title is a reference to Colin Campbell.

Notes

1 Heilke 22-27, 56-59, 81, 106-107. Fischer-Lichte expands on the impact–and shock value–of Nietzsche's *Birth of Tragedy*:

> [I]t was the statement that ancient Greek theatre originated in the Dionysian principle, which was manifested in and enacted by a chorus of satyrs, the original dithyrambic chorus. It is this principle which annuls individuation, transposes individuals into a state of ecstasy, and transforms them into members of a dancing, singing community – a community in which the boundaries separating individuals are dissolved. This idea was a total contradiction in an age in which there was a cult, a celebration of the individual. (*Theatre, Sacrifice, Ritual* 17-18)

Nietzsche's view of tragic theater as originating in the Dionysian ritual of dismemberment was adopted by Jane Ellen Harrison, who, as the head of the Cambridge Ritualists, centered on the ritual of death and rebirth (Fischer-

Lichte, *Theatre, Sacrifice, Ritual* 39-40). Harrison exerted her influence on Eva's circle, especially on Susan Glaspell and George Cram Cook. I thank Martha Carpentier for helping me to establish these connections. For an in-depth analysis of Harrison's modernist influence, see Carpentier.

2 The name "Sikelianoi," the Greek plural for "Sikelianos," is used throughout to refer to Angelos Sikelianos and Eva Palmer Sikelianos collectively.

3 For a recent discussion of Nietzsche's influence on the Sikelianoi, see Roilou 104-107. Roilou's extensive chapter three (89-130) focuses on the couple's concept of Greekness or "Hellenikotita" and on how it inspired a new performance style for revivals of ancient tragedy, which would subsequently help to constitute Greece's symbolic capital (in Bourdieu's terms). Leontis presents an excellent picture of the Zeitgeist in which especially Eva Sikelianou lived and worked ("American in Paris"). See also her "Mediterranean *Theoria*" 105, 110, as well as her cultural biography of Eva (in progress).

4 For some critics, the Sikelianoi's vision was too profound and contrived, and therefore too elitist. Detractors called the festivals vehicles for Angelos's narcissistic self-promotion and, at best, a noble, be it naïve and doomed, effort. The poet Kostas Karyotakis, for instance, struck an ironic note in his poem *Delphic Festival* (1927). The theater critic Alkis Thrilos wrote several long reviews, including one tellingly called "The Mute Pythia," in which she claimed that Sikelianos was not in communion with Delphi. In the periodical *Ellinika Grammata*, the left-wing author Vasilis Rotas branded the Delphic Effort as "estheticist" and unconvincing. Other negative assessments appeared in derivative articles (e.g., by Fotos Politis). Pertinent bibliographical references are included under the names of the authors mentioned above in the section "Works Cited." For further bibliographical items related to the Delphic Festivals, see Van Steen, "Aeschylean Tragedy" 391-392, and "When to Stop Performing?"

5 Nearly all commentators praised Eva's innovative work

with the chorus, which transformed theatrical content as well as form. Sideris 359; see also below. For perhaps the most detailed technical studies of Eva's choruses, see Glitzouris, "Delphic Festivals" and " 'Resurrecting' Ancient Bodies." For a short biography of Eva Palmer-Sikelianou, see Glitzouris, *Stage Director's Art* 661-663.

6 Nietzsche identified with the Aeschylean Prometheus. In the ninth chapter of his *Birth of Tragedy* (1872), he compared the myths of Prometheus and Adam. He concluded that the human race might achieve its loftiest goal, but only by actively committing sacrilege and then bearing all the consequences, including the misery inflicted by offended deities (Ziolkowski 116-117). Nietzsche famously called Aeschylus's tragedy a "hymn to impiety" and its hero's "offense" the "virtue" of "active sin," which, for him, commanded pride and dignity (ch. 9).

7 See further Falasca-Zamponi; Foss; Stone; Wyke. See recently Lasansky, who devotes ample attention to the performative aspects of Mussolini's appropriation of antiquity.

8 The bibliography on Nazi aesthetics and politics is large and growing. See especially Spotts. See also, however, Flashar for the connection with Germany's revival tragedy (164-180). For recent insightful discussions of the 1936 Olympics from various national—and dramatic--perspectives, see Fischer-Lichte, *Theatre, Sacrifice, Ritual* 69-86, and "Resurrecting Ancient Greece"; Krüger and Murray. Such studies build on the path-breaking analysis of the 1936 Games and the "fascist aesthetic" by Richard Mandell, who also coined the phrase "Nazi Olympics" in his 1971 book by that title. In the preface to his 1987 edition, Mandell stated: "the beautification of mindless, masculine physical power is, in fact, highly supportive and perhaps a part of totalitarian ideology" (xvi-xvii).

9 See also Fischer-Lichte, *Theatre, Sacrifice, Ritual* 68, 75-76, 79-82, 85-86, 200, 204. Katie Fleming raises important theoretical points about our own recurring characterization of "abuse" where fascist and Nazi appropriations of the clas-

sical tradition are concerned: the label of "abuse" lacks theoretical justification and further impedes a better understanding of the historical and ideological contexts of interwar totalitarianism and of its theoreticians' and sympathizers' participation in far more diverse modes of relating to the past, which may have been far removed from ideological and political opportunism. She states, in particular:

The horrors of this [Fascist and Nazi] period of European history force the use of the idea of "*mis*appropriation" and abuse, and the surety of the postwar moral consensus against fascism renders it fairly secure. To criticize fascist uses of the past as misappropriation is, at first sight, a straightforward affair: we are none of us, surely, fascists... .

> [T]he use of a vocabulary of "misappropriation" and "abuse," while still seen as politically and morally necessary, might nevertheless be theoretically and intellectually unnecessary. The challenge posed by fascism's use of the past, then, lies in our engagement with it: simply to dismiss, explicitly or implicitly, the appropriation of antiquity in the fascist regimes of the twentieth century as abuse is to understand neither the dynamics of that appropriation nor, ultimately, the regime that made it. (129, 137)

10 On the Italian fascist culture of the body and on its ideological underpinnings, see, for instance, Gori.

11 Krüger 32; Mandell 284; Petrakis 235 n. 73. Metaxas exploited the pretext of an impending communist takeover and of the dangers of social disruptions caused by general strikes announced for 5 August 1936. Petrakis 208 n. 16. Connections between Metaxas's regime and Hitler's Germany abound. Petrakis *passim*. For those who reject any link between the Delphic Festivals and the 1936 Olympics, there is the unfortunate fact that Koula Pratsika, the Greek dancer and choreographer who functioned as Eva's right hand, acted as the female "high priestess" at the torch-lighting ceremony that opened the Nazi Olympics. Kitroeff 101, 109.

12 On EON, the *Ethnikos Organismos Neolaias*, or Metaxas's

National Youth Organization, see further Petrakis 4 and *passim*. The juxtaposition with the Greek army as well as the choice of highly charged, military terms or metaphors such as "phalanxes" indicate that Metaxas recognized the potential that a well-trained youth held as a future combat army. Petrakis 221 n. 101. Petrakis further explains the propagandistic aim of the public appearances of large numbers of EON members in uniform:

> EON's participation was a necessary function in every orchestrated manifestation projected by the state-commissioned newsreels. However, their most significant participation was during the celebrations of the anniversaries of the "Fourth of August" regime in the Athens Stadium. (224 n. 147)

13 Vasileiou 61 n. 162, 326-327, 341-343, 364-366; Van Steen, *Theatre of the Condemned* 42-50. Vasileiou explains the success formula that made for the decades-long popular attraction of the didactic, "historical," and patriotic modern Greek plays: these works fictionalized Greek history by resorting to the tried components of fictional drama itself, such as adventure plots and "pitiless persecutions" of the good heroes by the bad ones; they bestowed divine justice on the good guys and delivered paradigmatic punishment to the enemies "of different nations and religions" (122). On the all-encompassing, insidious power of the Metaxas propaganda mill, see recently Petrakis, who devotes special attention to "theatre propaganda" (chapter four).

14 See further Wiedmann, and Witt 32-88, or her chapter two, titled "D'Annunzio's Nietzschean Tragedy and the Aesthetic Politics of Fusion." Fischer-Lichte expands on the elitist nature of the "theories of ritual" from the early twentieth century:

> [T]hey betray a particular mentality which, in some respects, seems to be typical of the *élite* in European culture of the time. True, they did not close their eyes to the problems of the day. However, they hoped to find a solution for the future by searching for origins,

by going back to a distant, mostly misty past which it was by no means possible to illuminate sufficiently. Thus, the past was treated as a kind of plane of projection for their visions of the future... .

The most effective and successful forms were those which were passed off for ancient Greek theatre and ancient Greek ritual, or which were understood as a rediscovery, reinvention or revival of them. (*Theatre, Sacrifice, Ritual* 44, 45)

15 For a milder evaluation of Sikelianos's emphasis on Greek race and blood and on a "purely" Greek culture, see Roilou 97-103.

16 Recently affirmed by Katie Fleming (133) and Heather Pringle (44-45, 143). The latter studied some of the state-sponsored scholarly circles of the Nazi regime and their pet "scientific" projects. See also Mandell for an example of how the foundation myth of Greece as the work of Nordic immigrants entered the rhetoric surrounding the Nazi Olympics (151). The constructed nature of the Aryan-*Dorian* Greek connection is, of course, a prominent theme in the (much-maligned) first volume of Martin Bernal's *Black Athena*. Bernal traces the origins of this construct back to its roots in older, neohumanist German scholarship (late eighteenth century – nineteenth century), which predates by several decades the abuse that Hitler and some contemporary classicists made of the artificial link (1:292-294, 330-336, 388-392, and *passim*). Spotts 23-23. Twenty years after the publication of Bernal's first volume, classicists can better fathom that Enlightenment and Romanticist thinkers invented an ancient Greece in the image of their own spiritual but idealized forebears. Sikelianos, too, envisioned an expressly "Doric" university at Delphi, where the superior Apollonian intellectual spirit would be revived and the Delphic generation of "neo-Dorians" would be reborn (Sideris 403). It must be repeated, however, that the association of the Doric or Spartan Greeks with Aryanism and with "racial and national purity" was not Sikelianos's original idea—or

even Hitler's—but was commonplace in the contemporary social ideology (Fleming 133). On the widespread, uncritical admiration for Sparta in the 1930s, see further Cartledge 169-170.

17 Palmer-Sikelianou, *Upward Panic* 106; Leontis, "Palmer's Distinctive Greek Journey" 175-177; Van Steen, "Aeschylean Tragedy" 375 and *passim*.

18 In 1930, Eva was once more impressed with the efficient assistance of the Ministry of War:

> ... this time it was Mr. Sophoulis, whom I had never seen before.
>
> "The Army knows," he said, "what Anghelos and Eva Sikelianos have done for Greece. She had only to appoint a time with me, and come to tell me what she wants."
>
> I was both embarrassed and overjoyed. Again the army! Why?
>
> ... The army took over the whole responsibility of the Stadium. (*Upward Panic* 133)

19 For further references to international reviews of and reactions to the Delphic Festivals, which were translated and published in *To Eleftheron Vima*, see Vasileiou 45 n. 98. Vasileiou's own discussion of the Delphic Festival productions is, unfortunately, limited to less than five pages (45-46, 283-284). The laudatory letter by the French critic and Wagnerian, Edouard Schuré, excerpted and translated in *To Eleftheron Vima* of 1 November 1927, may serve as a telling example. Indicative, too, is that Schuré's enthusiastic letter was invoked by the anonymous journalist and translator to silence some of the "incorrigible" Greek critical voices. The 1930 Delphic Festival provided another occasion for *To Eleftheron Vima* to feature foreign, preferably French, opinions, such as Mario Meunier's statement published on 9 May 1930 (written 5 May 1930).

George Cram Cook's
*Road to the Temple**

Linda Ben-Zvi

George Cram "Jig" Cook is a name little known today outside the annals of American theatre history where he is acknowledged as the founder and guiding force behind the Provincetown Players, the country's first indigenous theatre company which, in its seven years of existence, from 1915-1922, laid the foundation for modern American drama.[1] Jig Cook's importance, in fact, goes far beyond his work with the Players. In the first two decades of the twentieth century, he was a central figure in the two-pronged battles waged by the radical Greenwich Village community of writers, artists, journalists, and political and social reformers against pervasive Victorian values and mindsets as well as newly-instituted Progressive-era capitalist institutions and practices. However, unlike others in this group, including John Reed, Max Eastman, Mary Heaton Vorse, Djuna Barnes, Theodore Dreiser, Charles Demuth, Emma Goldman, and his wife Susan Glaspell, Cook did not leave a unified body of work or accomplishments behind to seal his place in American cultural history.

*Sections of this essay are based on my biography *Susan Glaspell: Her Life and Times* and Susan Glaspell's biography of her husband George Cram Cook, *The Road to the Temple*, which I edited.

He wrote in various forms—fiction, poetry, essays, critical reviews—on a wide range of subjects that interested him. Of his three novels, *In Hampton Roads* (1899) and *Roderick Taliaferro* (1903) were historical romances, the first based on the famous navel battle between the Monitor and the Merrimac, the second on Juárez's government in Mexico. Only his third, *The Chasm*, set out the contemporary battle in which he was personally engaged: between the philosophy of individualism inspired by his reading of Nietzsche and Cook's adherence to socialism, which he embraced in 1907.[2] His work for the *Chicago Evening Post*, between 1911 and 1915 was equally diverse. As the Associate Editor of their influential *Friday Literary Review* (1911-1912), he wrote extensive reviews and essays on the flood of modernist writing arriving from Europe by writers including Nietzsche, Strindberg, d'Annunzio, and H.G. Wells. His later essays in the *Post* and in New York journals (1912-1915) took up issues ranging from the importance of socialism, the need for a labor union to protect the rights and free speech of university professors, and the possibility of a cultural revolution spurred by a cadre of a hundred intellectuals (See Ben-Zvi, *Susan Glaspell* 114-15).

As diverse as Cook's output was, the constant element that drove his writing, theatre work, and personal life was his love for ancient Greece: its philosophers, artists, culture, and language. He believed that what marked the Golden Age of Pericles was the existence of a community of like-minded people who could, through their shared commitment to ideals of beauty, harmony, and art, shape the society as a whole; and he believed that his role was to be the inspiration for the establishment of such a new age in twentieth-century America. As Glaspell put it, "Beauty which came through another was as authentic as beauty that came from himself... What he wanted was to shape life into a form most hospitable to the creative thing in us all. That was why he loved Athens and Delphi of long ago" (*Road* 27). His greatness lay in his ability to fire others with his vision, their successes becoming the validation of his dream. His tragedy sprung from his failure to erect a lasting monument to his own genius, and, thus, secure the place in American letters that he sorely wanted.

For seven years, the Provincetown Players gave him the opportunity to forge this "beloved community of lifegivers"—as he called them—whom he believed would change the direction of American theatre and, by so doing, would serve as a beacon for new ideas and new possibilities not only in the arts but in the cultural, social, and political life of the country. When it ceased to be the community he imagined, he left New York and, with Glaspell, fulfilled another lifelong dream: to see Greece and experience firsthand the vestiges of its Golden Age still visible, he believed, in the daily lives and rituals of simple peasants who still herded sheep and toiled the fields around Delphi, in the shadow of Mount Parnassus. He wanted to live among such people, eating what they ate, living in accommodations similar to their houses, sharing with them the rhythms of their daily lives.[3] It was a rhythm, life style, and ideal that Jig Cook had sought throughout his life. His was always a journey on "the road to the temple," the title Susan Glaspell wisely chose for her biography of him. In her 1927 Preface to the book she wrote: "This is the romance of an American brought up on the Mississippi and buried beside the Temple of Apollo at Delphi. It is the story of a promised land that was entered" (19).[4]

What I want to explore in this essay is not "the promised land" entered—which Glaspell describes so vividly in *The Road to the Temple*—but the ways in which the Delphi vision of beauty and harmony shaped Cook's work and life in America, his love for Greece transferred to native soil. One criticism he had of Henry James was that his writing lost much potential vigor when he severed his ties with his native land. This never happened to Cook. His ancestors, culture, and history went with him to Greece, just as his heroes from classical Greece took up residence in Davenport, Iowa, his birthplace, and in Greenwich Village and Provincetown, Massachusetts, his adopted homes. Throughout his life, Jig would repeat the habit of looking back over his shoulder at the place from which he had come, comparing the past to the present locale in which he found himself. In Iowa he talked of Greece, in Greece of Iowa, in Provincetown of both. For example, around a campfire at Kalania, on the slope of Mt. Parnassus, where he and Glaspell joined the exodus from Delphi each summer, he would regale the shepherds with tales of life on the American plains and the exploits of Indians; in America he would read to friends from Plato and try to convince them that they too could find nobility through art. "Greece begins in Iowa," Glaspell claimed, describing the structuring principle of *The Road to the Temple*. It was his mother who had told him when he was a youth, "I think America is a good place to metamorphose Greeks. Emerson was about that" (*Road* 62), and adding the names Whitman and Thoreau. Like his friend and fellow Hellenophile Isadora Duncan, Cook took what he loved about Greece and grafted it to American masters and forms, hoping to enrich America by making it more Greek.

The Poetry of Living

When Babette Deutsch reviewed *Greek Coins* (1925), a posthumous collection of Cook's poetry that Glaspell edited, she noted, "The poetry of living, not the poetry of words, was his, and his poems are great where they catch the reflection of his life" (quoted in Tanselle 1). This life started in Davenport, Iowa, where Cook was born October 7, 1873, the younger of two sons in one of the most respected and established pioneer families in the town. His father, Edward Cook, was a noted lawyer from a long line of prominent Cook antecedents in America going back to Francis Cooke, the seventeenth signer of the Mayflower compact, and Ebenezer Cook, a drummer in the Revolutionary War, whose gold coin received for services rendered remained a family legacy. Jig's love of American history and democracy were associated with his illustrious forebears just as his fascination with pioneering and Western lore was connected to stories of Native Americans, particularly Blackhawk, whose heroic demeanor and humility in victory or defeat made a lasting impression on him and whom he conflated with Greek heroes in his play *The Spring* (1921).

The rectitude of the Cook side of the family was tempered in Jig's life by his mother, Ellen Dodge, whom everyone called Ma-Mie. She was the only child of a riverboat captain, and spent her childhood on the family plantation in Buffalo, outside of Davenport, reading Greek and German mythology and poetry. In staid middle-class Davenport, at the end of the nineteenth century, she was considered "queer"—that positive appellation that Glaspell's characters bear because of their unwillingness to conform to the status quo. One mark of Ma-Mie's "queerness" was her act of moving a cabin, inherited from her father, from inland to the banks of the Mississippi river and there creating a haven for local writers, artists, and thinkers, who were invited to visit and read from her vast library.[5] It was she who initiated Jig into ancient Greece, reading to him from Plato and Greek tragedies, in addition to German poetry, thereby instilling in him at a young age a love for literature and beauty, as well as a sense of individualism and pride in his intellect. In a letter to him chronicling her own life she explained, "If I had lived a hundred, two hundred, three hundred years ago and more I should have been burned as a witch—if I had lived two thousand years and more ago I should have been a Sybil with a tripod. If I had lived seven thousand years and more ago I should have been a priestess of the Temple of Isis."[6] "She was the significant pioneer," Glaspell writes, "for she broke a trail of self out of the life around her" (*Road* 68). She would also have an impact on her future daughter-in-law, who first visited the Cabin at the invitation of Mrs. Cook before she married her son.

At age seven, Jig built the city of Troy out of sand on a beach in Nantucket, where the family vacationed. At fifteen, already a college freshman at the University of Iowa, while reading Plotinus in the college library he suddenly had an epiphany about his oneness with the universe and the relationship of all natural and physical life. At Harvard, where he went in his final year of college, he studied classical Greek art under Charles Eliot Norton and forged a close friendship with John Alden, with whom he hoped to travel to Greece after graduation. His letters to Ma-Mie from Cambridge detail his growing enthusiasm. "All this year Greek has been unfolding its beauty. The country is becoming for me, as for so many others, as a lost Fatherland" (*Road* 71). "I sit here and dream of Greece. I hear—see—the blue waves of the Aegean eating on the shore (*Road* 72). "In Greece one's eyes can still be glad" (*Road* 22, 24, 244).

Jig was unable to accompany Alden; family financial reversals prevented it. But when he finally traveled to Greece at age fifty, he still followed the plan he had written out at nineteen: "Why not a Greek Thoreau, living with Homer and the mountains, the olives, the grapes, the fish, the shepherds, the sailors, and the sea? Winter in Athens with scholars and people and the Parthenon!" (*Road* 88). In the interim, he lived his Greek dream in America.

Planting Greek Roots in American Soil

Instead of going to Greece in 1897, Cook traveled to Europe for eighteen months, studying at the Universities of Heidelberg and Jena, and returned to take up the position of instructor in the newly-formed English department at the University of Iowa. There he formulated the role he saw himself best suited to perform, based on his Greek ideal: "I do not aspire to be, in the great sense of the word, a scholar. I hope to prove some day, writing and teaching, a person of tastes and talent, able to help people understand and love rightly the things which are beautiful" (Ben-Zvi, *Susan Glaspell* 64). Although he soon became disenchanted with his students ("the facts of the inner life and the facts of poetry, of imaginative beauty, elude the Iowan") (*Road* 71), and despaired of the direction of the university ("a scientifically minded university in the midst of a methodistically minded population") (*Road* 71), he never lost his desire to inspire others.

After trying his hand at teaching in the English department of Leland Stanford University and finding it still was not what he desired, he returned to his farm in Buffalo with his new wife and there took up the life of a truck farmer, selling produce in the summer to support winters spent writing poetry and fiction. Here, too, he attempted to live out his dream of agrarian life imbued with Greek spirit. When a local newspaper carried a story about him, the caption under an idyllic photo of the young couple noted, "The two seem like a youth and the maiden who might have stepped down one day from Keats' Grecian Urn or the Frieze of the Parthenon" (Davenport newspaper clipping). Ever a fine carpenter, he built a greenhouse on the property and decorated it in gold paint with designs of ancient Greece, and Greek dithyrambs explaining, "You will look between golden bars through nice clear glass and see the green things growing against the black background" (Ben-Zvi, *Susan Glaspell* 65). Glaspell would pattern Claire Archer's greenhouse in *The Verge* on it.

By 1904 Cook's first marriage had ended. "A young woman of social gifts who has married a university man has perhaps a justifiable grievance when she finds herself the wife of a farmer" (*Road* 74), Glaspell generously noted in her biography. Now living alone on the farm, unsure of what direction his life should take, he was buoyed by the arrival of Floyd Dell, then 16, already showing promise of the important writing and editing career ahead of him, and already a committed socialist. Dell soon became Cook's work hand and mentor—"like a St. Bernard following a little terrier around" (*Road* 153) Ma-Mie Cook remarked— the younger leading the older to Marx and Engels. Greece was also part of the relationship. As the two made the ten mile trip by wagon from Buffalo to Davenport to sell their produce, they would chant dithyrambs back and forth. They also discussed Nietzsche, socialism, and the possibility of cobbling them together, as Cook attempted to do in his novel *The Chasm*, whose genesis was his ongoing debate with Dell. For epigraphs to the book, he chose, "I love those who sacrifice themselves to the earth, that the earth may be one day the Superman's" from Nietzsche's *Thus Spake Zarathustra* and "Come shoulder to shoulder ere earth grows older! The Cause spreads over land and sea" from William Morris's *The Voice of Toil*. In the course of the novel, Cook arrives at a philosophy that embraces socialism while retaining the idea of superior individuals able to create a higher order of social good and beauty that would enrich the lives of the many.

That Cook was drawn to the philosophies of Nietzsche and Marx, as well as Greek culture, was not an individual enthusiasm. Isadora Duncan also drew from these seemingly disparate sources and similarly anchored such new ideas in American soil. For both, Nietzsche provided the figure of the intellectual who stood in counter distinction to the bourgeois societies of their youth and his championing of the Dionysian as complementary, not antithetical, to the Apollonian was very much in keeping with their own predilections and those of the modernist period of which they were such an integral part. Like Cook, Duncan desired to "break with the narrow, bankrupt morals and values of a Christian civilization and to harness the expansive, life-affirming creativity of the Superman" (Daly 29–30). Duncan too sought "to bridge that tension between individualism and collectivity in her performances. She wanted movement to suggest not individual expression but a collective social presence," likened to socialism, the experience of the individual embodying "the collective social presence" (Francis 21)—the theme of *The Chasm*.

Another important influence on Cook at the time, which reinforced his sense of the oneness of self and world, of body and spirit—first realized by his reading of Plotinus—was the writing of Ernst Haeckel, a scientist who also had a considerable influence upon Isadora Duncan and her work. Today Haeckel's theories of biogenetics based on the premise that "ontogeny recapitulates phylogeny," (that individual physiological development relates to the physiological history of the race), are identified with the Third Reich's usurpation of such theories; and has, thus, fallen out of favor.[7] However, in the first decade of the twentieth century, he drew a considerable readership among those who sought ways to overcome the dualities between body and soul, and nature and religion. Emerson's transcendental conception of the universe in which "mind is a part of the nature of things" and "there is something of humanity in all, and in every particular"(Emerson "Nature," *Essays and Poems*, 1, 41) [a Whitmanesque idea as well], were taken up by Haeckel and given a biological grounding, "as part of the process of evolutionary transformation," the nature of which was provable if one followed Darwin, who substituted "an intelligible natural law for unintelligible miracles" (Bölsche 28).

Haeckel's term for this unity was monism, a theory in which Darwinian evolution was not diametrically opposed to, but rather complementary to, religion. Monism appealed to Cook, who had come across similar ideas in his earlier reading of Emerson and German transcendentalism, as well as Greek philosophy. Duncan, too, found inspiration in Haeckel's writing, which seemed to reinforce her own study of Greek models and their applicability to her experiments with movement and the body as related to nature and the individual soul. For her, like Cook, Haeckel's scientific writing provided "a little of that divine continuity which gives to all of Nature its beauty and life" (Duncan 99).[8]

Cook, committed like Duncan to Americanizing European arts and theories, joined with Dell in 1907 to form a Monist Society in Davenport, based on Haeckel's writings. It drew together, as Glaspell—a member—describes it, those "who were out of sorts with what we were supposed to believe" (*Road* 160), and who together became "pioneers indeed, that pure, frightened, exhilarating feeling of having stepped out of your own place and here, with these strange people, far from your loved ones and already a little lonely, beginning to form a new background" (*Road* 161). For Cook, the group became the first testing ground for his Delphi vision of beauty and harmony, an enclave of idealism in a society alien to such ideals, with himself as leader and inspiration. The Provincetown Players would be his second.

Cook and Duncan both record similar experiences when they first saw Greek tragedy and immediately understood the power of the performance to move people. In her autobiography, *My Life in Art*, Duncan describes how she and her brother Raymond, on a trip to Paris in 1900, by chance attended a performance of *Oedipus Rex* featuring the great actor Mounet-Sully. "Raymond and I from our place in the tribunes caught our breath. We grew pale. We grew faint. Tears streamed from our eyes, and when finally the first act was over, we could only hug each other in our delirium of joy"

(Duncan 89-90). Jig Cook describes similar emotions when he saw *Lysistrata* in New York: "I sat there in the darkness of the second balcony with the tears streaming. Something in the play (its beauty, its coming from so far away in time, its revelation of man and woman as they were two thousand years ago...struck something tremulous in me" (*Road* 201). He wrote this to Glaspell in 1913, a few months before their marriage, while they waited for his second divorce to become final so they could wed.[9] Again, he harkened back to the need for a Greek revival in America and what the two of them and a small group of like-minded people might be able to create:

> An American Renaissance of the Twentieth Century is not the task of ninety million people, but of one hundred. Does that not stir the blood of those who know they may be of that hundred? Does it not make them feel like reaching out to find each other — for strengthening of heart, for the generation of intercommunicating power, the kindling of communal intellectual passion?" (*Road* 184)

The Beloved Community of Lifegivers

Greenwich Village in 1913 was already under the sway of classical Greece, as seen in the clothing and shoes worn by Bohemian women, such as the social activist Harriet Rodman; the new awareness of the body and movement Isadora Duncan introduced; and the general sense of optimism and change that pervaded the experimentation that brought modernism to America. As Glaspell's persona Ruth Holland proclaims in her novel *Fidelity*: "There were new poets in the world; there were bold new thinkers; there was an amazing new art...everywhere the old pattern was being shot through with new ideas" (*Fidelity* 29). Or as Floyd Dell recalled, "we had something which it seemed all bourgeois America—sick to death of its machine-made efficiency and scared respectability—wistfully desired to share with us: we had freedom and happiness" (*Intellectual Vagabondage* 117). When Cook moved to Greenwich Village in 1913, he found an ideal climate to nurture his Greek vision; and at last he found a concrete project in which he could channel his gargantuan thirsts for life, art, wine, and shaping twentieth-century America to resemble fifth century BCE Greece: the Provincetown Players.

In the summer of 1915 Cook, Glaspell, and their friends—summering in Provincetown, Massachusetts, a small, predominantly Portuguese fishing village on the tip of Cape Cod—began to amuse themselves by writing and putting on plays in a building on a wharf used during the day by fishermen. Although all enjoyed the diversion, only Cook took it as more than a pleasurable way for friends to spend time during a long summer vacation. He believed that this theatre could be a concrete way of establishing his "beloved community of lifegivers" in America, and through theatre, as the Greeks had done, to change the values of the country at large. He wrote the following note during that summer:

> One man cannot produce drama. True drama is born only of one feeling animating all the members of a clan—a spirit shared by all and expressed by the few for the all. If there is nothing to take the place of the common religious purpose and passion of the primitive group, out of which the Dionysian dance was born, no new vital drama can arise in any people. (*Road* 203)

From such lofty ideas the Provincetown Players, and with it modern American drama, were born. Not everyone who worked on the productions on the wharf shared Jig's sense of mission or zeal, but all could be swayed, if only for a short time, by his fervor. While the others who were part of the beginnings of the Provincetown Players, including Glaspell, Dell, Neith Boyce, John Reed, Louise Bryant, Max Eastman, artists Charles Demuth and Marguerite and William Zorach, might have been absorbed for the moment, Cook devoted all his energies to this end, convinced that if he built a place where it was possible to work free of monetary constraints, playwrights would come. Eugene O'Neill did in the summer of 1916. Others he hoped would follow. Cook also believed that such a theatre required a special type of audience. He had first formulated the idea when he saw *Lysistrata* in 1913. "One thing we're in need of," he wrote at the time,

is the freedom to deal with life in literature as frankly as Aristophanes. We need a public, like his, which itself has the habit of thinking and talking frankly of life. We need the sympathy of such a public, the fundamental oneness with the pubic, which Aristophanes had. We are hurt by the feeling of a great mass of people hostile to the work we want to do. (*Road* 201-02)

In September 1916, at the end of their second summer season, Cook decided that the group should take their theatre with them when they returned to Greenwich Village. He was certain that the Players could draw supporters willing to see whatever the untried American playwrights presented, and would not be put off by the theatre's notoriously uncomfortable seats or miniscule stage, ten feet by twelve, in the group's first theatre at 133 MacDougal Street, slightly larger when they moved two years later to 139 MacDougal Street, a former stable and brewery. Whenever spirits flagged among the Players, Jig would schedule a party, and when the alcohol was in danger of running low, he would shout, in Dionysian approximation: "Give it all to me... and I guarantee to intoxicate all the rest of you" (*Road* 212). And he usually did.

Cook not only oversaw the Players, he also acted in many of the productions, particularly those written by Glaspell, which he usually directed. In addition to co-authoring two one-acts with her—*Suppressed Desires* and *Tickless Time*, both parodies of their own avant-garde group—he wrote two full-length plays: *The Spring*, drawn from stories about ancient Indian rites and pioneer history; and *The Athenian Women*, an anti-war work directly inspired by, and infused with, his Greek passion. *The Athenian Women* was a radical undertaking for the Players because of its production values and political message. Up to this point, the company had presented only one-act plays with few characters and little scenery. *The Athenian Women*, which opened in March 1918, was their first full-length production consisting of three acts with six scenes requiring scene changes, and a cast of 27 playing 33 speaking parts. Only Cook, a dreamer who never let the realities of time and place limit his vision, could have believed that the Players could successfully mount such a work on their tiny stage. Although it was set during the time of Pericles, its stirring anti-war speeches were clearly addressed to the contemporary American audience of 1918, embroiled in World War I. Cook believed the war was a capitalist struggle, and, therefore, had no legitimacy for American socialist interests. Many in the Greenwich Village community agreed; and because of their beliefs, they had been harassed by the U.S. government.[10] That *The Athenian Women* was allowed to run uncensored, while other political and cultural activities espousing similar positions and themes were closed, is probably due to the fact that Cook set his protest in 445 BCE Greece, and dressed his protestors in Greek costumes. Yet, he carefully built parallels between Pericles's renunciation of imperial conquests and his willingness to engage in a thirty-year peace treaty to end the Peloponnesian War and the need for America to end its participation in the current war. The specific inspiration for the play was his reading of Thucydides. "With almost incredible foreknowledge Thucydides knew that he was writing in little the history of a greater war, 'In all human probability these things will happen again,' the Greek wrote centuries ago" (*Road* 215). Cook believed that his generation felt these words more than any other generation (*Road* 215).

If Thucydides as well as Plutarch gave him the historical grounding for the play, Aristophanes, albeit without his comedy and satire, provided the dramatic form, particularly the use of relations between women and men to alter historic events. In Cook's modern version of *Lysistrata*, Pericles has left his wife, Kalia, and now lives with Asphasia who prods him to turn his back on war and conquest. It is she who is the true hero of the play and who has the most stirring speeches, saying at one point to Kalia:

> O Kalia, do you not know in your heart that there is no other such disaster as this war of exhaustion which has become the nightmare of our lives. The evil brought into the world by such a war outweighs a thousandfold the good which victory can bring to either democracy or aristocracy. Take heed lest ten or twenty

years from now, with Athens and Sparta bleeding to
death, their splendid vital energy forever gone, their
generous spirits grown hateful with long hatred, you
are compelled to look back at this night and say—"I
might have prevented this!" (*Road* 216-17)

Making the analogy between the Greek war and the
present war, Cook has her also say to Pericles:

Not one hour undarkened by this threat which lies
like a nightmare on the clear soul of Greece. Will they
who come after us know how dark it was? If the light
of Greece goes out, what will there be but darkness? Is
the future to be shaped in the coarse and cruel minds
of Carthaginian or Roman, and not in the sensitive
strength of the beautiful mind of Greece. (*Road* 216)

While *The Athenian Women* falls far short of Greek models, it does reveal the extent to which Cook conflated Greece with America, and could extract lessons for the country of his birth from the history and vision of the country of his spirit.

The very nature of the Provincetown Players was predicated on his belief that a small group of people dedicated to beauty could make a positive change, that a beloved community of lifegivers could show by their own work and commitment the possibilities that lay undiscovered in the America of their time. It was his belief, energy, and total commitment that created the Provincetown miracle, and it was a miracle. With virtually no money, no press agent in the first years, and no advertising, a group of amateurs, virtually none of whom had ever worked in theatre before,[11] succeeded in putting on 100 original plays by 52 American playwrights,[12] including two bound for greatness: Eugene O'Neill and Susan Glaspell, whose successes validated his beliefs.

Ironically—or perhaps inevitably—the very success

of his theatre destroyed Cook's dream. As O'Neill's and Glaspell's works became known, subscriptions poured in, and productions such as *The Emperor Jones*, sold out on MacDougal Street, they were transferred "uptown" to Broadway, and eventually sent across the country in traveling companies.[13] Thus, the fragile organization that Cook had created began to unravel; it became less a community and more a commercial enterprise, a product of the changing times. In 1913 Cook was among others who dreamed of a new world in America, where beauty, love, joy, and harmony would thrive. By 1922, the idealistic fever had run its course; the Jazz era was beginning, and Jig Cook was considered by many an anachronistic holdover, chastising those with "little willingness to die for the thing we are building." It is no wonder that many of the newly-arrived Players found him at best out of step, at worst a befuddled nuisance.[14] Cook knew this. In what Glaspell calls one of his bravest hours, when squabbles over receiving salaries commensurate with their growing stature were rife, Jig convened the Players and read to them passages from Plato about community. It didn't help. Tired, disillusioned with the group, and hurt by what he felt was the rejection of his dream and himself, he told Glaspell "it's time to go to Greece." They intended to go for one year and then return refreshed. In the interim the theatre was rented and the company took a year's sabbatical.

In March 1922, twenty-five years after he had first planned his visit, Jig Cook finally arrived in Greece. When asked by those he met why he had come, he would reply, "Ancient Greeks said something to me, something I can still see across blurred centuries." He explained:

> I wanted before my moment was gone, to walk where their feet walked and see what their eyes saw. But I wanted more than that...I wanted you. I love so much the Greek words that I wanted for my friends men who have never spoken any other. Greek is not dead, I told myself. It lives and is spoken on Parnassus today. I will say all the common things, I will say "good morning and good night and give me some bread and let us sit down under the tree in words that said those things long ago. (*Road* 253)

The prized possession he brought with him was a copy of the huge Liddel and Scott Greek dictionary. Given his considerable linguistic talents, he was soon able to converse with local residents and read newspapers in Modern Greek just as he had earlier mastered classical Greek. He and Glaspell were also able to make a home for themselves in Delphi, as he had imagined. They rented a simple house that still stands at 29 Pavlou and Freiderikis Street, the main street of Delphi. The lot slopes so precariously that the house, which opens onto the street, angles down two stories in the back to the gardens sloping even further, affording a magnificent view of the valley of olive groves, the imposing, rounded mountain directly across, and, slightly to the right, and far below, the small town of Itea and the Corinthian Bay. Today the space they occupied is taken up by a gift shop, in the window of which are modern reproductions of Greek and Roman heroes; but the balcony behind the house is the original, and the view is still spectacular. In the summer, Cook also fulfilled his dream of ascending Parnassos and living with shepherds, the repositors, he believed, of life, language, and customs of the ancient Greeks. It was there in Kalania that he felt closest to his Greek dream.[15]

Although his Delphi stay was often marked by bouts of depression, particularly feelings of failure over the Provincetown Players, he still retained the absolute belief in those "radiant moments" that beauty and art can bring forth, and in the possibility of a community working to create them. While in Greece, he began talking of starting a Delphi Players, perhaps creating, he told his visiting friend Bill Rapp, another Oberammergau. He even outlined a trilogy he would write to open this new theatre to be situated in the ancient Delphi theatre. The first play concerned the evolution of life in Delphi, beginning thousands of years before classical Greece, when shepherds, antecedents of those still working in Kalania, tended their flocks and fought any attempts at encroachment. The second play would be set in the Hellenic world, the stones of the earlier time now taking on mythic import as they became part of rites codified and expanded in classical Greece. Finally Delphi of 1892 would emerge in the third part, with the old city now buried by the new and the modern Delphi, at the beginning of the twentieth century, resisting being moved from the ancient site to allow archeologists to rebuild the old city.

By the summer of 1923, Cook's plan for his Delphi theatre started to take shape and was even heard of abroad. A reporter from the *Philadelphia Enquirer* came especially to Delphi to write a story on the project and a young Athenian volunteered to be the theatre's stage manager. However, the plays were never presented. Cook's health had been compromised by his accelerated drinking in Delphi; and he was unable to ward off a case of glanders, a rare disease he contracted from his dog. He died in Delphi on January 11, 1924. Although Cook had been in Greece only two years, he had already won the hearts of the locals, and they insisted on performing the last rites for the man they called Kyrios Kouk, washing his body with wine and dressing him in his rouka, the traditional Greek costume that he had begun to wear. With his long white hair, it had suited him so well that when a fellow Iowan entering a taverna in Delphi in 1922 saw him, he wrote home that he had found "the personification of Greek power and beauty just as he had always imagined" (Ben-Zvi, *Susan Glaspell* 66). Cook would have been pleased.

His reputation was not confined to Delphi. In Athens, a special service was held in his honor, with Leandros Palamas, son of the Greek national poet, reading portions of *The Athenian Women* that Cook had begun translating into Greek and which Palamas completed. Palamas also organized a George Cram Cook Club, and on the following Easter led a group to his grave. In addition, the Greek Writers' Union petitioned the government, and they agreed for the first time to have a stone from the Temple of Apollo to be used as a headstone. On a slab of marble, which covers Cook's grave is the last stanza from his poem "At Fifty I Ask God": "I hear the mountain stream/Pouring in beauty/That rhythmic water/Does not need to be/More than itself,/But I,/Spirit,/Have no reason for living unless, somehow, for spirit/somewhere,/Life is immortal" (*Greek Coins* 132). Under it in larger letters is carved George Cram Cook, and under that is the figure of a small bird, part of the legend already spreading of Jig's taming of a small robin, a *kombojanne*, in Kalania, which flew to Delphi when he was dying. Directly behind the grave, on the huge stones of the back wall of the cemetery, are two other plaques. On one are two stanzas from his poem "The Shining Rocks." the second of which reads:" More deeply here/In the heart that is us all,/ The instinct of the hollow of the hills,/Not knowing its own aim,/Built blindly for the Greece which could not be" (*Greek Coins* 80). On the other, placed there by Nilla Cook, his daughter, twenty years later are the names of his mother, Ma-Mie; Nilla's mother, Mollie Price; and Susan Glaspell.

When the word reached America that Cook had died, condolences and obituaries were numerous. The most moving was the anonymous article in *The Nation*, which ended thus: "George Cram Cook was a Greek of the Periclean age, strayed somehow out of his place and time into our more timid age; and after bruising himself by working a lifetime against realities which he was too eager to reshape, he strayed back again to what must have seemed his own country" (*Nation* 23 January 1924).

There is a footnote to Cook's Delphi dream. In 1923 Glaspell, Cook, and Nilla had spent the month of May in Xylokastro, a seaside town near Corinth, with their friends Eva Palmer and her husband Angelos Sikelianos—later to be the national poet of Greece—his sister, Penelope, and her husband, Raymond Duncan, brother of Isadora Duncan.[16] During the month the group talked about their shared dream to reclaim ancient Greek culture and folk art, and to renew the Delphi Festival: Palmer hoping to resurrect the art of classical weaving, and Sikelianos to reconstitute Greek Drama, "not the trifling exertions which gather little crowds to little theatres but the great drama which helps masses, fifteen, twenty, thirty thousand people in the pursuit of great poetry, great music, great dancing" (Palmer 103). Like Cook, Sikelianos believed in action, not talk, about the Delphi vision. He also believed, like Cook, that "to reach below the surface where speeches cannot penetrate, our actors must be organically connected with the roots of the Greek people" (Palmer, 103).

In May 1927, Eva Palmer and Angelos Sikelianos finally arranged to hold a Delphi Festival, just as Cook had dreamed. Besides staging *Prometheus Bound*, they organized an exhibition of Greek folk art, and a performance of klepthic ballads. They also held the Pythian Games in the ancient stadium, and dedicated them to Cook. Nilla, who had returned to Delphi a year after her father's death, and at seventeen had married Nikos Proestopoulos, a cousin of Sikelianos, worked with Palmer and Sikelianos to create the festival. At their house in Phaleron near hers, Nilla learned to weave the ancient Greek silk fabric that would fall in perfect folds for the authentic costumes they created. She watched as workers embroidered designs taken from ancient vases, depicting Dionysus, attic images, and dolphins, the sign of Apollo. She also was part of the Oceanides group that presented Greek dances at the festival, accompanied by their own singing.

In her description of the festival, however, she makes special mention of the athletic games, dedicated to her father:

> With a clash of shields and blare of trumpets they danced the Pyricheion, the ancient war dance for fallen heroes, in memory of Kyrios Kouk. The drums and trumpets rang in the cliffs and the cheers of the stadium when the white silk banner with his name in gold letters was carried around it. What he would have liked best, I thought, was that the eagles came down from the peaks of Parnassus to see what was going on. (Nilla Cook 60)[17]

The games were held again in May 1930 and were

equally successful, drawing over 3,000 participants from around the world. However, try as they might, Sikelianos in Greece and Palmer, who subsequently divorced him and returned to America, could not get further backing for the event, although she spent the remainder of her life trying to interest Americans, including Eleanor Roosevelt, in sponsorship, so that the Delphi ideal of world understanding through beauty and moderation would not "fall from the high lookout where we had placed it."[18] In 1950 she returned to Greece; Sikelianos died that year, and she the year after. She is buried one grave away from Cook, along the same ancient wall.

Cook's part in the reinstitution of the Delphi festival, however, has blurred with time, just as the letters carved on his grave have faded. In 1997, on the 70th anniversary of the first event, the European Cultural Centre at Delphi sponsored an international symposium honoring the festival. Although there were papers, exhibits, and performances concentrating on the work and life of Eva Palmer and Angelos Sikelianos, and the Sikelianos museum honoring the couple and the festival was officially opened yards from the old cemetery, there was no mention at all of Cook. His name still does not appear in the museum today. Like so many instances in his life, his inspiration and influence on others, as well as his own work have gone unacknowledged. It is time to rectify this erasure, for if there ever were a person faithful to the Delphi dream it was George Cram Cook.

Works Cited

Banks, Charles Eugene. Assisted by George Cram Cook and Marshall Everett [pseudonym of Henry Neil]. *Beautiful Homes and Social Customs of America: A Complete Guide to Correct Social Form and Artistic Living*. Chicago: Bible House (Henry Neil), 1902. Print.

Ben-Zvi, Linda. *Susan Glaspell: Her Life and Times*. New York: Oxford University Press, 2005. Print.

_____., ed. *The Road to the Temple* by Susan Glaspell. Jefferson, North Carolina: McFarland and Company, 2005. Print.

Bölsche, Wilhelm. *Haeckel: His Life and Work*. Translated by Joseph McCale. Philadelphia: George W. Jacobs, 1907. Print.

Cook, George Cram. *The Athenian Women*. With the original text and a modern Greek translation by the author and revised by C Carthais. Athens: Printing House "Estia," 1926. Print.

_____. *The Chasm: A Novel*. New York: Frederick A. Stokes, 1911. Print.

_____. and Charles Eugene Banks. In Hampton Roads: A Dramatic Romance. Chicago Rand, McNally, 1899. Print.

_____. *Roderick Taliaferro: A Story of Maximilian's Empire*. Illustrated by Seymour M. Stone. New York: Macmillan, 1903. Print.

Cook, Nilla. *My Road to India*. New York: Lee Furman, 1939. Print.

Daly, Anne. *Done into Dance: Isadora Duncan in America*. Bloomington: Indiana University Press, 1995. Print.

Dell, Floyd. *Homecoming: an Autobiography*. New York:

Farrar and Rinehart, 1933. Print.

———. *Intellectual Vagabondage*. 1926. Reprint. Edited by Douglas Clayton. Chicago: Ivan R. Dee, 1990. Print.

———. *Moon-Calf*. New York: Knopf, 1920. Print.

Deutsch, Helen and Stella Hanau. *The Provincetown: A Story of the Theatre*. New York: Russell and Russell, 1931. Print.

Duncan, Isadora. *My Life*. Garden City, New York: Garden City Press, 1927. Print.

Emerson, Ralph Waldo. "Nature," *Essays and Poems*. Edited and with an Introduction by Peter Norberg. New York: Barnes and Noble Classic Series, 2004. Print.

Francis, Elizabeth. *The Secret Treachery of Words: Feminism and Modernism in America*. Minneapolis: University of Minnesota Press, 2002. Print.

Glaspell, Susan. *Fidelity*. Boston: Small, Maynard, 1915. Print.

———., ed. *Greek Coins: Poems by George Cram Cook*. New York: George Doran, 1925. Print.

———., ed. *The Road to the Temple*. New York: Frederick A. Stokes, 1927. Reprint. With a new Preface by the author. New York: Frederick A. Stokes, 1941. Reprint. Edited and with an Introduction by Linda Ben-Zvi. Jefferson, North Carolina: McFarland, 2005. Print.

Kemper, Susan. "The Novels, Plays, and Poetry of George Cram Cook, Founder of the Provincetown Players." PhD diss., Bowling Green University, 1982. Print.

Kenton, Edna. "The Provincetown Players and the Playwrights' Theatre" (1931). Edited by Travis Bogard and Jackson R. Bryer. *Eugene O'Neill Re-*

view 21.1-2 (Fall 1997): 15-160. Print.
Palmer-Sikelianos, Eva. *Upward Panic: The Autobiography of Eva Palmer-Sikileanos*. Edited and with an Introduction by John P. Anton. London: Harwood Publishers, 1993. Print.
Richards, Robert J. *The Tragic Sense of Life: Ernst Haeckel and the Struggle over Evolutionary Thought*. Chicago: University of Chicago Press, 2008. Print.
Sarlós, Robert Károly. *Jig Cook and the Provincetown Players*. Boston: University of Massachusetts Press, 1982. Print.
Tanselle, Thomas. "George Cram Cook and the Poetry of Living, with a Checklist." *Books at Iowa* 24 (April 1976). Print.
Williams, Maynard Owen. "New Greece, the Centenarian Forges Ahead," *National Geographic* December 1930. Print.

Notes

1 On the history of the Provincetown Players, see Deutsch and Hanau; Kenton; Sarlós; and Ben-Zvi, *Susan Glaspell: Her Life and Times* and *The Road to the Temple*.
2 On Cook and his writing, see Tanselle and Kemper.
3 For their experiences in Greece, see *The Road to the Temple*, particularly 243-339.
4 The biography was republished in 1941, largely because of Cook's prescient comments, written in 1922 in Delphi yet pertinent to people living in the shadow of World War II:

    The oracle at Delphi which still speaks
    To whomso cares to listen
    Gives Europe
        "Till 1941."
    Europe then will die
    Of Nietzsche's philosophy—

> As the eagle and lion die,
> Being for themselves alone.
> The lone hand loses.
> Pity their magnificence.

The third edition appeared in 2005, which I edited to supplement my biography of Glaspell.

5 The Cabin, usually referred to with a capital letter denoting a proper name, was actually a plantation, a rambling two-story house with dark red roofs, built in the 1830s. In 1902, Cook, assisting his friend Charles Eugene Banks in writing the book *Beautiful Homes and Social Customs of America*, provides a photo and a description of the "elegant" atmosphere and "cozy room of Mrs. Cook." For other descriptions, see *The Road to the Temple* and Dell, *The Homecoming* and *Moon Calf*.

6 This and all other quotations of non-published material, appear in Ben-Zvi, *Susan Glaspell*.

7 In light of the focus on Charles Darwin during the bicentennial of his birth, there is new interest in Haeckel. See, for example, Richards.

8 For the influence of Haeckel on Duncan, see Daly and Richards. Richards describes Duncan's invitation to Haeckel to attend one of her performances in Berlin (420).

9 Around the time Cook started the Monist Society, he met a young anarchist journalist from Chicago, Mollie Price. They married in 1909, despite the growing friendship between him and Glaspell. After two years of marriage and two children, Nilla and Harl, he and Glaspell declared their love for each other, but had to wait for two more years to wed, until his second divorce became final.

10 In one of the most famous cases, the editors of the socialist journal *The Masses*, John Reed, Floyd Dell, Max Eastman, and artist John Sloan—all close friends of Cook—who were tried twice and finally acquitted for advocating and dispensing information concerning draft evasion. Even Eugene Debs, four-time candidate for president on the socialist ticket was arrested as well.

11 When trained director Nina Moise first joined the Play-

ers, she found that the working arrangement was "If people stood in front of each other and bumped each other in a room, why not do it on the stage, which was exactly what they were doing. I didn't know much about stage direction, the rest of them knew less."

12 Cook was adamant about producing only American writers and original plays. Only two non-American playwrights were staged: Arthur Schnitzler and Gustav Wied, both during time when Cook was not involved in the program or on sabbatical leave from the Players.

13 For a discussion of the end of the Provincetown Players, see Ben-Zvi, *Susan Glaspell*, 251-62.

14 For controversy surrounding Cook's direction of the Players in 1922, see Ben-Zvi, 251-55.

15 See Glaspell's descriptions of Delphi and Kalania in *Road*, and my summary of this period in *Susan Glaspell* "Interlude 2."

16 For details about the time spent in Xylokastro, see Nilla Cook, 19.

17 For descriptions of the Delphic Festival, see also, «A Delphic Festival,» *Morning Post*, 13 May 1925, and Maynard Owen Williams, "New Greece, the Centenarian Forges Ahead," *National Geographic*, December 1930.

18 Information about Palmer from the Museum of the Delphi Festival.

The Value of Home: Susan Glaspell's *Fugitive's Return* as a Response to F. Scott Fitzgerald's *The Great Gatsby*

Barbara Ozieblo

Susan Glaspell's fifth novel, *Fugitive's Return* (1929), begins with a failed suicide attempt, and yet it ends with the protagonist returning to her home in the West, full of hope for the future, having rejected easy solutions in favor of a positive stance and a readiness to labor for the "other," a labor that promises personal salvation. This essay will explore Glaspell's attitude toward home and America in her modernist novel *Fugitive's Return*, in juxtaposition to the widely acclaimed and taught *The Great Gatsby* (1925) by F. Scott Fitzgerald, one of "that enduring triad, the 'big three' of Hemingway, Faulkner, Fitzgerald," as novelist and critic Nicholas Delbanco dubbed them in a 1999 interview (238).

Before looking in greater detail at these two novels and comparing their vision of the American future and the value of self and home, an inevitable question requires at least minimal consideration: why did that "triad" endure and make it into the second half of the twentieth century when Glaspell did not? On publication in 1929, *Fugitive's Return* earned words of praise from the *New York Herald Tribune* book reviewer Virgilia Peterson Ross, who admired the "soaring quality" of the novel, and noted that *Fugitive's Return*, as it follows "a woman's stream of thought and memory [,] ... swells, surges, recedes and rises again in a fine rhythm. Like the sea, it awes you." For critic Arthur Hobson Quinn, writing in 1936, *Fugitive's Return* was a novel of "distinction" (716) and Glaspell "a novelist of high rank" (717). Not only was *Fugitive's Return* well-received by the critics; it ranked fourth on bestseller charts that placed Ernest Hemingway's *A Farewell to Arms* first. However, no critic claimed it to be an "American" novel in its portrayal of a distraught woman who has lost her husband and her adored daughter and yet fights her way through to survival.

On the other hand, Fitzgerald's novel of adultery, murder, and suicide was declared by Harry Hansen to be "American to the core, modern to the hour, sophisticated" (Bryer 231), and it garnered earnest praise from critics such as Gilbert Seldes writing for the prestigious *Dial*, or William Rose Benét who claimed that the novel was "disillusioned" and "mature" (Bryer 219). These critics were praising what they saw as Fitzgerald's development from a chronicler of college love affairs in *This Side of Paradise* to a novelist of mature technique in story and style; H. L. Mencken recognized the "charm and beauty of the writing" (Bryer 212) while Seldes, acknowledging that the characters and the setting were "specifically of Long Island," claimed nonetheless that they were "universal" and that "the spirit underneath" was American (Bryer 240). Curiously, both Ruth Snyder writing in the *New York Evening World* and Ruth Hale of the *Brooklyn Daily Eagle*, whom Susan Glaspell had known in her Provincetown Players days, were annoyed by *The Great Gatsby*.[1] For Snyder, Fitzgerald was "evidently attempting to 'degrade the American girl' by covering her with imaginary vices" (Bryer 195), while Hale dismissed the novel with an exasperated: "The boy is simply puttering around" (Bryer 197).

Many reasons can be put forward as to why Glaspell's voice was silenced after her death in spite of the Pulitzer Prize for drama in 1931 and the critical and popular acclaim that her novels had won. Martha Carpentier has argued convincingly in an essay comparing Willa Cather's and Susan Glaspell's novels that there are many reasons why Glaspell's oeuvre was so easily dismissed: she reminds us of Paul Lauter's statements on canon formation as a masculine, nationalistic endeavor, of the establishment of American modernism as typically male territory, and of the disadvantages of Glaspell's style, which, "embracing as it does psychological realism, naturalism, and expressionism, does not accord with the New Critical aesthetics which dominated literary taste … through the 1960s" ("The Deracinated Self" 152). More importantly, however, Carpentier points to yet another reason why Glaspell's work was dismissed while, as she indicates, Cather's novels have been allowed into the canon. Although, as Glaspell herself admitted (see Rohe), she was not interested in political activism, she did believe in a writer's political responsibility and reflected her political and social ideas in her oeuvre. Carpentier points to "Glaspell's adherence to progressive political ideals well past the end of the Progressive era" and concludes that: "Both Willa Cather and Susan Glaspell are American myth-makers, but Glaspell presents the most sacred of American myths as contested – it is the plurality of choices and ways of being that to her are inherently American, rather than a hegemonic monomyth of personal and national destiny" ("The Deracinated Self" 152).

Noelia Hernando-Real has argued in similar terms. In a 2007 article on the play *Inheritors*, Hernando-Real focuses on Glaspell's role in the development of the concept of "cultural pluralism" as "she deconstructs the universalism of the United States, offering instead a feminist and multicultural revision of its identity" (65-66). Such a "feminist and multicultural" revision, however, was not appreciated by critics throughout most of the twentieth century while Fitzgerald's ability to capture what was interpreted as a whole era of American history in his novels was joyfully embraced – indeed, Jeffrey Steinbrink even attributes the "spirit of the 1920s" to Fitzgerald, stating that "he helped to create [it]" (159). Steinbrink identifies the period as entropic and dominated by frustration, disappointment, and disenchantment:

> The New Jerusalem envisioned by our Puritan fathers was never to be realized; the possibilities of a spiritual regeneration in a boundless New World were fatally diminished by the closing of the frontier ... The very impetus or direction of American history came repeatedly into question, and what once had appeared ... an ascending spiral curve now became a steady downward sweep toward the void of nonexistence. (158)

Given this depressing situation, Steinbrink identifies Fitzgerald's position on "the course of human experience, whether individual or societal ... as a long downward glide" (158), so that Gatsby's dream of returning to the past is necessarily doomed. This pessimistic vision is only heightened by Fitzgerald's attitude to the West, as described by William R. Handley. According to Handley, Fitzgerald rejects Frederick Jackson Turner's concept of the Frontier as a leveling of classes and races and stresses the materialistic approach: "Immigrant experience is erased in favor of a seeming 'natural aristocracy,' and instead of Turner's composite American, the victors to whom belong the spoils are the Anglo-Saxons, Nick and Tom" (Handley 163). Indeed, Tom, the first time we see him, identifies himself as a "terrible pessimist" who believes that "civilization's going to pieces" (19);[2] he has absorbed the ideas of Goddard as expressed in *The Rise of the Colored Empires* and insists that: "It's up to us, who are the dominant race, to watch out or these other races will have control of things" (*The Great Gatsby* 19).[3]

Glaspell's attitude toward the American West and other races is far from Fitzgerald's pessimism and racial superiority. As Carpentier has argued, Glaspell "celebrated the ideals that drove immigrants to make a new life in America" ("The Deracinated Self" 141) in *Inheritors* and in novels such as *The Morning Is Near Us*. In *Fugitive's Return*, the protagonist Irma Lee learns to accept those she had initially considered inferior and to be positive about her roots and the future. Irma's family goes back to the earliest settlers – "Great-grandfather Lee had come there the year Iowa was opened for settlement, and this gave a certain position" (110) – even though the gradual loss of family fortunes had upset their social ranking and their part of town had become less desirable. The link between the early settlers and the new immigrants is made explicit in the move of Irma's family from the old home to one of the row houses her father had built to rent to the Irish, the Swedes, and the Germans who had come into the area. As a child, Irma views the immigrant laborers as inferior, but as she grows older, she learns to accept them and their role in the life of the community. By the time her brother marries one of the Swedish girls, she is ready to drop her superior tone and participate in the young family's meals, "sharing their ice-cream" and their dreams for the future (*Fugitive's Return* 154). At the novel's end, after her sojourn in Delphi, which Carpentier identifies as an "inspirational return, to use the Bergsonian term, to *origines*" ("The Deracinated Self" 137), she is able to redefine her concept of identity, family, and community: her vision of the American future, as of her own, is not a "downward glide" but a reaffirmation of purpose.

Other interpretations of the *The Great Gatsby* also help to emphasize the different attitudes displayed by Fitzgerald and Glaspell. Nicole Guetin focuses on Fitzgerald's Irish-Catholic background and sees Gatsby's desire to recover Daisy's love as a "holy mission." Gatsby then becomes a "wealthy worshipper" and his house a "richly adorned temple dedicated to Daisy as his celestial queen" (22). This of course implies a spirituality or unearthliness that places Daisy above and beyond sexuality; she is indeed presented to the reader as dressed in virginal white, almost "p-paralysed with happiness" and "her face was sad and lovely with bright things in it" (*Great Gatsby* 15) – like the jewels that adorn statues of Madonnas, we might say. Gatsby's quest, "the following of a grail" (*Great Gatsby* 155), according to Nick, becomes a spiritual mission, not an adventure of passionate love, and Gatsby himself is a Platonic creation. For Guetin, the novel depicts "a spiritual world where men and women are disincarnated" (23). Indeed, in *The Great Gatsby*, passion is linked to adultery and violence, rather than to Gatsby's love for Daisy or Nick's attraction to Jordan. Glaspell's position on love and passion is much less Victorian. In the play *The Verge*, her protagonist is married, has a lover for whom she is "a fascinating hostess" (62) under her husband's roof, and incites another man to make love to her (87). The novels *Fidelity* and *Brook Evans* (the latter made into a film significantly entitled *The Right to Love*) also have protagonists who surrender themselves to Dionysian love, rejecting the "spiritual" or "disincarnated" Apollonian concept of such emotions. As in all her writing, in *Fugitive's Return*, Glaspell creates a protagonist who learns to accept that passion and desire are a part of her being (see Carpentier *Major Novels*, 101). Love is linked neither to adultery, procreation, or social betterment but to a truly "orgastic" (*Great Gatsby* 187) or "ecstatic" Dionysian release, in which "passion and tenderness had wed, and there was the new-born ecstasy" (*Fugitive's Return* 284).[4]

Bert Bender, rather than attribute the lack of sexuality in *The Great Gatsby* to its author's religious upbringing, points in the direction of Darwin, Haeckel, and Fitzgerald's interest in evolutionary biology, as he understood it, particularly in Darwin's theory of sexual selection as governing social hierarchies: "As a story of modern love, *Gatsby* is squarely within the tradition of American fiction that began to appropriate Darwin's theory of sexual selection immediately after *The Descent of Man*, beginning with W. D. Howells's *A Chance Acquaintance*" (Bender 404). Such a reading allows Bender to consider Nick as being "repelled by the chaotic nature of sex" (415) and to reduce Gatsby and Daisy to beings propelled by the "force of beauty" (407) toward one another, the instinct to multiply thwarted only by Tom's brute force supported by his superior social standing (404).

Contrasting with the racist, eugenicist, and asexual perspective that these critics have identified in Fitzgerald's novel, Glaspell's vision of America, of the West, and of personal relationships was based on quite other premises, although she too was not only an admirer of Haeckel, but also of Nietzsche. Kristina Hinz-Bode, in her essay "Susan Glaspell and the Epistemological Crisis of Modernity," draws attention to Haeckel's "holistic philosophy (a kind of scientific pantheism) that attempted to reconcile the contemporary knowledge of the origin of species and the evolution of man with the need for religion he observed in Western societies" (93), a strain of Haeckelian thought that Scott Fitzgerald apparently did not take into account. This "mixture of Romantic natural philosophy and empirical Darwinian science" as Hinz-Bode indicates, "obviously appealed to Glaspell" (93) who had joined the Monist Society of Davenport as a young woman in 1907, preferring its meetings to church-going and finding in it "a welcome outlet for her frustrations [with traditional Davenport society] and ideas" (Ozieblo 2000, 38). Monism would be influential in most of her writing; as Hinz-Bode rightly claims:

> Many of her works deal directly with Haeckel's philosophy of the 'oneness' of all things, which Glaspell combined with an idealist notion of evolutionary progressivism. Metaphorically, her hope for a progressive development of humankind is often represented by what she calls the 'leap' – the evolutionary jump made by the first primitive life forms from water to land. In this step, for Glaspell, lies the cradle of the pioneer spirit, the *daring to change life and make it better*. (94, my emphasis)

Glaspell believed in the constant upward curve of humanity, in a constant progression toward perfection and a renewal of the capacities of nature and humankind, and thus, *Fugitive's Return* can be read as a response to *The Great Gatsby's* pessimism as to America and her future. Indeed, it would be safe to claim that, while always aware of the failings of humankind, her whole oeuvre labors to bring out our affirmative aspects and possibilities – especially those of women. In the play *The Verge* (1921), the protagonist Claire, a botanist who is researching new life forms, believes that destruction can engender renewal:

> Plants do it. The big leap – it's called. Explode their species – because something in them knows they've gone as far as they can go. Something in them knows they're shut in to just that. So – go mad – that life may not be poisoned. Break themselves up into crazy things – into lesser things, and from the pieces – may come one sliver of life with vitality to find the future. How beautiful. How brave. (70)

Claire even sees the Great War as "another gorgeous chance" that was lost; it was an opportunity to "Break up. Push. Harder. Break up. And then – and then – But we didn't say – 'And then –' The spirit didn't take the tip" (70). Glaspell does, however, question the price of such dramatic renewal. Her protagonist in this play breaks through into new forms when she creates a plant called "Breath of Life" that is "stronger … and more fragile" and whose "form is set" (96); but a price has to be paid for breaking out into what is new because the inevitable loss of novelty leads to stagnation that will again imprison life. Nonetheless, the attempt to break out has to be made as it is the only future for the progress of humankind – progress that is never won by going back to the past as Gatsby is determined to do. As *The Verge* ends, Claire is judged insane by her family and friends; her spirit has gone beyond the limitations imposed by society and therefore beyond the bounds of sanity. Glaspell leaves her on "the verge" of society, her future open to the audience's interpretation.[5]

In *Fugitive's Return* Irma Lee is drawn to death by the loss of her daughter – Claire too had lost a young son – and becomes incapable of acceptable functioning within society. Irma's momentary madness leads to a thwarted suicide attempt and a psychosomatic muteness; the resulting isolation, both geographical and psychological, added to the loss she has suffered, is the price she pays for her epiphanic realization that she must return to labor in her grandfather's vineyard. The form of the novel, in particular Glaspell's use of a third-person stream-of-consciousness narrative that moves backward and forward in time, permitted Glaspell to develop her argument further than she could go in *The Verge*. Irma, having experienced the violent break-up of ambitions and desires founded on love for the husband who has left her and the child who has died, eventually finds strength and inspiration to re-create herself anew among the ruins of the sacred temples of Delphi. In contrast, neither Nick nor Gatsby attain renewal. Nick, bored with the West after his war experiences felt that in the East his life "was beginning over again" (*Great Gatsby* 10) and put his hopes on his financial and social career. Gatsby, who "sprang from his Platonic conception of himself" (105) when he abandoned his life in the West as a beachcomber, arrived in New York imprisoned in his dream of recovering Daisy. Both, as we know, were doomed to fail. Monetary gain and the ethereal image of Daisy, the only incentives Fitzgerald could offer them, were not sufficient to sustain regeneration. Irma's struggle to re-identify herself as a valuable member of the human community succeeds because it is founded on a realization of her own worth, an inner strength built out of pain and directed toward a meaningful objective, that of helping another.

Glaspell's philosophy of "evolutionary progressivism" was based on her faith in human courage to go beyond the accepted patterns of social life, and she had no qualms in taking for women what Nietzsche had claimed for men. Margit Sichert believes that Glaspell "would have shocked Nietzsche" (272) by her appropriation of Zarathustra's "I will" for Claire in *The Verge*; I would go further and claim that she would do so for all her women protagonists. In Irma's case, the condition of outsider during her exile in Delphi and the inability to communicate through speech allow her to live in a state of pseudo-nirvana, negating the past and unaware of the present. It is only when she recovers speech that she recognizes her own pain. Sichert, expanding on how Glaspell had appropriated Nietzsche's thought, quotes the philosopher's derisive "Pain makes hens and poets cackle" (274) from his discourse on the pain of creation in *Thus Spoke Zarathustra*. As Claire in *The Verge* recognizes the anguish of bringing new forms to life, so Irma knows the agony of sorrow and the agon of rebirth that is essential if one is to go on living, a process summarily denied to Gatsby through the agency of Myrtle Wilson's husband and one of which Nick is simply incapable.

Having re-found her voice, Irma can no longer stifle her feelings; sitting on one of the stone seats in the ancient theater of Delphi, she struggles with her memories: "Until now she had remained quiet. That long quiet broke, and she was sobbing, crying out her anguish, the mother mourning for her child" (217). Irma is unsure whether her life in Delphi is real or a dream, whether perhaps she had taken the overdose she had already prepared when her cousin Janet walked into her bedroom and arranged for her to go to Greece, and she is tortured by that timeless existential question of the meaning of life. She asks for a sign: "There was something she wanted to know. She wanted to know who and where she was. And why? Why?" (229). And it is then, at this crucial moment when Irma is searching for peace and understanding that the deformed shepherd girl, Constantina, appears before her: on the ancient stage where countless plays had been performed, Constantina's head came up from between the stones and then disappeared. Although Irma knows that Constantina's appearance is easily explained by a passage underneath the stage, she interprets the girl's emergence from the stones as the sign of life she had been asking for: "now she knew who and where she was. Constantina had told her it was not a dream. Constantina had told her it was life" (230). She thus links Constantina and the Delphic Oracle. Martha Carpentier, when she interprets this critical moment as a birth image – "Constantina can represent both a daughter born to Irma and Irma herself reborn as a child" (*Major Novels* 98) – highlights the complexity of the novel and the multiple meanings it encloses.

On another occasion, wandering among the ruins of the ancient temples, Irma had found the "hollowed place" from which the Oracle had spoken and where Constantina "had been ravished" by the handsome shepherd Andreas. In this spot, Irma again turns to the Oracle, this time questioning its very existence: she initially sees the concept as "a childish idea. Man wanting to be directed. Man getting up a play. Give me wisdom, man said. Show me the way… . *Wisdom was to point the way for himself, and he did not know that wisdom is that which looks on*" (93, my emphasis). With these words, although still unconsciously, Irma is accepting the peace that comes with the ability to value self as an independent and yet integrated being. And so, when she settles herself in the hollow, "it was as if something opened underneath" and she finds herself talking to the Oracle, at first scoffing its male-oriented wisdom: "Oracle, what did you ever know – beyond the way to win a battle?" But then she urges the Oracle to respond to her queries in more personal terms:

> Why do we never reach what we know is there to find?
> Why do we cease to seek what we were born to treasure?
> What is it lets us know our days are passing and we not in them?
> Wake now – be voice for us!
> Be shepherd's voice, for man is lost.
> Silent? Still silent?
> Too easy.
> Silence may be emptiness. Pretensions. Fear. *I* know.
> Oracle, so you know Constantina?
> Tell me – I cannot tell it – *are* you Constantina? (96)[6]

The last lines of the monologue: "Sometimes we feel we have not far to go,/ But we do not know that little way" (97), state clearly Irma's quest for peace and acceptance of self as she struggles for wisdom at the site of the Delphic Oracle.

Even as a child, Irma had found it difficult to accept her position in life and society. The impoverished circumstances of her parents had made her feel like an outsider in their Midwestern town, and then her husband's desertion had emphasized this sense of not belonging within society. Thus Irma can identify with Constantina and is fascinated by the girl from the moment she first sees her, reaching out to her, and gradually winning her confidence. Constantina, born deformed and ugly, was cursed by her father who had wanted a son. As soon as she was old enough, he sent her out into the mountains to mind the sheep where she suffers not only the horror of rape but also the ignominy of the boy's refusal to marry her. Andreas, who had preferred prison to marriage to Constantina, was now to marry Theodora, the beautiful refugee from Turkey in Irma's service. Constantina, watching the courting couple among the sacred ruins, tips over a rock that crashes on Andreas and kills him, and the villagers, who had always mocked the girl, turn against her, for "There was no punishment too great for a woman who killed a man in Greece" (299).

Irma saves Constantina by helping her escape from her pursuers and cross the mountain on foot. Relatively safe in the train that will take them westward, away from the scene of the murder, she hears a voice: "And the wonder was the greater, for the clear voice was her own. From the very heart of that which was herself, she heard a voice that was her own, and the voice said: 'I am going home'" (323). Her struggle has given fruit, and not only can she now communicate with others, but, more importantly, she can hear her own voice. She is now able to "point the way for [her]self" (93) and accept, as she had understood when she had previously questioned the Oracle among the ruins, that wisdom must come from oneself, and not from a soothsayer, even one disguised as an innocent, hurt child. Although Irma had had moments of homesickness as a young woman when living with her aunt after her parents' death (131, 153), she had never fully known what "home" meant; now she understands: "Slowly it rose – that which gave meaning to all her days. The old house on the hill ... waited – patient, ready" (323-4). As the novel ends, Irma Lee does not know what the future holds. The last lines of the novel: "She did not see all that was between, but the goal she saw – inevitable, benign, as day. She would labor in her vineyard. In her own vineyard would she labor" (324). These lines can only be read as a positive statement about going home, a determination that the modernists of the Lost Generation were not able to embrace.

Throughout the novel, the house in which Irma had been born and lived in as a child, and to which she is now returning, bears symbolic meaning. It is a ruined "house on the hill" (110), with its unkempt vineyards, and thus resonates with the biblical phrase "You are the light of the world. A city set on a hill cannot be hid," from the Sermon on the Mount, and with Winthrop's "city upon a hill," a phrase that has been used and abused by politicians and that has done so much to mythologize the significance of America. As Hernando-Real has shown, Glaspell de-mythologizes this image in the play *Inheritors*, and in *Fugitive's Return* she invests it with new, highly personal, meaning. In *Inheritors*, Silas Morton builds a college on his prime land, a hill, in order to educate the boys and girls of the prairies. This college, as Hernando-Real has argued, loses its symbolic value when it becomes a place of "confrontation ... based on race, class, or gender" (75) as it is about to receive financial aid from the state. But the protagonist, Madeline, refuses to let her grandfather's spirit die when she insists on following her conscience, on pretending "just for fun – that the things we say about ourselves [as Americans] are true" (139), even though she is aware that her action will result in a prison sentence. In *Fugitive's Return*, Glaspell allows Irma to achieve the wisdom and voice necessary to value her "house on the hill" as she embarks on the return journey, full of hope after her experience of life on the slopes of Parnassus, to a future that draws active inspiration from her past, rather than mere nostalgic yearning for a lost Eden.

In *Fugitive's Return*, home is a welcoming place, in which Irma, even as a child who resented the unfashionable, old family house that did not have an indoor toilet (110), was happy listening to her father's stories of the first settlers when "it was just themselves, just here at home" (117). No such idyllic family scenes appear in *The Great Gastby*: Nick's memories of home are full of "cold vestibules" (182), "hard-boiled" portraits of ancestors, and a "clan" of potentially disapproving "aunts and uncles" (9) in a town full of gossip and rumors. The novel is dominated by Tom Buchanan's "red-and-white Georgian Colonial mansion" (12) and Gatsby's "colossal affair by any standard – a factual imitation of some Hôtel de Ville in Normandy" (11). Gatsby's father, who appears briefly, is awed by the "height and splendor of the hall and the great rooms opening out from it into other rooms" (174), but seems to prefer the photograph of the house that his son had sent him. By the end of the novel, both houses stand empty (186), incapable of sustaining life or love, of harboring positive memories, or of promising a future.

In contrast to the houses in *The Great Gatsby*, all the homes in *Fugitive's Return* are sites of warmth, security, and companionable living, even the cramped row house that Irma's family is forced to move into after the fire that destroyed their home; and "the house beside the temple" (48) in which Irma lives in Delphi is more of a home than any of the houses in Fitzgerald's novel. Irma finds books there that are waiting for her to read, learn from, and enjoy; Gatsby's library only pretends to be a real library, just as the house is merely the pretence of a home. As the man with "owl-eyed spectacles" marvels when he picks up a book: "It's a bonafide piece of printed matter. It fooled me. This fella's a regular Belasco. It's a triumph. What thoroughness! What realism! Knew when to stop, too – didn't cut the pages" (*The Great Gatsby* 51-52). The counterfeit of home works on another level in *The Great Gatsby*: the servants, butlers, chauffeurs and gardeners are legion but impersonal and sometimes "villainous" (119). Irma Lee, even when she does not speak, is surrounded by people she comes to love and who care for her wellbeing: Vascelo, who does the cooking, and the refugee maid Theodora both live in the lower part of the house, and the three women form a community that, in spite of the rivalries between Vascelo and Theodora, acts as an extended family. There is no satisfying sense of family or community in *The Great Gatsby*, neither in the West where Nick and Daisy come from, nor in the East.

As Irma sets out for the Midwest in *Fugitive's Return*, so also *The Great Gatsby* ends with Nick returning to the Midwest; his return, however, signals the recognition of the "ruined promise of the East" (Ornstein 59) or, more bluntly, as Gary J. Scrimgeour puts it, "[Nick] Carraway's distinctiveness as a character is that he fails to learn anything from his story" (78). On leaving for the East, he thought he was going "permanently" because the "Middle West now seemed like the ragged edge of the universe" (9). But his eastern experience makes him reject all "riotous excursions with privileged glimpses into the human heart" for the straight-laced "uniform" and "moral attention" (8) he had always associated with the West and had considered himself superior to. As Janet Giltrow and David Stouck argue, Nick returns to his "Midwestern origins" in search of "an ideal of lost innocence" (144) – a disconsolate contrast to Irma Lee's new understanding.

Glaspell, true to her positive, progressive outlook on humanity and America, still saw in the West a locus of promise – the possibility of "continually beginning again" as Frederick Jackson Turner had identified the significance of the frontier (81). Irma, by returning to the Middle West, brings together the old pioneer spirit of adventure and the traditional desire for home and community, and, through Constantina, adds to the multiculturalism and plurality of her town. The West is a real place for her, a ruined house she can rebuild and a vineyard, both figurative and literal, that requires her attention. Glaspell did not view the settlement of America as a failed enterprise nor did she share the disenchantment of the Lost Generation that led Steinbrink to say of the 1920s: "Possessed of what seemed an irrelevant past, Americans faced an inaccessible future" (157). Glaspell's protagonist understands her past thanks to the experience of the sacred ruins of Delphi, of an ancient culture and a mythology that survives among the remains of the temples and, fortified by Constantina's need of someone to care for her, she can rebuild the ruins of her life. William R. Handley has argued that for Fitzgerald the West did not have a "clear positive referent" (176) and so could only "produce desire through both its promise and poverty of signification" (177). The Middle West that Gatsby comes from is "unlocatable as a space on the American continent" (Handley 171); he defines it carelessly as "San Francisco" (71) and it is left to Nick, in one of his editorial explanations of the action of the novel, to identify it as North Dakota, Lake Superior and Minnesota (104-06) at different moments of Gatsby's life. Unfortunately, as Handley clarifies: "In *The Great Gatsby*, to 'go West' has nothing to do with a magnetic compass and everything to do with a moral compass galvanized by the need to leave the scene of the crime" (Handley 180).

Fugitive's Return, as the title suggests, is structured around the concept of return; not a Gatsby-like dream of return to a past love, but the reality of a woman whose acceptance of mythic ritual embodied in Dionysian passion and renewed Demetrian motherhood permits her to return to her roots, to her "house on a hill." This house is a beacon that shines out in the night, drawing Irma back; in Fitzgerald's novel Gatsby looks out across the bay toward the "single green light, minute and far away" (29) on Daisy's dock, signifying her home and symbolizing what could only be an unreachable "dead dream" (141). The green light loses its symbolic value halfway through the novel, when Gatsby and Daisy are reunited and "His count of enchanted objects had diminished by one" (100). The home that Irma is returning to was never limited to a reductive symbol nor was it ever enchanted; throughout the novel she has grappled with memories of an unhappy past toward her final conception of "the house on a hill," built by her grandfather, as a place of peace, love and acceptance.

Glaspell creates, in *Fugitive's Return*, a novel that offers an answer to the Lost Generation's rejection of the value of their homeland. Gatsby had "believed in the green light, the orgastic future that year by year recedes before us. It eluded us then, but that's no matter – to-morrow, we will run faster, stretch out our arms further ... And one fine morning – So we beat on, boats against the current, borne back ceaselessly into the past" (187). Fitzgerald, appealing to the reader's sense of romance, does not allow for a reconciliation of the past and the present, but Irma Lee, almost miraculously transported into the sacred past that is Delphi, is reborn in it or through it and, strengthened by her experience of the ancient past that had aroused her "wonder" can return to her native land, not in search of a chimera of love, but prepared to work "in her own vineyard" (324). Gatsby teaches that the past cannot be returned to, and so we understand that the "enchanted moment" when the Dutch sailors contemplated the "green breast of the new world" and the possibilities it offered, had gone for ever. Haeckel, Darwin, and Nietzsche led Glaspell to an interpretation of America's past and future that could look to positive change in spite of loss thanks to the capacity of renewal inherent in its pioneer spirit, whereas Fitzgerald focused on the romantic, superficial sensibilities of the Jazz Age mistaking them for signifiers of the American identity.

Nina Baym, in "Melodramas of Beset Manhood" has argued that the New Critics developed "the idea of essential Americanness" (71) on which they based the American literary canon, disregarding all writers whose work did not reproduce this "inherently male" (70), though highly romantic, essence, as did Delbanco's "enduring triad." Critics, perpetuating a Gatsbyesque myth of America, excluded – and continue to exclude – the writing of American women that reflected the stark reality of an individual's struggle, psychological or physical, but always within society, to overcome disappointment and sorrow. The enduring predominance of novels such as F. Scott Fitzgerald's *The Great Gatsby* as a parameter of "great" American fiction continues to affect resistance to Susan Glaspell's more positive vision of the American individual and society, and to the inclusion of her fiction in the canon. Murder is, after all, much more exciting and romantic than failed suicide and recovery.

Works Cited

Anon. "The Color of a Life." *New York Evening Sun* 7 Dec. 1929. Print.

Baym, Nina. "Melodramas of Beset Manhood: How Theories of American Fiction Exclude Women Authors." *The New Feminist Criticism*. Ed. Elaine Showalter. New York: Pantheon, 1985. 63-80. Print.

Bender, Bert. "'His Mind Aglow': The Biological Undercurrent in Fitzgerald's *Gatsby* and Other Works." *Journal of American Studies* 32:3 (1998): 399-420. Print.

Black, Cheryl. *The Women of the Provincetown Players, 1915-1922*. Tuscaloosa and London: University of Alabama Press, 2002. Print.

Bryer, Jackson R. ed. *F. Scott Fitzgerald: The Critical Reception*. Burt Franklin & Co., 1978. Print.

Carpentier, Martha. *The Major Novels of Susan Glaspell*. Gainesville: University Press of Florida, 2001. Print.

_____. "The Deracinated Self: Immigrants, Orphans, and the 'Migratory Consciousness' of Willa Cather and Susan Glaspell." *Studies in American Fiction.* 35:2 (2008): 131-55. Print.

Delbanco, Nicholas. "The Situation of American Writing 1999." *American Literary History.* 11 (1999): 215-353. Print.

Fitzgerald, F. Scott. *The Great Gatsby.* Harmondsworth, Middlesex: Penguin, 1967. Print.

Gainor, J. Ellen. *Susan Glaspell in Context: American Theater, Culture, and Politics, 1915-1948.* Ann Arbor: University of Michigan Press, 2001. Print.

Giltrow, Janet and David Stouck. "Pastoral Mode and Language in *The Great Gatsby.*" *F.Scott Fitzgerald in the Twenty-first Century.* Eds. Jackson R. Bryer, Ruth Prigorzy, and Milton R. Stern. Tuscaloosa and London: University of Alabama Press, 2003, 138-52. Print.

Glaspell, Susan. *Inheritors. Plays by Susan Glaspell.* Ed. C. W. E. Bigsby. Cambridge: Cambridge University Press, 1987. 103-57. Print.

_____. *The Verge. Plays by Susan Glaspell.* Ed. C. W. E. Bigsby. Cambridge: Cambridge University Press, 1987. 57-102.

_____. *Fugitive's Return.* New York: Frederick A. Stokes, 1929.

Gospel according to St. Matthew. "The Sermon on the Mount." 5:14-16. *The Holy Bible.* King James Version 2000. University of Virginia. Web. 20 August 2008.

Guetin, Nicole. "Icons and Myths in *The Great Gatsby.*" *A Distant Drummer: Foreign Perspectives on F. Scott Fitzgerald.* Eds. Jamal Assadi and William Freedman. New York: Peter Lang, 2007. 21-28. Print.

Handley, William R. *Violence and the Nation in the American Literary West.* West Nyack, NY, USA: Cambridge University Press, 2002. Ebrary. Web. 10 October 2008.

Hernando-Real, Noelia. "Drama and Cultural Pluralism in the America of Susan Glaspell's *Inheritors.*" *Interrogating America through Theatre and Performance.* Eds. William W. Demastes and Iris Fischer. New York: Palgrave Macmillan, 2007. 65-80. Print.

Hinz-Bode, Kristina. "Susan Glaspell and the epistemological Crisis of Modernity: Truth, Knowledge, and Art in Selected Novels." *Susan Glaspell: New Directions in Critical Inquiry.* Ed. Martha C. Carpentier. Newcastle: Cambridge Scholars Press, 2006. 89-108. Print.

Hutchinson, Percy. "A Sensitive Novel by Susan Glaspell." *New York Times Book Review,* 11 October 1929.

Koster, Katie de. Ed. *Readings on* The Great Gatsby. San Diego, CA: Greenhaven Press, 1998. Print.

Noe, Marcia. "*The Verge*: L''Ecriture Féminine at the Provincetown." *Susan Glaspell: Essays on Her Theater and Fiction.* Ed. Linda Ben-Zvi. Ann Arbor: The University of Michigan Press, 1995. 129-44. Print.

Ornstein, Robert. "Scott Fitzgerald's Fable of East and West." *Twentieth Century interpretations of The Great Gatsby.* Ed. Ernest Lockridge. Englewood Cliffs, NJ: Prentice-Hall, 1968. 54-60. Print.

Ozieblo, Barbara. *Susan Glaspell. A Critical Biography.* Chapel Hill: University of North Carolina Press, 2000. Print.

———. "Silenced Mothers and Questing Daughters in Susan Glaspell's Mature Novels." *Disclosing Intertextualities: The Stories, Plays, and Novels of Su-*

san Glaspell. Eds. Martha Carpentier and Barbara Ozieblo. Amsterdam: Rodopi, 2006. 137-58. Print.

———. and Jerry Dickey. *Susan Glaspell and Sophie Treadwell*. London and New York: Routledge, 2008. Print.

Quinn, Arthur Hobson. *American Fiction: An Historical and Critical Survey*. New York: Appleton and Century-Crofts, 1936. Print.

Rohe, Alice. "The Story of Susan Glaspell." *New York Morning Telegraph* 18 December 1921. Print.

Scrimgeour, Gary J. "Against *The Great Gatsby*." *Twentieth Century Interpretations of The Great Gatsby*. Ed. Ernest Lockridge. Englewood Cliffs, NJ: Prentice-Hall, 1968, 70-81. Print.

Sichert, Margit. "Claire Archer – a 'Nietzscheana' in Susan Glaspell's The Verge." *REAL: Yearbook of Research in English and American Literature*. Ed. Herbert Grabes. Tübingen: Gunter Narr Verlag, 13 (1997): 271-97. Print.

Steinbrink, Jeffrey. "'Boats Against the Current': Morality and the Myth of Renewal in *The Great Gatsby*." *Twentieth Century Literature* Summer 26:2 (1980): 157-70. Print.

Turner, Frederick Jackson. "The Significance of the Frontier in American History." *A Nineteenth-Century American Reader*. Ed. M. Thomas Inge. Washington D.C.: United States Information Agency, 1987. 81-85. Print.

Virgilia Peterson Ross. "'Fugitive from Life' Review of *Fugitive's Return*." *New York Herald Tribune Books*. 10 Nov. 1929.

Winthrop, John. "A Model of Christian Charity." University of Virginia. Web. 20 August 2008.

Notes

1 For Susan Glaspell and the Provincetown Players see Black, and Ozieblo 2008.

2 Tom, of course, is not Fitzgerald's mouthpiece. When *The Great Gatsby* is read as a criticism of the mores of the times, it does exude a pessimistic view of American society.

3 Bender identifies this book as Lothrop Stoddard's *The Rising Tide of Color Against White-World Supremacy* (164) while Guetin prefers to emphasize the "religious connotation" of the name "Goddard" (25).

4 Edmund Wilson "corrected" the spelling of "orgastic" believing it should be "orgiastic"; however, as Fitzgerald explained to Max Perkins in a 1925 letter, he had meant "orgastic," because "it expresses exactly the intended ecstasy" (quoted in Koster 117).

5 For interpretations of Claire's insanity and future see Hinz-Bode 170 and Gainor 162.

6 This poetic monologue reminds us of Claire's speeches in *The Verge*, which Marcia Noe has read as an example of *"écriture féminine"* before its time. The novel was in fact praised by the reviewer of the *New York Evening Sun*, who, considering Glaspell to be a poet, saw *Fugitive's Return* as "possibly the finest exemplification of the poet's success with the novel" (Anon. 1929).

The Influence of George Cram Cook's Delphic Spirit on Eugene O'Neill

Mike Solomonson

Lewis Sheaffer once wrote of George Cram Cook: "Poor Jig, not a good writer, not a good actor, not a good director, yet a genius of sorts, the one who lit the flame in the Provincetown Players and did the most to keep it burning" (401). The "genius" aspect that Cook possessed was his unique vision of the Delphic spirit, which he used as a motivational means to inspire others. Linda Ben-Zvi wrote of Cook's final months in Greece: "Drinking, talking, dancing to the music of local fiddlers and pipers during that long, beautiful autumn, he was in turn Apollo and Dionysus, the two mythic inhabitants of Delphi, the gods of poetry and wine" (281). Years earlier he had harnessed that Delphic passion to motivate the artists of the Provincetown Players to new artistic heights. In particular, Cook's inspirational powers influenced Eugene O'Neill's work. In examining this influence, I will examine Cook's philosophical ideas and demonstrate how they were manifested in O'Neill's work.

Susan Glaspell said Cook defined his theatrical philosophy by proclaiming:

> One cannot produce drama. True drama is born only of one feeling animating all the members of a clan—a spirit shared by all and expressed by the few for the all.

> If there is nothing to take the place of the common religious purpose and passion of the primitive group, out of which the Dionysian dance was born, no vital drama can arise in any people' ... He came home and wrote it down as an affirmation of faith. (Cargill et al. 30)

The fact that Dionysus was prominently mentioned was not coincidental. It was central to his philosophical outlook, which had a deep connection to Greece and, in particular, his obsession with Dionysus. In his own dramatic works Cook used certain devices aimed at communicating the essence of his notion of the Delphic spirit. These included the use of rhythm to create an emotional connection, an emphasis on the concept of spiritual unity, and stage characters who yearned to transcend their given circumstances. By examining Cook's play *The Spring* one can see how he tried artistically to use these three aspects of his philosophy.

When Glaspell was writing her husband's biography she relied heavily on scraps of paper that contained Cook's insights (vi). Among the scraps were notes pertaining to *The Spring*. They contained phrases like: "Make play the imaginative impulse to the new religion" (225). "The scalp-dance. The passionate oneness of the warriors, all excited by the same rhythmic ecstasy" (226). "The religion of the oneness of men supplanting class-struggle, the oneness of matter and mind, the oneness of all men's minds in the human mind" (227). Based on these preliminary notes, it becomes clear how portions of his philosophy were firmly entrenched in his mind as he approached the writing of the script.

However, he tried to communicate his vision by using fringe psychological theories, such as telepathy, automatic writing, and telepathic hypnosis. Unfortunately, these were not sufficient for him to ignite the spirit of Delphi in dramatic form. The play had a mixed reception. *New York Times* reviewer Alexander Woolcott panned the play: "Thus has Mr. Cook achieved less a play than a séance. He has been so engrossed with his psychic phenomena that he has had no time or room for much else... ." (2).

Despite the play's problems, it is still helpful in clarifying Cook's intentions for later comparison with O'Neill's works. First, the play tries to make tangible use of rhythm. The prelude shows how the ancestor of the Robbins family makes peace with Native Americans, including Nam-e-qua who begins the play practicing crystal gazing. "She takes crystals and kernals, and with self-hypnotizing rhythm sets them in a magic pattern" (10). Much of the later action involving Elijah's hypnosis of Esther could also be considered rhythmic, particularly when the sounds of the spring are included, since the spring itself was apparently intended to serve a hypnotic function. Glaspell quoted Cook as saying, "'It will hypnotize the audience,' he said, 'and make it easier to reach that deep level where I am you and you are me!'" (228). Cook hoped that the audience viewing his play would enter into the same collective mindset through the influence of the sounds of the spring and the stage action. Not only does that quotation reflect his emphasis on rhythm, but also spiritual union.

He introduces that element in the play's prelude section. After Robbins attempts to kill Black Hawk, they are reconciled. Black Hawk initiates a symbolic smoking of the peace pipe, which ends with Black Hawk proclaiming: "As my smoke and your smoke become one smoke, so shall your spirit and mine be one!" (22). Cook's interest in the spiritual shows up in subtle ways, such as a stage direction that describes Professor Chantland as "spiritually arid" (25). Cook also showed he could be less subtle. A speech by Elijah clearly demonstrated Cook's idealism and yearning for harmony: "If we felt this hidden oneness of all men—could there be war? A keen new sense of the identity of human beings—that is the heart of a great new living religion. Spiritual communism!" (39-40). Another speech in *The Spring* reaffirms his concern for spiritual union, but also hints at his interest in transcending the norm. Elijah says: "I'll give you an idea wilder still. A conscious mind like mine directing unconscious powers like yours—two such as we might grow to be one person—one person in two minds—gifted as no one mind has been gifted—a new kind of genius—the end of loneliness!" (40).

In many ways, *The Spring* concretely reflected the transcending ideal of Cook's Delphic vision. Throughout the play, Elijah battles Chantland's traditional views and entreats the professor to be open to new possibilities. In the end Chantland's inadvertent death seals Elijah's fate, but it does not conquer his dreams of transcending. Elijah says to Esther: "Hold! Hold—and we will live through even this. Even though we wait ten years we will yet sail into ourselves—we will yet see the shore of our new world!" (108).

There is evidence that Jig's play became a point of contention between himself and Eugene O'Neill. Cook challenged O'Neill to explore theatrical devices that would transcend the theatrical norm. Robert K. Sarlos described how O'Neill took exception to Cook's motivational appeals. "Gene turned to Jig and said, 'well, you did it, and look at the result! Your *Spring* as a play is not what it was on the dunes when you told it to us!'" (*Theatre Survey* 44). Based on this evidence, it is clear that Cook had communicated to O'Neill portions of playwriting philosophy and that O'Neill was familiar with what Cook had attempted to do with *The Spring*.

In considering *The Spring* as an influence on *Marco Millions* it is intriguing to notice how O'Neill, like Cook, uses crystal gazing. As previously mentioned, Nam-e-qua used crystal gazing in *The Spring* to see the near future. In *Marco Millions*, O'Neill wrote a scene where Kublai uses a crystal to see Marco's return to Venice (426). O'Neill also incorporates hypnotic suggestion into his play. As Kukachin makes a final attempt to win Marco's favor, she urges him to look into her eyes. "He looks for a moment critically, then grows tense, his face moves hypnotically towards hers, their lips seem about to meet in a kiss" (414-415).

Also, the use of rhythm is present in *Marco Millions*. In act one, the stage directions read: "From the darkness comes the sound of a small Tartar kettledrum, its beats marking the rhythm for a crooning, nasal voice, rising and falling in a wordless chant" (373). In act two, another strong rhythmic image is offered. The slaves are loading bales in a mechanical fashion. "By the side of the shed, a foreman sits with a drum and gong with which he marks a perfect time for the slaves, a four-beat rhythm, three beats of the drums, the fourth a bang on the gong as one slave at each end loads and unloads" (400). Also in act two, the "sailors lower and furl the sail of the mizzenmast, every movement being carried out in unison with a machinelike rhythm" (407). Later, after the princess dies, the voices of the mourners are described as rising "together in a long, rhythmic wail of mourning" (433).

The idea of spiritual union is brought out in a number of different ways. Kublai asks spiritual leaders of different religions if they can conquer death. Each leader provides a unified chorus by simply saying, "Death is" (434-435). The different cultures that Marco encountered in the scenes of act one also help to create a sense of spiritual unity (Robinson 110). The third scene of act one features the Mahometan people. The next scene features Buddhists, but the stage direction reads: "Otherwise, the scene, in the placing of its people and the characters and types represented, is the exact duplicate of the last except that here the locale is Indian" (369). Thus, O'Neill set up a contrast between the spiritual unity of the different cultures, despite their varied beliefs, and the culture represented by the Polos.

The use of characters who desire to transcend their circumstances is also present in *Marco Millions*. Kublai is presented as wanting to transcend the philosophical posturings of the various world religions and reach the truthful core. The first line he speaks in the play presents his quest: "I bid you welcome, Messr. Polo. But where are the hundred wise men of the West who were to dispute with my wise men of the sacred teachings of Lao-Tseu and Confucius and the Buddha and Christ?" (378). O'Neill also plays with the transcendence of overcoming death in the brief reanimation of Kukachin who revives from the dead to speak the following: "Say this, I loved and died. Now I am love, and live. And living, have forgotten. And loving, can forgive" (352). The stage direction completes the idea: "A sound of tender laughter, of an intoxicating, supernatural gaiety, comes from her lips and is taken up in chorus in the branches of the tree as if every harp-leaf were laughing in music with her" (352). The laughter is descriptively close to the type O'Neill later depicted in *Lazarus Laughed*, which has the strongest connection to Cook's inspiration and influence on O'Neill.

Robert Sarlos made a compelling case for Cook's influence on *Lazarus Laughed*. Jig's daughter Nilla reported to Sarlos that before Cook and Glaspell sailed to Greece they met with the O'Neills. Cook and O'Neill had a heated debate over the idea of O'Neill giving up traditional theatre and concentrating on dithyrambic theatre. Two years after Jig's death, O'Neill contacted Nilla after he had finished writing *Lazarus Laughed*. He told her he wanted to learn Greek and music. She reportedly told Sarlos: "Lazarus is definitely the outcome of the attacks Jig made on Gene for sticking to the conventional after the *Emperor*, which had opened the way to new forms" (*Theatre Survey* 42-43).

Also, a January 8, 1928, article in the *New York Times* quoted O'Neill as saying that he got the idea for *Lazarus Laughed* while researching *The Fountain* (2), which he began writing near the time *The Spring* was produced. According to Travis Bogard, Cook's play may have been a subconscious influence on O'Neill (*Contour* 234). The newspaper article also credits a March, 1925, O'Neill letter to critic George Jean Nathan as the earliest mention of *Marco Millions*. The evidence suggests that near the time of Cook's sudden death O'Neill's mind was occupied with both *Marco Millions* and *Lazarus Laughed*.

If those facts are accepted, it is plausible that the memory of Cook was an intangible factor as O'Neill approached the task of writing the plays, and it could be true that Cook's ideal of dithyrambic theatre inspired O'Neill's attempt to transcend traditional dramatic form in *Lazarus Laughed*. The play made heavy use of masks, choral refrains, and supernatural laughter, and one scene was set in Athens. While it can be argued that these theatrical devices are an outgrowth of earlier experiments, the tone of the play has a distinctive feel of dithyrambic ecstasy in many scenes, which is consistent with the urgings Cook made to O'Neill. The play opens just after Lazarus's resurrection. Throughout the play, Lazarus meets characters who are conflicted about whether to fully enter into Lazarus's laughter, which would lead them to a transcendent moment, or whether they should deny his laughter and the corresponding experience. In Rome, the disciples of Lazarus follow his laughter, which leads to their death. Their deaths, however, can be interpreted as a victorious release. Miriam also trusts Lazarus and meets her death with a feeling of assurance. Other characters, such as Caligula, consistently rebel against fully accepting the transcendent experience and they meet their own tortured fates.

The play reflects other aspects that are reminiscent of Cook's Delphic philosophy such as numerous references to rhythmic laughter or a rhythmic cadence as some characters speak. The second scene begins with the sounds of a rhythmic dance. Throughout the play, stage directions contain many rhythmic references. The chorus, in particular, accomplishes this task. Act two, scene one, serves as an example. The chorus is described as "chanting in a deep, rhythmic monotone" (303).

Another meaningful connection to Cook was O'Neill's references to Dionysus. In the first scene of act two, Lazarus is described as having a countenance like Dionysus (307). The chorus also chants "Dionysus, Son of Man and a god!" (299). Even Lazarus's laughter has its roots in Dionysian ecstasy. Edwin Engel wrote: "His laughter is the direct expression of joy in the Dionysian sense, the joy of a celebrant who is at the same time a sacrifice in the eternal process of change...." (178).

The idea of spiritual unity is also present in the play. Those who accept Lazarus are propelled by a joyous unity of laughter. When the laughter is not accepted or ceases, it leads to spiritual disharmony. For example, when the people of Lazarus's village split between following him or Christ, a riot breaks out and many villagers die in the upheaval.

In his own way, O'Neill was consciously attempting to attain a sense of unity. *The Unknown O'Neill* includes a memorandum written by the playwright detailing the use of masks in *Lazarus Laughed*. O'Neill wrote:

> I was visualizing an effect that, intensified by dramatic lighting, would give an audience visually the sense of the Crowd, not as a random collection of individuals, but as a collective whole, an entity. When the Crowd speaks, I wanted an audience to hear the voice of Crowd mind, Crowd emotion, as one voice of a body composed of, but quite distinct from, its parts. (409)

The above quotation was also reminiscent of the group unity that Elijah hoped to achieve through his experiments with Esther, as well as Cook's concept of group unity that he articulated for the Provincetown Players.

Sarlos suggested that guilt over Cook's death may have influenced O'Neill to write *Lazarus Laughed* (*Theatre Survey* 45). O'Neill often dealt with his guilt by writing plays dealing with the wronged individual. Obviously his family was a source of guilt that led to the writing of some of his plays. Other people who caused significant guilt in his life eventually became subjects in his plays. Kitty MacKay was the model of Eileen in *The Straw* (Bogard, *Contour* 112). *Abortion*, according to Bogard, may have dealt with the pregnancy of O'Neill's first wife (*Contour* 23). It also is clear that Cook became a source of guilt. After Cook's death, O'Neill wrote a letter to Susan Glaspell in May 1924, where he tried to assuage his guilt:

> When I heard of his death, Susan, I felt suddenly that I had lost one of the best friends I had ever had or ever would have—unselfish, rare, and truly noble! And then when I thought of all the things I hadn't said, the others I had said and wished unsaid, I felt like a swine, Susan. Whenever I think of him it is with the most self-condemning remorse. (Ben-Zvi 298)

I believe that following the unexpected death of Cook, O'Neill felt compelled to develop a drama that would live up to the expectations of his mentor, as well as providing a means of expiating his guilt over how he treated Cook. I also agree with a number of scholars, including Doris Alexander, who credit Cook with partially shaping O'Neill's personal vision. Also when he articulated his theatrical philosophy in interviews, he often sounded like Jig Cook. For instance, O'Neill said he desired a theatre that was:

> a legitimate descendent of the first theatre that sprang, by virtue of man's imaginative interpretation of life, out of his worship of Dionysus. I mean a theatre returned to its highest and sole significant function as a Temple where the religion of a poetical interpretation and symbolical celebration of life is communicated to human beings, starved in spirit by their soul-stifling daily struggle to exist as masks among the masks of the living! (Bogard, *Unknown O'Neill* 410)

Eugene O'Neill continues to loom as an imposing figure with his collection of Pulitzer prizes and copious amounts of scholarly attention. Jig Cook has received little acclaim since his talent was not the type that would leave a lasting dramatic work. We are told that

Cook's gift was "inspiration," but what that means is somewhat nebulous after all of these years. Perhaps in the words of M. Eleanor Fitzgerald, who was the executive director of the Provincetown Players, might we get a sense of Cook's motivational power. Writing in 1929, Fitzgerald recalled a memorable lunch with Cook and its lasting effect on her:

> Jig talked of the theatre as it was, as he hoped to make it... At first I was at the theatre only in the evening. Then I came for full-time, to do press, subscriptions, business managing, everything and anything. That first flare of enthusiasm, that flame of Jig Cook, has never died. That vision of what could be done for writers who had something to say, for artists who had something to show, for all new creative talent in theatre, still holds me today. (Fitzgerald)

Perhaps what Fitzgerald felt was the influence of Delphi. It seems that Cook could draw upon the poetic influence of Apollo to imagine the artistic possibilities, and the unquenchable Dionysian urge to bring to life that which seemed impossible. It was that desire to create that which did not yet exist, which led Cook to his cajoling, pestering ways that ultimately made him such a memorable person to his contemporaries, and that quite conceivably influenced Eugene O'Neill's creation of *Marco Millions* and *Lazarus Laughed*.

Works Cited

Alexander, Doris. *The Tempering of Eugene O'Neill*. New York: Harcourt, Brace and World, Inc, 1962. Print.

Ben-Zvi, Linda. *Susan Glaspell: Her Life and Times*. Oxford University Press, 2005. Print.

Bogard, Travis. *The Unknown O'Neill: Unpublished or

Unfamiliar Writings of Eugene O'Neill. New Haven: Yale University Press, 1988. Print.

_____. *Contour In Time*. New York: Oxford University Press, 1988. Print.

Cargill, Oscar, N. Bryllion Fagon and William J. Fischer, ed. *O'Neill and His Plays—Four Decades of Criticism*. New York: New York University Press, 1961. Print.

Cook, George Cram. *The Spring*. London: Ernest Benn Limited, 1925. Print.

Engel, Edwin A. *The Haunted Heroes of Eugene O'Neill*. Cambridge: Harvard University Press, 1953. Print.

Fitzgerald, M. Eleanor. "Valedictory of an Art Theatre." *New York Times*. 22 Dec.1929, page XI. Print.

Glaspell, Susan. *The Road to the Temple*. London: Ernest Benn Limited, 1926. Print.

O'Neill, Eugene. *Lazarus Laughed*. *The Plays of Eugene O'Neill*. Volume 3. New York: The Modern Library, 1982. Pages 271-371. Print.

_____. *Marco Millions*. *The Plays of Eugene O'Neill*. New York: Random House, 1967. Pages 343-439. Print.

"O'Neill and His Plays". *New York Times*. 8 Jan. 1928, sec. 8:2. Print.

Sarlos, Robert Karoly. "Write a Dance: Lazarus Laughed as O'Neill's Dithyramb of the Western Hemisphere." *Theatre Survey*. 29 (May 1988): 37-49. Print.

Sheaffer, Lewis. *O'Neill: Son and Playwright*. Boston: Little, Brown and Company, 1968. Print.

Woolcott, Alexander. "Second Thoughts on First Nights." *New York Times*. 6 Nov. 1921, sec. 6:2. Print.

Susan Glaspell's Delphi and the Legacy of Jane Ellen Harrison

Martha C. Carpentier

Susan Glaspell's relationship to Delphi was embedded in the *archai*, the very stones of the place, as she wrote in an unpublished poem among her papers at the Berg collection. Although poetry is the only genre in which Glaspell did not excel, she expresses her sentiment effectively:

I stood in what had been a temple,
My hand upon a broken column; ...
It was my hand ... upon the broken column—first felt another moment....
What did he feel—that Greek of long ago—the day the rising
column stood at what is now the break?
Perhaps a hand lay where mine lies ...
Loving the living moment of flowers in grass and sails on sea;
And because that hand was very still and was forgotten,
And mine was still and was forgotten,
I live again in what lived then,
And what lived then moves now in me.

This relationship to the stones of Delphi was a mystical connection to the past she shared with her husband George Cram Cook, but despite his urging she would not commit herself to learning the Greek language –

she preferred not to subject her experience of Greece to the *logos* (or word) but to treasure it as a mystical semiotic. This delighted Jig and he would "boast" about her unique approach: "She says she doesn't know it, but she understands everything.... Let her begin where she will. I have seen Susan stand before those old stones as if they had something to say to her" (313-14). Indeed, Glaspell's love of the Greek inscriptions on the fallen stones echoes the feminist semiotic she created in her most famous play, *Trifles*, a play that has been justly celebrated by critics and scholars since Annette Kolodny's ground-breaking essay, "A Map for Rereading: Gender and the Interpretation of Literary Texts."

In her biography of Cook, *The Road to the Temple*, Glaspell wrote, "Now that the Temple was so much a part of my life, I would have its secrets," and after walking among the ruins she wrote down fragmentary inscriptions for Cook to decipher:

"Woman, what have you brought home?" [he teased]
"Brought home?"
"This inscription of yours. It is the most indecent thing I have ever seen upon paper – I mean upon stone."
You could read the inscription one way, the usual way, and it was commending the virtue of a certain hero of Herod. But you could juggle it a little, not violating inscription technique, and behind this perfunctory tribute lurked a sensational accusation of unchastity. What of the other inscriptions? There too did the Oracle hide words within her words? Had these stones held secrets through the centuries? Were they laughing deep laughter? The Oracle must have said a good deal the authorities of the Temple did not care to repeat, yet they would be fearful about refusing it. A mysterious place – Delphi; perhaps we had not found out how mysterious. (314)

From this wonderful passage – with its own eerie oracular prediction of Hélène Cixous' "Laugh of the Medusa" – it is clear that Glaspell does not only read the "usual" way, but seeks to read the "secret," the silenced "unchastity," that is the mother's body hidden behind the "perfunctory tribute" to the Roman tyrant. By attributing this semiotic transgression and its "deep laughter" to the Oracle, Glaspell reinscribes the Temple of Apollo as a maternal space and, indeed, throughout her novel *Fugitive's Return*, temple, theater, and sacred way are all portrayed as the set of a feminist drama enacting the daughter's return to the mother.

This return of Delphi to the matriarchal past of Greek religion is based on a radical feminist rereading of classical tradition that Glaspell inherited from an intellectual foremother she shared with Virginia Woolf: Jane Ellen Harrison. In an intriguing observation probably derived from Nilla Cook's memoir, Marcia Noe describes Glaspell's reading material on a return voyage to Greece after visiting her mother as Jane Harrison's *Prolegomena to the Study of Greek Religion*, originally published in 1903 and just reissued in a third edition in 1922 (50). Recently referred to as "one of the most archaeologically sensitive classical scholars of her age" (Dyson 715), Harrison was one of the earliest students and later a teacher at the first women's college at Cambridge, Newnham, the founding of which in 1872 Woolf so eloquently describes in *A Room of One's Own*, where she also pays tribute to Harrison, who had just died when Woolf gave the lecture that became *A Room of One's Own* to Newnham students in 1928.

When I first discovered Susan Glaspell, I was uniquely positioned to understand Harrison's influence on her work. I had just finished and published my dissertation: *Ritual, Myth, and the Modernist Text: The Influence of Jane Ellen Harrison on Joyce, Eliot, and Woolf.* Indeed, my work on Harrison formed my own "Prolegomena" to my study of Susan Glaspell. Both were innovative woman writers, radical and influential in their own days but subsequently overshadowed and marginalized by the "great man" or "solitary genius" approach to intellectual history. In the case of Glaspell, I refer to the attribution of the birth of modern American drama to Eugene O'Neill, and in the case of Harrison, the attribution of the "ritual theory" quite inaccurately, to Sir James George Frazer, author of the compendious 12-volume *Golden Bough* immortalized for all literary scholars to come by T.S. Eliot's notes to *The Waste Land*. Frazer was Harrison's contemporary at Cambridge; her major books, published from 1890 to 1913, were contemporaneous with, not influenced by, the three editions of *The Golden Bough*, and she was far better trained and more scientifically oriented than Frazer, who "had never been on a field trip," culling all his comparative anthropology from the research of others (Vickery 83). In contrast, after graduation Harrison spent two decades in London studying archaeology and lecturing on Greek art at the British Museum, and during this time she traveled to all of the major archaeological digs in Europe: Athens, the Peleponnesos, Crete, Delphi, Olympia, Eleusis, Sicily.

Harrison worked particularly closely with Wilhelm Dörpfeld, the great German archaeologist who took over the excavation of Mycenean Troy after the death of Schliemann and headed the German excavations at and around the Acropolis. In 1890 in *The Classical Review* she defended Dörpfeld's "startling and original" view, based on his excavation of the Theater of Dionysos at Athens, that "down to Roman date the chorus and actors stood on the same level" on a dominant circular orchestra, as opposed to the then orthodox opinion that they performed on a smaller, twelve-foot high proscenium. For Dörpfeld "the *proskenion* of the Greek theatre is simply the decorative wall ... in front of which the acting went on," its height corresponding to the "ordinary Greek house" (274-5). By 1895 his excavations of the various strata of the Dionysian theater in Athens had thoroughly proved his point that the "floor of the *paradoi* was upon the same level as the ancient orchestra" (Marquand 538), and this later played a key role in Harrison's 1913 book *Ancient Art and Ritual* – a book I am convinced influenced George Cram Cook's vision of the theater as a "Beloved Community of Life-Givers" (*Road* 203) every bit as much as Nietzsche.[1] In *Ancient Art and Ritual* Harrison succinctly formulized the "ritual theory" connecting drama in its origins to the "*dromenon*," meaning "things done" in communal ritual – the rhythmic dances and dithyrambs chanted by worshippers, as the incipient chorus on the great circular orchestra at the spring Dionysia in Athens:

> The history of the Greek stage is one long story of the encroachment of the stage on the orchestra ... As the drama and the stage wax, the *dromenon* and the orchestra wane.... The shift in the relation of the dancing-place and stage is very clearly seen in ... the Dionysiac theatre at Athens. The old circular orchestra shows the dominance of ritual; the new curtailed orchestra of Roman times and semicircular shape shows the dominance of the spectacle. (*AAR* 143)

As religious faith waned, Harrison further theorized, "the ritual mould of the *dromenon* [was] left ready for new content" (140) and "the new wine that was poured into the old bottles of the *dromena* at the Spring Festival was the heroic saga" (146). The "great innovation" of sixth-century Athens was the coming of Homer and "out of Homeric stories playwrights began to make plots" emphasizing, instead of the communal death and rebirth "of the life-spirit," the sagas of "human individual heroes." (145)

But it was Crete and Delphi that inspired Harrison's *Prolegomena to the Study of Greek Religion* and her 1912 book, *Themis*. In 1894 Oxford archaeologist Arthur Evans had been deciphering stone seals found on Crete, proof to him of the "prevalence of a new alphabet" predating the Mycenean (E.A.G. 232), and in 1900 he began excavating the massive palace of Knossos. Harrison wrote: "I shall never forget the moment when Mr. Arthur Evans first showed me ... a clay sealing ... representing the Great Mother standing on her own mountain with her attendant lions, and before her a worshipper in ecstasy.... Here was this ancient ritual of the Mother and the Son which long preceded the worship of the Olympians: here were the true Prolegomena." By 1904, when she returned to Crete, much of the palace was excavated and the archaeologist R.C. Bosanquet showed her a fragmentary "Hymn of the Kouretes found in the temple of Diktaean Zeus" which reaffirmed for her "the magical rite of the Mother and Son, the induction of the Year-Spirit who long preceded the worship of the Father" (*Reminiscences* 72).

Like Susan Glaspell, who noted in an interview that although she was "interested in all progressive movements, whether feminist, social, or economic," she could "take no very active part other than through [her] writing" (quoted in Ozieblo, 138). Jane Harrison's feminism was not overtly political, but it was nonetheless powerful. She was not a suffragist, but by her life of education, travel, scholarship, and publication, she exemplified the turn-of-the-century "New Woman" just as Glaspell did twenty years later by graduating from Drake University in 1899 (where she also studied classical languages and literature), pursuing a career in journalism, attending graduate school, founding a theater, and writing eleven innovative plays and nine successful novels over her lifetime. Both Harrison's and Glaspell's writings were infused with a vigorous covert feminist sensibility that has been characterized as "pre-oedipal"; that is, both attempt to subvert patriarchy by elevating the mother-child connection, in which, as Julia Kristeva has established, the primal semiotic is grounded. As early as 1903 in the *Prolegomena to the Study of Greek Religion*, Harrison began a lifelong quest to re-establish the primacy of indigenous matriarchal cults over the later imposition of the anthropomorphic Olympian patriarchy – that is, to reassert the primacy of mystery (the semiotic) over rationality (the *logos*). "The religion of Homer," she wrote in *Themis*, "was no more primitive than his language. The Olympian gods ... seemed to me like a bouquet of cut flowers whose bloom is brief, because they have been severed from their roots. To find those roots we must burrow deep into a lower stratum of thought, into those chthonic cults which underlay their life and from which sprang all their brilliant blossoming" (xi).

Nowhere is this "burrowing" more evident than in her discussion of the Temple of Apollo, the Pythian Oracle, and the Dionysiac worshippers at Delphi. In 1888 Harrison concluded the annual summary of "Archaeology in Greece" for the *Journal of Hellenic Studies* with "the expression of a hope":

> The great archaeological disappointment of the year has been the delay of the excavations at Delphi. Preparations are however now actually in hand for the removal, at the expense of the Greek government, of the village which occupies the site. Surveyors were already at work when I visited the place on April 10, but I could not learn when the excavations would actually begin. Kastro, which has grown up in such beautiful and natural fashion round the few scant ruins that are above ground, must be destroyed; this is a hard necessity, but the harvest hoped for is a plentiful one, and no archaeologist can afford to shrink when the sickle is put in. (133)

By 1894, another correspondent to the *Journal of Hellenic Studies* enthused:

> The excavations of the French School at Delphi are now in full activity. They have been looked forward to for years with the keenest interest [and] now that the work has actually begun, it has proved that even the most sanguine anticipations were not unfounded. The find in inscriptions and in sculpture is of extraordinary richness and interest, and will form an epoch in the history of archaeological discovery no less important than those marked by the excavations of Olympia and the Athenian Acropolis. (E.A.G. 224)

He went on: "after long negotiations and tedious delays, the village of Castri has at last been almost entirely removed to its new site," and he described the "most elaborate system of inclined tramways at different levels ... down these the trucks run of themselves, to be hauled up again by horses when they reach the end." The French archaeologists, under the direction of M. Théophile Homolle, had by then reached the temple itself, uncovering thus far the treasure houses of the Sicyonians and the Siphnians, the treasury of the Athenians, and a "great mass of rock projecting in the midst, [which] ... must, as M. Homolle has observed, be the rock of the Sibyl." The observer concluded, "There are still large areas and great masses of earth to be excavated, so that the promise of this site, richly as it has been fulfilled, is as yet by no means exhausted" (E.A.G. 228-9).[2]

Thirty years later, when Glaspell and Cook arrived in the spring of 1922, the archaeological site at Delphi, once the hub of activity, seemed abandoned. All the ferment and fervor of digging and discovering prior to the Great War was long gone and Glaspell and Cook wandered at will with their little dog over the Sacred Way and the Theater of Dionysos; they picnicked in the Temple of Apollo. Glaspell writes of watching a woman in the bushes "gathering something. She explained that when the village stood upon the Temple this had been her mother's garden; she still came back each year to get the berries. The bells of her goat and lamb, grazing while she worked, were thin, broken music in the old theater. 'We could give a play here to-morrow,' Jig cried" (*Road* 311). But in the end it was Susan, not Jig, who wrote the play for the silent stage and she wrote it in the form of a novel, a novel that captures both the mythic past and the post-war reality of Greece in its vision of the lawless deracination, particularly of women and children, that is caused by war.

Susan Glaspell was profoundly affected by the thousands of Greek refugees sent from their homes in Smyrna by the Turks in 1922. Staying with friends in Salonika (now Thessaloniki), a port on the Aegean Sea, she had helped them distribute supplies to the refugees. She wrote in letters to her mother of the "heartbreaking experience. They were crowded around the shed where we were working, many of them women with babies and little children, all holding up their slips [of paper] anxious to be taken at once, for fear the things would run out. And they did soon begin to run out." When another ship arrived carrying 10,000 more refugees who could not be accommodated, Glaspell wrote:

> It was of course packed with people, mostly women and children, as the men are held prisoner by the Turks. There was simply nothing to be done about them ... nothing for them to do but lie down in the streets, and nothing for them to eat. It was the saddest thing I ever saw in my life, and I shall never forget it.

Even Edenic Parnassos was subject to post-war lawlessness and chaos. One night while Glaspell, Cook, and friends sat around a fire at their summer campsite on the mountain, they heard gunshots: Demetrius Komblss, one of the "richest shepherd[s] of Parnassos" had been shot by bandits. They ran to try to help him as he bled to death in his tent and were told that five years ago his son Alekos had been kidnapped and, although he'd paid the ransom, his son had never returned. After debating their own safety, they decided it was time to go back down the mountain to the relative safety of the town. Weeks later on a "quiet November afternoon" while Glaspell sat in the theater thinking of "the places of the dancers of the odes still marked in unfading stone," she saw "two women ... about to cross the stage, the one supporting the other who was crying. When they saw some one was there, they halted. But they saw it was I, and I went up to them. It was the wife of Alekos Komblss who was crying. We stood there holding each other's hands" (*Road* 320).

This vision of suffering women on the ancient stage, revenants perhaps of the great Greek tragic heroines, inspired Glaspell's novel, *Fugitive's Return*, a modernist masterpiece in which she attempts to give form and meaning to contemporary post-war life through allusions to a mythic past, on a par in that regard with T.S. Eliot's *The Waste Land,* Pound's *Cantos,* or even Joyce's *Ulysses.* It is also one of Glaspell's most overtly feminist works; she identified deeply with the orphaned children and homeless mothers of Greece and, like *Trifles, Fugitive's Return* represents a subtle exploration of female revenge – a tale of women uniting in a silent sisterhood against patriarchal violation. Here Glaspell's fearless transgression of generic boundaries is most evident: she goes so far as to attempt a Greek tragedy in prose fiction, a reincarnation of Aeschylus's *Eumenides* or Euripides's *Bacchai* in a twentieth-century realist novel. Just as Joyce, building on his Homeric substrate, updated the *nostos* (homecoming) of father and son, Glaspell used the myths of Procne and Philomela, Demeter and Persephone, and the ritual worship of Dionysos at Delphi to tell her story of mother and daughter reunion.

Glaspell's tribute to Harrison's influence is evident from the start of the novel with the character Miss Mead, an "archeologist, stout, energetic woman who made a business of digging up the past," no doubt modeled on Harrison herself. Miss Mead gives the protagonist Irma – a fugitive from her own past of divorced husband and dead child – a book to read on board ship to Greece, just as Glaspell had read Harrison's *Prolegomena* on her return trip: "All about the past, this book," Irma thinks, "a long dead past...." As she reads, she imagines "Broken columns, in great stillness ... a broken column on a mountain by the sea" much like the imagery of Glaspell's poem (*FR* 28).

This "broken column" has great significance for Irma, just as it did in Glaspell's poem, for it is Miss Mead who first begins identifying Irma with the Thyiades, the female worshippers of Dionysos at Delphi, by taking her "to a shop where women wove Greek silk. She watched them at their looms.... liking the rhythm of these movements, as the beautiful fabric was made – ivory, it was – it gave her the folds of an old beauty" (45). Once dressed in the garment, Irma is "so near the color of stones that had once been temple that when she walked among them she seemed of them.... She was not only the Kyria now. She was the Kyria of the Archai" (50). The particular broken column that had been Glaspell's inspiration must have been the acanthus column, excavated in 1896 and still magnificently on display in the museum in Delphi. While the meaning and purpose of the column have been debated by archaeologists, one of the most common attributions of it is described by Spyros Meletzis: "The luxuriant leaves symbolize fertility which is said to return each year when the God [Dionysos] awakens. The girls are presumed to be thyiades, priestesses of the god, and are performing a cult dance" (xvii). Indeed, later in the novel Glaspell describes Irma and her lover John Knight visiting the museum in Delphi, just as Glaspell and Cook did, where, she writes, "they were looking at the column of dancing women, those devotees who in the snows of high Parnassos would dance themselves into a frenzy for their god Dionysos" (*FR* 253).

Harrison cites Pausanias describing the Thyiades as "Attic women who go every other year with the Delphian women to Parnassos and there hold orgies in honour of Dionysos" (*Prolegomena* 391). The Thyiades, Harrison continues, "are the historical counterparts of the Maenads of countless vases and bas-reliefs ... they are the same too as the Bacchant Women of Euripides" (393) and "it is at Delphi that we learn most of their nature and worship, Delphi where high on Parnassos Dionysos held his orgies" (389). Another source was of course Aeschylus, whose Apollonian bias in the *Eumenides* Harrison repeatedly scorns. But most of her background for the worship of Dionysos came from Plutarch, himself a priest at Delphi "intimately acquainted with the ritual of Delphi, and a great friend of his, Klea, was president of the Thyiades at Delphi" (392, 439). "Dionysos," Harrison emphatically states, "has just as much to do with Delphi as Apollo himself, a statement rather startling to modern ears" (439).

In addition Harrison "translated and edited works by French scholars ... and was clearly shaped by their approach to classical archaeology" (Dyson 715); she had met M. Théophile Homolle, the director of the French excavations at Delphi, and her discussions of the temple, theater, and oracle are based on her firsthand familiarity with the site itself as well as her profound knowledge of vase-painting, sculpture, and inscriptions with which she always validated her arguments and enlivened her books. From these two vases, for instance, she derives a distinctly feminist reading of the religious history of Delphi:

> It was not only the Olympian Father Zeus who victoriously took over to himself the cult of the Earth-Mother and the Earth-Maidens. Even more marked is the triumph of the Olympian Son, Apollo. The design in fig. 91 is from a rather late red-figured amphora in the Naples Museum. A wayfarer, possibly Orestes, has come to Delphi to consult the god; he finds him seated on the very omphalos itself, holding the laurel

> and the lyre in his hands…. The vase-painter knows quite well that it is really a priestess who utters the oracles. Only a priestess can mount the sacred tripod, and he paints her so seated, the laurel wreath on her head and the sacred taenia in her hand, but he knows also that Apollo is by this time Lord of All….
> But even [in Aeschylus's *Eumenides*], so stately and yet so pitiful are the ancient goddesses that our hearts are sore for the outrage on their order. And on the vase-painting, when we remember that the omphalos is the very seat and symbol of the Earth-Mother, that hers was the oracle and hers the holy oracular snake that Apollo slew, the intrusion is hard to bear. (*Prolegomena* 319-21)

From a vase in the Hermitage Museum Harrison also discerns "a brief epitome of the religious history of Delphi" as the story of shifting power-struggle over the omphalos of Gaia, portrayed in the foreground while "higher up in the picture are other divinities superimposed on this primitive Earth-worship. Apollo and Dionysos clasp hands while about them is a company of Maenads and Satyrs." Harrison concludes:

> In this vase-painting, which dates about the beginning of the fourth century B.C., all is peace and harmony and clasped hands. The Delphic priesthood were past masters in the art of glossing over awkward passages in the history of theology. Apollo had to fight with the ancient mantic serpent of Gaia and slay it before he could take possession, and we may be very sure that at one time or another there was a struggle between the followers of Apollo and the followers of Dionysos. Over this past which was not for edification a decent veil was drawn. (390-91)

Glaspell retells in fiction Harrison's story of the conflict at Delphi between Apollonianism and Dionysianism, between patriarchy and matriarchy, logos and semiotic, through her characters in *Fugitive's Return*, all of whom are avatars of the Greek mythic past. I have elsewhere discussed the influence of Nietzsche on this novel, but I feel that Glaspell derived her understanding of these two gods and what they represent more directly from Harrison who, unlike Nietzsche, stressed that Apollo stole the Oracle from the ancient vatic earth-mothers, a violation that Glaspell personifies in the rape of the Greek shepherd girl, Constantina, by the handsome young shepherd nicknamed the "New Apollo."[3] For Harrison, Apollo was always "all for the father," whereas "the relation of Dionysos to his father Zeus was slight and artificial.... It is at once a cardinal point and a primary note in the mythology of Dionysos that he is the son of his mother ... 'child of Semele' " (*Prolegomena* 401-3). Semele was an "Earth-goddess in her agricultural aspect as Demeter, Corn-Mother" (416) and, just as in the rituals of Demeter and Persephone at Eleusis, Dionysian ritual at Delphi told of death, rebirth, and the return of child to mother. From Plutarch, who describes the Thyiades worshipping a baby in his cradle and identifying Dionysos with Osiris, Harrison concludes, "at Delphi there were rites closely analogous to those of Osiris and concerned with the tearing to pieces, the death and burial of the god Dionysos, and his resurrection and re-birth as a child" (401, 439).

John Knight, hardly Irma's "knight" in shining armor, but a son/lover who asks her to be his "understanding mother," has never been a sympathetic character to contemporary feminist readers, but when read as a supplicant to the Delphic oracle, his is perhaps not an inappropriate way of addressing a living avatar of the Thyiades. Writing a book about Delphi, Knight tells Irma: "I do not feel we have ever found the secret

... of why Delphi was. Why there were voices here. For there were, you know.... It has seemed to me the place itself holds the secret, and if one tried patiently, trustingly, it would give up its secret'" (*FR* 246). Under the tutelage of Knight, and unlike Glaspell herself, Irma's "desire to learn Greek became a passion." In particular she studies Pindar, "for she who lived within the sacred precinct at Delphi should know the Pythian Odes" (242). Taking the path to the theater, John and Irma linger on the stage and it is easy to hear Harrison's voice behind these lines:

> "It is said," [Knight] remarked, "that the heart of Dionysos is buried under this stage."
> "Would you," [Irma] asked, "have been a follower of Apollo, or follower of Dionysos?"
> He considered it but only said, "I wonder," as if he did not know. "You would have been a follower of Apollo," he affirmed.
> "I fear so," she said.
> "Fear?"
> "So much of life seems with Dionysos. He wanted life – for them all. Fullness of life, and joy."
> "Apollo was a noble god," he defended, "despite a good deal of treachery and dirty work." (255)

In Irma, Glaspell portrays a woman who has repressed the traumatic episodes from her past, in particular her divorce and the death of her young daughter from infantile paralysis, to such an extent that she has become mute. By withdrawing from language she evades expressing the inexpressible – the rage and pain that she feels. Once in Greece, however, she becomes immersed in a nonverbal realm of signs that opens to her a sisterhood of Thyiades and results in a Dionysian catharsis, a renewed sexuality, and the return of a daughter as, at the end of the novel, she adopts the unwanted rape victim, Constantina. *Fugitive's Return* is as grounded in place as a novel can get, as each major character is identified with and personifies the *archai* just as Irma becomes the "Kyra of the Archai" and one of the Dionysian Thyiades.[4] But while all of these characters have mythic aspects that reflect Delphi's past, they were inspired by people Glaspell and Cook actually met, reflecting at the same time Greece's post-war present.

In *The Road to the Temple*, Glaspell describes Athanasius, the waiter who left his job at the Pythian Apollo Hotel to work for Glaspell and Cook in Delphi, just as the fictional Irma is served by "old Elias who did so well for himself at the Pythian Apollo" (*FR* 47-8). Athanasius's sister was Stamula, who lived with her family "in the house just above" Glaspell and Cook's (*Road* 436), and in *Fugitive's Return*, Elias's sister, also named Stamula, becomes Irma's closest friend and an avatar of Apollonianism. Calm, creative, and rational, Stamula is referred to in the novel as "'Handmaiden of Apollo'" (253). Glaspell identifies her with this locus in the *archai* as Stamula shows Irma "where her father's house had been when the village was there. For this she led the Kyria inside the temple. It seemed almost in the center of the Temple of Apollo Stamula had been born" (70). Because she is Apollonian, Stamula's friendship provides a calming safe haven for Irma and, as she teaches her how to weave with their looms set up on the Dionysian stage, Irma's "greatest pleasure was in the old theater, weaving with Stamula. Making the little plays together, as they must, to communicate, was ... engagement, encounter, amusement, but like a fire controlled, or like the play it was, it could not run where one would not have it go" (99). How can Stamula, the "Handmaiden of Apollo" also be, with

Irma, a Thyiades on the Dionysian stage? Because, first, making plays is a subversive act, as no one knew better than Susan Glaspell. As the women tell stories silently through acting, Stamula mocks her husband and both women laugh – hardly a "Dionysian orgy," but certainly an eroticized bodily semiotic as Irma begins to find out "how to let her hands, her body, do things for her" and the women become "more deeply acquainted with each other than if they had been able to talk with words" (65). Secondly, and more importantly, Stamula's birthplace, the center of the Temple of Apollo is rendered by Harrison and Glaspell both as a potent binary locus because it is also the site of the Oracle. It is the hole, the opening, the silenced mother at the center of the father's house.

Like Stamula, Constantina is also associated with these archaic loci – her birthplace is the Dionysian stage through association with her mother, just as Stamula's birthplace in the temple had been identified with her father: "the house where Constantina's mother was a little girl had rested upon the very stones where the Kyria and Stamula now wove" (54-5). Recalling the village woman Glaspell had met harvesting berries in the *archai*, she portrays Constantina going to the stage to gather her legacy from her dead mother's garden, "making sure no other took a ripening fig or berry … She would fight for her fruit, just as, in the temple below, she had fought for her own virtue" (55-6).[5] For in this "lowered place, as a cellar, though small; as a grave, though large" in the temple of Apollo where she hid from the villagers, Constantina was raped by the shepherd nicknamed the "New Apollo" (69). The real-life Constantina, an eleven-year-old shepherd girl whom Glaspell and Cook had met in their mountain camp, had "since she was seven years old, [been] many nights alone on the mountain with the sheep." "Looking into her face as she leaned to our fire," Glaspell wrote in *The Road to the Temple*, "we would feel something older than Greece" (348). In her fictional portrayal of this girl Glaspell represents the orphaned refugees she had seen in Salonika, as well as Persephone, the ravished daughter of myth and ritual, and further, she is "something older than Greece," the silenced voice of the Oracle: "There was a hollowed place in the temple. One climbed down the stones into tall grasses and thistles. There the little shepherd girl, Constantina, had been ravished. There the Oracle once spoke" (*FR* 94). "[P]erhaps you are the Pythian Priestess," John Knight says to Irma, but she shakes her head and replies, "No, if the Pythian Priestess is here, she is Constantina ... Was it not a shepherd girl in the beginning?" (247).

There is no question as to which god triumphs at Delphi, for either Jane Harrison or Susan Glaspell. For Harrison, Dionysianism was "a religion which conquered Delphi [and] practically conquered the whole Greek world (*Prolegomena* 390-91), while for Glaspell, Constantina's revenge – pushing a huge stone (was it the rock of the Sibyl? or perhaps the omphalos itself?) over a ledge and crushing the "New Apollo" in his temple (*FR* 296) is an act of ritual nemesis against patriarchal violation of women on a mythological scale comparable to the Furies' pursuit of Orestes in Aeschylus, or the Bacchantes' rending of Pentheus in Euripides. Glaspell writes, "That night there was again life in the secret precinct of Delphi" (299). In her novel *Fugitive's Return* Glaspell exemplifies T.S. Eliot's "mythic method ... manipulating a continuous parallel between contemporaneity and antiquity" (177-78) by portraying a new play enacted on the ancient stage as the Thyiades, Irma and Stamula, plot together to save Constantina, whose hiding place after the murder is no longer in the temple of Apollo but beneath the stage of Dionysos, once the site of her mother's home:

> [Irma] reached the stage, and a moment stood there upon it, trembling now, less from fright, than with the excitement of what she might soon come to know. It came into her mind – The heart of Dionysos was buried under this stage. Was Constantina disturbing the heart of Dionysos? Would it be good to her – strange heart of Dionysos? ... She fancied she could hear the beating of a heart. There was no other sound. (303)

Glaspell included a photo of Jig Cook emerging from the underground passage beneath the stage of the Dionysian theater at Delphi in the 1927 edition of *The Road to the Temple* (reproduced in Linda Ben-Zvi's recent edition on page 312). She was already intrigued with this aspect of stagecraft; for instance, the set of her 1921 play *The Verge* features a trap-door in the floor of a greenhouse through which the protagonist's assistant enters and returns to a subterranean laboratory. In *Fugitive's Return*, Irma first observes the outcast Constantina in a birth image as a head emerging from the hiding place "right there on the old stage before which she sat – as if it had come up through the stones" (229). It was Dörpfeld, Harrison's mentor, who first discovered the secret passages underneath the Dionysian stage in Athens (Marquand 538), yet another uncanny connection between these two women writers who were both so inspired by the *archai* at Delphi.

Although a generation apart, Jane Ellen Harrison and Susan Glaspell each exemplified in her own way the turn-of-the-century "New Woman," becoming educated, traveling, working, and expanding the borders of female experience and intellectual achievement. Both inspired important movements that provided direct and living links with ancient Greek drama and ritual; Harrison through her influence on the Cambridge Anthropologists, and Glaspell through her co-founding of the Provincetown Players. Both found in the unearthed ruins at Delphi a rich and fertile metaphor for the cultural and historical "burial" of female experience, and both were empowered by the inscriptions they read in the stones and relics to inscribe their own feminist visions in their works.

Works Cited

Dyson, Stephen L. "Review of *The Invention of Jane Harrison.*" *American Journal of Archaeology* 105.4 (2001): 715. JSTOR. Web. 13 June 2008.

E.A.G. (Gardner). "Archaeology in Greece, 1893-4." *The Journal of Hellenic Studies* 14 (1894): 224-232. JSTOR. Web. 13 June 2008.

Eliot, T.S. "*Ulysses*, Order and Myth." *Selected Prose of T.S. Eliot.* Ed. Frank Kermode. New York: Harcourt, Brace, Jovanovich, 1975. 175-78. Print.

Glaspell, Susan. *Fugitive's Return.* New York: Frederick A. Stokes Company, 1929. Print.

———. Letter to Alice Keating Glaspell, 28 September 1922. The Berg Collection of English and American Literature, The New York Public Library, Astor, Lenox and Tilden Foundations. Print.

———. *The Road to the Temple.* Ed. Linda Ben-Zvi. Jefferson, N.C.: McFarland & Company Inc., 2005. Print.

———. "Stones that once were [a] temple." Typescript

of a poem, with the author's ms. corrections, unsigned and undated. The Berg Collection of English and American Literature, The New York Public Library, Astor, Lenox and Tilden Foundations. Print.

Harrison, Jane Ellen. "Archaeology in Greece, 1887-1888." *The Journal of Hellenic Studies* 9 (1888): 118-133. JSTOR. Web. 13 June 2008.

_____. "Delphika. – (A) The Erinyes. (B) The Omphalos." *The Journal of Hellenic Studies* 19 (1899): 205-251. JSTOR. Web. 13 June 2008.

_____. "Dr. Dörpfeld on the Greek Theatre." *The Classical Review* 4.6 (1890): 274-277. JSTOR. Web. 13 June 2008.

_____. *Prolegomena to the Study of Greek Religion*. New York: Meridian Books, 1955. Orig. Cambridge: Cambridge University Press, 1903. Print.

_____. *Reminiscences of a Student's Life*. London: Hogarth Press, 1925. Print.

_____. *Themis*. Cleveland and New York: The World Publishing Co., 1912, 1927. Print.

Marquand, Allan. "Archaeological News." *The American Journal of Archaeology* 10.4 (1895): 538. JSTOR. Web. 13 June 2008.

Meletzis, Spyros and Helen Papadakis. *Delphi Sanctuary and Museum*. Chicago: Argonaut Publishers, 1968. Print.

Noe, Marcia. *Susan Glaspell: Voice from the Heartland*. Western Illinois Monograph Series 1. Macomb: Western Illinois Press, 1983. Print.

Vickery, John B. *The Literary Impact of the Golden Bough*. Princeton: Princeton University Press, 1973. Print.

Notes

1 For instance, compare Cook's "One man cannot produce drama. True drama is born only of one feeling animating all the members of a clan – a spirit shared by all and expressed by the few for the all. If there is nothing to take the place of the common religious purpose and passion of the primitive group, out of which the Dionysian dance was born, no new vital drama can arise in any people" (*Road* 203) with Harrison from *Ancient Art and Ritual*: "So long as people believed that by excited dancing, by bringing in an image or leading in a bull you could induce the coming of Spring, so long would the *dromena* of the Dithyramb be enacted with intense enthusiasm, and with this enthusiasm would come an actual accession and invigoration of vital force. But, once the faintest doubt crept in, once men began to be guided by experience rather than custom, the enthusiasm would die down, and the collective invigoration would no longer be felt" (137). Part of this similarity in their ideas about the primitive, collective, and inspirational nature of drama may derive from both Cook's and Harrison's familiarity with the work of Bergson, Durkheim, and Lévi-Bruhl.

2 It is fascinating to follow the unfolding drama of these, as well as other, excavations during this period. The *Journal of Hellenic Studies*, published by the Cambridge Society for the Promotion of Hellenic Studies (of which Harrison was a lifetime member) produced an annual summary of the progress of "Archaeology in Greece," a job taken on after Harrison by E.A. Gardner from 1890-95 and then R.C. Bosanquet through 1902. In addition, the *American Journal of Archaeology* published the "Archaeological News" quarterly, a thorough review of progress at archaeological sites around the world, in the 1890s with reports usually submitted by A.L. Frothingham, Jr. or Allan Marquand.

3 See my "Apollonian Form and Dionysian Excess in Susan Glaspell's Drama and Fiction" in *Disclosing Intertextualities: The Stories, Plays, and Novels of Susan Glaspell*. Eds. Carpen-

tier and Ozieblo. Amsterdam & New York: Rodopi, 2006. 35-50.

4 Another Dionysian Thyiad is introduced with Theodora, Irma's servant, a beautiful dancing-girl. This character is modeled on Glaspell's and Cook's actual servant Theodora, a Greek refugee from Turkish Smyrna, whose lively antics and babbled stories entertained them. In the mountain camp they had to supply her with a bonfire each evening so that Theodora could "jump over it – or through it, indeed. It was as some mad rite in which she could not be restrained" (*Road* 383-4).

5 Like Alice Walker in her archetypal feminist essay, "In Search of Our Mother's Gardens," Susan Glaspell consistently associates gardening with mothers and with female creativity. In *Fugitive's Return* Irma recalls her father saying, "You know the first time I ever saw your mother? She was picking flowers in their garden. Oh, I'd seen her before— but not to *see* her" (140). See also, for example, Glaspell's novels *Brook Evans*, pp. 59-60; *Ambrose Holt and Family*, pp. 1-6; and *Judd Rankin's Daughter*, p. 101. This analogy might be paralleled with Jane Harrison's lengthy discussion in the *Prolegomena to the Study of Greek Religion* of women's fertility and harvest festivals such as the Thesmophoria and Haloa, precursors of the rituals at Eleusis.

Female Charioteers in Susan Glaspell's Plays: Re-visiting The Spirit of Delphi and Aristotle's *Poetics* in *Inheritors, The Verge*, and *The Comic Artist*

Noelia Hernando-Real

> "What we really should do is go to Greece. Wouldn't you like to go to Delphi, Susan? Maybe we could live there. We could go up and see the shepherds." (Cook quoted in Glaspell, *The Road to the Temple*, 235)

Greece, and particularly Delphi, had always stood in George Cram Cook's mind as an earthly Olympus available for poor American mortals. When the Provincetown Players, the little theatre group George Cram Cook and Susan Glaspell co-founded and which revolutionized the American stage, deviated toward Broadway commercialism, Delphi appeared as the only redeeming place. "It's time to go to Greece" said Cook to Glaspell. Although this dream was primarily Cook's, for Glaspell too "Greece offered a haven ... since it presented the extra appeal of history and culture" (Ozieblo 195), and before setting off for Delphi, Greece had long lived in Susan Glaspell. Even though the question of whether Glaspell's personal experience in Delphi was completely satisfying or not is still an issue in Glaspell scholarship, the influence that Greece had always exerted on her cannot be denied. Her own interest in classical art, Greek drama, and, obviously, her marriage to George Cram Cook, "a fanatical Hellenist" (Carpentier *The Major Novels* 28), paved the way for the multiple "references and allusions to Socrates, Plato, Aeschylus, Sophocles, and Euripides" we find in Glaspell's works (Molnar 37). As Ozieblo also points out in her biography of Glaspell, in Delphi "Glaspell delighted in walking up the hill, studying the fallen columns of ancient temples, the stone seats of the theater, and the uneven paving of the streets" (202). And as Glaspell herself confided in *The Road to the Temple*, she admired profoundly the Greek people, who "have a charm our lives have not; their lives have the flavour of the ages" (*The Road to the Temple* 264). Diving into these ancient Greek charms, this essay discusses Glaspell's revision of Aristotle's *Poetics* and his tragic conventions for the modern North American stage by focusing on three of Glaspell's female protagonists, Madeline in *Inheritors* (1921), Claire in *The Verge* (1921), and Eleanor in the lesser known and usually rejected *The Comic Artist* (1928), written in collaboration with Norman Matson. Susan Glaspell presents in these women modern American female charioteers, who comprise and revamp in different ways the Spirit of Delphi.

One aspect of Greek theatre that Susan Glaspell certainly approved of was the way drama was embedded within the structure and cultural system of the *polis*, since her theatrical experiments with the Provincetown Players aimed at this implantation in the very cultural heart of the United States of America, Greenwich Village. And within this experiment, the role of women took a fundamental position. Synnøve des Bouvrie affirms that "[i]n explaining the hypothesis that Greek tragedy is turning around central social institutions

– e.g. the *oikos*, family, marriage and legitimate succession – it becomes clear that women, being pivotal to those institutions, had to play a dominant part in drama" (32). Many recent studies on women's "dominant part" in Greek tragedy usually hint at the process of masculinization that many different tragic heroines experience. That is, in order to play this dominant part successfully, female characters adapt to the male heroic scheme, becoming for instance "vigorous and aggressive characters," as exemplified by the cases of Medea and Antigone (des Bouvrie 60).

It is precisely regarding female characters that the first and most obvious re-evaluation of Aristotle's *Poetics* in Glaspell's renewal of the American tragedy takes place. As Aristotle affirms, the "good woman" character can exist, even if she "is an inferior class," but the protagonist of tragedy has to be "manly," which means "strong or clever," qualities absolutely inappropriate in female characters (15). Glaspell, however, ignores Aristotle's tragic rules as she places strong and clever women center stage. Indeed, their strength and cleverness mirror a symbol of the spiritual and artistic grandness of Delphi: the Charioteer. Dedicated to the sanctuary as a tribute to Apollo for helping Polizalos, tyrant of Cela, win the chariot race during the Pythian games around 474 BCE, the Charioteer is the most famous sculpture at Delphi. Javier Sainz has described this magnificent work in the following terms:

> the Charioteer drives his chariot straight, with determination and a little naiveté; aware that he's being looked at, proud of what he represents [...] he holds the reins of the four horses, the reins of his starting life which he knows he can control, with the shyness of the beginner as things are new. But he is sure of

himself, of his strength and determination to achieve his vital objective, his goal.[1] (6, my translation)

Moreover, the Charioteer has been understood as a metaphor of both the artistic and rational awakening of the Greek world:

The Charioteer has raised his forearms in the shape of a right angle to hold the reins in the same way that the sun rises in the horizon, just as rational thought has been born among humans, as also symbolizing the emergence of the determination to control one's destiny, to be in charge of one's own acts, to assume responsibilities, both in happiness and disgrace.[2] (Sainz 9, my translation)

As the Charioteer does, Glaspell's female protagonists hold the reins with determination as they drive themselves against any obstacle, aware of the new life awaiting them and of the fact that they can find either happiness or disgrace when their goal is reached. But before starting their dramatic races, each of these women goes through the tragic processes of *peripeteia*, *anagnorisis*, and *pathos*. Respecting here Aristotle's canon, Glaspell creates complex plots revolving around "the change from one state of things within the play to its opposite of the kind described, and that too in the way we are saying, in the probable or necessary sequence of events" (Aristotle 11). The initial state of things in *Inheritors* is an idyllic pioneer community in the Midwest where settlers from different backgrounds, such as hard-working white Anglo-Saxons, noble Hungarian refugees, and humble Swedish immigrants, work together to tame the country and to make it a better place for their heirs. The opposite state is presented in the following acts, where Madeline, the protagonist and descendant of these pioneers, finds this place transformed by a xenophobic fungus and the old ideals have been subverted. In *The Verge* there is a change from Claire's control over her own house to her total lack of control. Claire, a modern woman, struggles from the very beginning to be released from the traditional roles of mother, sister, and wife. When the play opens she has turned all the heat of the house to her greenhouse, where she is experimenting with plants. All the other characters are forced to submit to her rules: she keeps the keys to all the doors and opens and closes them at her will. Events will show that her determination to be out has its costs, and Claire's best friend will find a tragic end. And in *The Comic Artist*, the initial state of things reflects a peaceful and protective home where Eleanor lives with her husband Stephen and their baby Wallop. A sudden reversal, triggered by the visit of Nina, her husband Karl, who is also Stephen's brother, and her mother, Luella, will make this house become a battle front where the sanctity of home is not respected. Nina will struggle to have Eleanor's husband, who had been her lover years before, back.

In order to create good complex plots, Glaspell is also sure to conform to Aristotle's *Poetics*, since during these initial states of things, and "attended by peripeties," Madeline, Claire, and Eleanor go through the process of *anagnorisis*, the unavoidable "change from ignorance to knowledge, and thus to either love or hate" (Aristotle 11). Significantly, the knowledge these female protagonists are awakened to is located in the very foundations of Greek philosophy. Glaspell constructs these characters, adopting and challenging for her feminist agenda some of the principles of the celebrated Seven Sages of Greece. The antique legend of the Seven Sages, originated circa the mid-sixth century

BCE and collected by different authors, points out that these *sophoi* "cover the domain of wisdom, cleverness, and poetic skill." The Seven Sages, whose number and names vary and include Bias of Priene, Chilo of Sparta, Solon of Athens, or Thales of Miletus, "were men involved with the problems of contemporary statecraft [... and who] expressed their thoughtful wisdom in pithy or Delphic mottoes" (Hornblower and Spawforth 1397). As Marie Delcourt describes, according to the legend, the Sages themselves engraved some of these mottoes, which encompassed Apollo's wisdom, in the Temple of Apollo at Delphi (208). Susan Glaspell's Madeline, Claire, and Eleanor embrace the knowledge necessary for their tragic developments through these maxims of the Spirit of Delphi: "A pledge, and ruin is near," "Nothing in excess," and "Know yourself."

In *Inheritors*, Madeline's *anagnorisis* relates to the Delphic principle "A pledge, and ruin is near." According to this motto, attributed to Chilon of Sparta (560 BCE), ruin hovers around pledges such as contracts or any other kind of financial agreements and transactions. Misfortune is near when money is involved. In the ideal state of things the play opens with, the pioneers' disregard for money and their hope for a better future materializes in the construction of Morton College. Very early in the play, one realizes that Silas cares much more about some kind of moral legacy than about willing large sums of money to his inheritors. When Smith, a real estate agent, tries to convince Silas Morton to sell a tract of his land, Silas refuses the offer without hesitating:

SILAS: What is it they want to buy – these fellows that are figuring on making something out of – expanse? (*a gesture of expanse, then a reassuring gesture*) It's all

right, but – just what is it?
SMITH: I am prepared to make you an offer – a gilt-edged offer for that (*pointing toward it*) hill above town.
SILAS: (*shaking his head – with the smile of the string man who is a dreamer*) The hill is not for sale. (108)

As Silas Morton says a bit later, "It's not for myself I'm holding it" (108), since he eventually gives up the best piece of his land, this hill that had belonged to the Sacs and which the Mortons, as many other early settlers, died for in the war. Silas's plan is to construct a college for everybody, boys and girls, rich and poor, white and red: "I give you this deed to take to rich men to show them one man believes enough in this to give the best land he's got. That ought to make rich men stop and think" (117). In the Morton College that Silas's granddaughter, Madeline, inherits, the poor are not welcome, immigrants are expelled, and girls use the library to learn jazz steps in their simplistic wish to hunt a good husband while they are still young and pretty. Glaspell shows very clearly that the reason for this complete denial of Silas Morton's dream is money. Complaining about the financial shortage the college is going through, Felix Fejevary, Madeline's uncle, tells Senator Lewis: "Let God give our students mammon. I mean, let the state appropriate" (120), something that will not happen unless the college is "one-hundred-per-cent American," that is, absolutely White Anglo-Saxon and Protestant. Hoping to expand Morton College, Fejevary is willing to go on ruining the essence of the place, reversing completely the initial state of things in the play.

Madeline's discovery is prompted by a key event: the vexatious treatment of Hindu students at Morton College. The young protagonist witnesses how these immigrant characters are insulted and hit when they reprove the United States' comfortable blindness as far as British rule in India is concerned. Aware that her grandfather's ideas have become just a phrase to repeat meaninglessly at the college foundation celebrations, Madeline courageously decides that she has to do something. She hits a policeman and is sent to prison for the first time. Presenting Morton College as a metonymy of the United States, Madeline realizes: "They're people from the other side of the world who came here believing in us, drawn from the far side of the world by things we say about ourselves. Well, I'm going to pretend – just for fun – that the things we say about ourselves are true" (139). Glaspell emphasizes her strength, unusual for a woman, as Madeline is warned that her political involvement in these immigrants' fight is "not a child's play – not today. You could get twenty years in prison for things you'll say if you rush out there now. (*she laughs*) You laugh because you're ignorant. Do you know that in America today there are women in our prisons for saying no more than you've said here to me!" (141). Careless of money – something that reminds the audience of Silas Morton – and as her twenty-first birthday approaches, Madeline will use the money Silas left her to get these immigrants out of prison: "if it's true that these strangers in our country are going to be abused because they're poor, – what else could I do with my money and not feel like a skunk?" (140). As the Seven Sages advise, Madeline understands the evil side of money. Madeline realizes the dangers of money in the case of Morton College, and how her uncle Felix Fejevary destroys the pioneers' dream for the sake of funds. However, as a strong political character, Madeline also understands and shows the good side of money, as she uses it to help those in need.

For Claire's discovery in *The Verge*, Glaspell revisits the maxim "Nothing in excess." According to this motto, attributed to Cleobulus of Lindos, measure and proportion must be observed so that irrevocable decisions are not made. For the female protagonist yearning to escape from given roles and forms, this principle becomes her personal punishment. As Carpentier says, "Claire seeks to break through Apollonian form into Dionysian excess" ("Apollonian Form" 47). Claire can indeed be seen as the incarnation of many of the key elements of the ruins of Delphi: she is the Charioteer, but she can also be regarded as the Pythia, the Sphynx of the Naxians, and even the Temple itself. As Panos Valavanis points out, the new Temple of Apollo (330 BCE) "integrated the mystic place and harmony of the Apollonian spirit and the inspired madness of the Dionysiac in a unique balance" (234). Similarly, Claire has created a place where she tries to keep this balance between being a woman and still having an identity of her own out of the ordinary traditional forms. This place is a tower. But not a common tower: it is "thwarted," "*a tower which is thought to be round but does not complete the circle. The back is curved, then jagged lines break from that, and the front is a queer bulging window – in a curve that leans. The whole structure is as if given a twist by some terrific force – like something wrong*" (78). Although other characters note that the tower "lacks form" (91), since "A round tower should go on being round," Claire "bought the house because" of the thwarted tower (79). As with the oracle of Apollo, this tower is Claire's location of vision. While Claire feels imprisoned within the walls of the house, representative of the earlier mentioned imprisonment in the roles of wife, sister, and mother, this tower provides Claire with the possibility of looking beyond. The tower has "a view" (79), but more significantly, the walls have pricks and slits to look through in a metaphorical way. The tower is *"lighted by an old-fashioned watchman's lantern hanging from the ceiling, the innumerable pricks and slits in the metal throw a marvellous pattern on the curved wall, like some masonry that hasn't been"* (78). Glaspell's use of lighting reproduces holes though which Claire solitarily dreams of looking beyond and of freedom: "never one of you – once – looked with me through the little pricks the gaiety made – never one of you – once, looked with me at the queer light that came in through the pricks" (82).

It is interesting to note that the geography of the stage space Glaspell creates in this play follows quite closely the Temple of Apollo. The *oikos* is the greenhouse where the people seeking the oracle wait, in the same way that all the characters wait for Claire to direct their lives. And there are, extraordinarily, two spaces functioning as the *antron*. The tower, as seen, is supposed to be Claire's private space, where she has her visions. This is unlike the Pythia's cave because this place is invaded. But as the Pythia's cave in the Temple of Apollo, Claire's tower also undergoes its own ritual. As the myth tells, Apollo had been wandering over several regions on Greece to found his first oracle for humans when he came to Delphi, where the place then called Pytho was guarded by a terrible female serpent called Python. After fighting and killing the Python, Apollo became the sole occupant of the place. Apollo's purification in the temple after killing the serpent seems to have rooted the tradition of his oracle. In *The Verge*,

Claire has her own Python to fight: her sister Adelaide. Adelaide intrudes the tower in her attempt to bring the protagonist back to tradition, and significantly, out of this queer tower. But Claire, as Apollo, fights this enemy and expels her from her temple. Then, Claire, as Apollo did, feels the need "to purify the tower" (84). Claire's second *antron* resembles the Pythia's cave in the Temple of Apollo, which was "probably at a slightly lower level" (Valavanis 261). Claire has a room of her own at a lower level in the greenhouse, accessible through a trap door whose only key Claire has.

But even as strong as Claire seems to be, her problem is her excess, a fault the Seven Sages warn about. Her yearning to reach and control "Otherness" will lead to her own collapse. Parallel to the way Claire denies behaving as a proper wife and mother, she experiments with plants, to create forms never seen before. Claire explains her vision of otherness: "these plants – Perhaps they are less beautiful – less sound than the plants from which they diverged. But they have found – otherness [...] They've broken from the forms they found themselves. They are alien. Outside. That's it, outside; if you know what I mean" (76). Claire's excess, however, becomes awareness. In a speech reminiscent of the Pythia's words, which were "usually ambiguous and unclear" (Valavanis 261), Claire admits:

(*and though speaking, she remains just as still*)
Breath of the uncaptured?
You are a novelty.
Out?
You have been brought in.
A thousand years from now, when you are but a form too long repeated,
Perhaps the madness that gave you birth will burst

again,
And from the prison that is you will leap pent queernesses
To make a form that hasn't been –
To make a person new.
And this we call creation. (*very lowly, her head not coming up.*)
Go away! (96)

This is the Pythia speaking, letting the audience know that the original form she has created "a thousand years from now [will be] but a form too long repeated." After realizing that transcending given forms is impossible, Claire's reaction to her *anagnorisis* will be extreme again. She murders the only true friend she has, Tom, in an attempt to save him from conventionality. As she says after strangling him: "Yes. I did. MY – gift" (100, emphasis in original), an act of liberation that will be discussed later on.

It is in this relationship established between Claire and death that the representation of this character as a modern version of the Sphinx of the Naxians comes to surface. The Sphinx of the Naxians, an important monument of archaic art dedicated to the sanctuary circa 560 BCE, represents "a monster of ancient mythology and art, with the body of a lion, the face of a woman, and the wings of a bird. [...] Its daemonic nature soon made it a symbolic adornment of tombs and a common dedication in sanctuaries" (Valavanis 215). Glaspell also constructs Claire by combining features of a woman, a lion, and a bird. In her strength and courage, Claire is an unusual lion woman who fights fiercely and is even able to kill. Claire's wings can be glimpsed in her obsession with flying:

To fly. To be free in the air. To look from above on

> the world of all my days. Be where man has never been! Yes – wouldn't you think the spirit could get the idea? The earth grows smaller. I am leaving. What are they – running around down there? Why do they run around down there? Houses? Houses are funny lines and down-going slants – houses are vanishing slants. I am alone. Can I breathe this rarer air? Shall I go higher? Shall I go too high? I am loose. I am out. (69)

If Claire actually had the Sphinx's wings, she could fly away from the house, the forms, and the roles that entrap her. But she knows that she has no wings. Tom's corpse is her only, though excessive, means of survival and empowerment.

In *The Comic Artist*, Glaspell revamps the importance of the maxim "Know yourself" to make Eleanor discover the new state of things in her house. This dictum, attributed to Thales of Miletus in 585 BCE, warns us against ignorance, for only the ignorant think they are clever. Only through self-knowledge will we be able to live wisely. As we are told, Eleanor had bought this house and decorated it to fit her own identity, that of a traditional and loving mother and wife:

> ELEANOR: My people were here long ago. They built this house in seventeen hundred and something. I feel my great-grandfather in the old forgotten roads, on the beach [...] I said: 'Let's look up the old place on the Cape.' It had been sold to Portuguese, but we bought it back. [...] We're buying back old things that were in it. [...] When I discover an old tool, they seem in life again. (13, 56-57)

Eleanor, in order to create and maintain an identity, buys the old house where her ancestors had lived, and endeavors to get back all the belongings that once were in the house, regaining thus the identity the house once had. But this self-made identity has submerged Eleanor into a state of numbness from which only a shocking *peripeteia* could awake her. The fear of losing her husband when the young and sexy Nina appears will make her react. This reaction, however, requires a process of self-discovery. In a first attempt, and atypically for a Glaspell female protagonist, Eleanor asks her husband to expel Nina from the house: "Oh, Stephen, keep me from doing that! Protect me – as a man should protect his wife" (79). Realizing that her husband will not help her to recover her house and her place, Eleanor decides to talk to Nina herself:

ELEANOR: I asked Stephen to do something for me. It was cowardly. I must do it myself. (*Pause*) Karl loves you. [...]
NINA: Am I to step back to Karl's love, and leave Stephen for you?
ELEANOR: Yes.
NINA: Yes! Why not? What a good idea? But what are we to do with the fact that Stephen loves me?
ELEANOR: Stephen does not love you, Nina. Stephen loves me. [...] Stephen feels you'll ruin his brother's life. He's doing this for Karl to see what you are. (80-82)

It is only when Eleanor recognizes that she is a strong woman, capable of defending what is hers, that she will tell Nina to go away and try to control her life. Although Eleanor does not convince Nina to love Karl and forget Stephen, at least she has left aside the passive role of the frail wife.

As suggested in my previous discussions on these three plays, Madeline, Claire, and Eleanor, experience tremendous *agons*. And adhering to the principles of Aristotle's *Poetics*, Glaspell places these tragic deeds within the family. As Madeline claims, "It's dreadful about families," "I hope I never have one" (148). This character, as Marie Molnar has pointed out, is a modern version of Antigone, and "having decided to which members of her family she owes her loyalty, must make the choice between protest and silence" (38). Loyal to her pioneer ancestors, Madeline will have to struggle against her father, cousin, aunt, and uncle, if she is to drive her own life. In *The Verge*, Claire is in constant conflict against her sister, daughter, and husband, because they want her to behave as a True Woman does. Her sister Adelaide unsuccessfully commands Claire to respect the family and "be the woman you were meant to be!" (79). And in *The Comic Artist*, Eleanor, as discussed, confronts her husband's infidelity in her attempt to keep the family tied together, as she says, to make the house "again be our house" (78).

The plots Glaspell presents onstage in these three plays include the ingredients to provoke those feelings of pity and fear Aristotle sought to arouse in the audience. Responding to the new times, Glaspell's pity and fear focus on modern women who suffer as they try to be themselves. Up to now, many aspects of Glaspell's reworked version of tragedy have been suggested regarding her female characters, but a key point that deserves special attention in this revision relates to language, power, and the subversion of patriarchal hierarchies. As Laura McClure has pointed out, "Tragedy, in its capacity as an 'official' discourse, has also reinforced the ideology of silence and seclusion for women promulgated by other texts even as it represented speaking females engaged in a diverse array of roles" (24). Borrowing McClure's words,

> the equation between power and speech [...] reflects a fundamental male concern about maintaining control

over the bodies and speech of perceived subordinates. For this reason, fifth-century literary resources frequently represent women's verbal activities as dangerous and subversive of political stability. (69)

As seen throughout this essay, the speeches Glaspell provides Madeline, Claire, and Eleanor afford them a means of resisting patriarchal hierarchical structures that attempt to control their lives. The audience of Glaspell's plays experiences pity and fear for the strong woman who dares to speak and act publicly against patriarchal institutions, be these family, marriage, government, or university. The struggle of these female protagonists reveals a sharp political denunciation the audience has to disentangle.

A final step in Glaspell's revision of Aristotle's *Poetics* concerns the aim of good tragedy: releasing purification. Catharsis should liberate us from the pity and fear seen onstage, which are representative of the real suffering in our lives. Glaspell's plays, however, do not end with this purification. The price Madeline, Claire, and Eleanor have to pay for daring to become female charioteers will be more suffering. Madeline disgraces her family, as she eventually decides to go on defending the immigrant characters. As the play ends, Madeline leaves the stage for prison. Although this end leaves the audience partly satisfied for the pleasure of having onstage a female character brave enough to confront family and government, the taste of prison with which she will rewarded is far from purifying.

In *The Verge*, Claire, unable to go on controlling her own life, after having discovered that she will always live subject to the rules society imposes, turns to violence. With her act of killing Tom, she empowers herself and becomes an avenging goddess, deciding humans' fates. After strangling her soul mate, Claire does not feel any remorse, instead she says: "(*speaking each word very carefully*) Saved – myself [...] Out. (*a little like a child's pleased surprise*) Out" (100). That is, she feels outside convention and thus in control of her life. Again, the audience can hardly feel purified, for the cost of what this female character had to do to feel herself does nothing but arouse more pity and fear. And in Eleanor's case, her discovery of her potential to drive her life will not find a happy ending either. Before she can expel Nina from the house, Nina's husband drowns in the sea attempting to rescue Nina, who had threatened to kill herself after her confrontation with Eleanor quoted earlier. After this event, it is hardly probable that Eleanor and Stephen will ever live happily again. As J. Ellen Gainor has pointed out, "Stephen and Eleanor are left with the wreckage of their marriage" (200). Eleanor discovered her potential, but just too late to leave the audience satisfied.

It could be said that Glaspell follows Aristotle's *Poetics* closely, but it is in her departures that her works become more significant. Instead of mimesis, the representation of the real, Glaspell provides what Elin Diamond calls a feminist mimicry, where "the relation to the real [is] productive, not referential, geared to change," and where "the tendency to tyrannical modelling (subjective/ideological projections masquerading as universal truths) are explored" (xvi). This is the reason why Glaspell does not close her plays with catharsis, a purifying resolution that could make the audience feel satisfied with the price paid for their tickets. On the contrary, this lack of purification is aimed to make us think that purification is not easily achieved in real life, and that, within the feminist discourse that frames Glaspell's works, universal patriarchal truths that have been guiding women's lives for ages must be explored, shown, and vanished.

In *The Road to the Temple*, Glaspell quotes Cook: "Americans spoil Greeks" (270). With this essay, I hope to have demonstrated that this transnational relationship could be more positive. Glaspell was one of those Americans who benefited from Greece, from Greek philosophy, and from Greek art. The memory of Susan Glaspell has lived in the heart of Delphi, in the same way that her plays, positively influenced by the Greek world, are being resuscitated on the world's stages. As discussed, Glaspell's protagonists are metaphors of modern Greek female charioteers placed in American contexts. There is, however, one main difference between the Delphic Charioteer and the female characters explored in this essay. As Valavanis has said, the Charioteer "is not depicted during the contest, for he would otherwise be shown in a more intense posture, but after his victory, as calm and happy, he makes a lap of triumph in the Hippodrome" (227). Instead of depicting Madeline, Claire, and Eleanor victorious and proud, Glaspell shows her female charioteers in real struggle, in the moments previous to and during the race, when the uncertainty of the result makes the audience's hearts, as the Charioteer's, beat rapidly.

Works Cited

Aristotle. *On the Art of Poetry*. Trans. Ingram Bywater. Oxford: Clarendon Press, 1920. Print.

Carpentier, Martha C. "Apollonian Form and Dionysian Excess in Susan Glaspell's Drama and Fiction." *Disclosing Intertextualities. The Stories, Plays and Novels of Susan Glaspell*. Eds. Martha C. Carpentier and Barbara Ozieblo. Amsterdam and New York: Rodopi, 2006. 35-50. Print.

———. *The Major Novels of Susan Glaspell*. Gainesville: University Press of Florida, 2001. Print.

Delcourt, Marie. *L'oracle de Delphes*. Paris: Payot, 1981. Print.

des Bouvrie, Synnøve. *Women in Greek Tragedy*. Oslo: Norwegian University Press, 1990. Print.

Diamond, Elin. *Unmaking Mimesis. Essays on Feminism and Theater*. London and New York: Routledge, 1997. Print.

Gainor, J. Ellen. *Susan Glaspell in Context. American Theatre, Culture, and Politics, 1915-48*. Ann Arbor: University of Michigan Press, 2001. Print.

Glaspell, Susan. *Inheritors. Plays by Susan Glaspell*. Ed. C. W. E. Bigsby. Cambridge: Cambridge University Press, 1987. 103-57. Print.

———. *The Comic Artist* (with Norman Matson). London: Ernest Benn, 1927. Print.

———. *The Road to the Temple*. London: Ernest Benn, 1926. Print.

———. *The Verge. Plays by Susan Glaspell*. Ed. C. W. E. Bigsby. Cambridge: Cambridge University Press, 1987. 57-101. Print.

Hornblower, Simon and Anthony Spawforth, eds. "Seven Sages." *Oxford Classical Dictionary*. 3rd edition. Oxford and New York: Oxford University Press, 1996. Print.

McClure, Laura. *Spoken Like a Woman. Speech and Gender in Athenian Drama*. Princeton, NJ: Princeton University Press, 1999. Print.

Molnar, Marie. "Antigone Redux: Female Voice and the State in Susan Glaspell's *Inheritors*." *Susan*

Glaspell: New Directions in Critical Inquiry. Ed. Martha C. Carpentier. Cambridge: Cambridge Scholars Press, 2006. 37-44. Print.

Ozieblo, Barbara. *Susan Glaspell. A Critical Biography.* Chapel Hill: North Carolina University Press, 2000. Print.

Sainz Moreno, Javier. *El vértigo del auriga de Delfos. Colección La Dialéctica en el Arte.* Pliegos Libres, nd. Print.

Valavanis, Panos. *Games and Sanctuaries in Ancient Greece. Olympia, Delphi, Isthmia, Nemea, Athens.* Trans. David Hardy. Athens: Kapon Editions, 2004. Print.

Notes

1 Javier Sainz Moreno, *El vértigo del auriga de Delfos. Colección La Dialéctica en el Arte* (place unknown: Pliegos Libres, date unknown), 6. The original reads, "*El Auriga conduce su carro muy derecho, con decisión y algo de ingenuidad, consciente de que le están mirando, orgulloso de lo que representa [...], lleva las riendas de los cuatro corceles, las riendas de la vida que comienza y que ve que va a poder dominar, con la timidez del principio y de todo lo nuevo, pero seguro de sus fuerzas, de su destreza y decisión para alcanzar su objetivo vital, la meta.*"

2 *Ibid.* 9. The original reads, "*El Auriga ha levantado los antebrazos en ángulo recto para sujetar las riendas de los corceles. Como se levanta el sol por el horizonte, tal como ha nacido el pensamiento racional entre los hombres, como emerge la decisión de manejar el propio destino, de ponerse al frente de los propios actos, de asumir las responsabilidades, en la felicidad y en la desgracia.*"

The Noble Peasant: Primitivism, Classicism, and the Epistemological Pivot in Susan Glaspell's Career

Michael Winetsky

While living in spruce huts, high on Mount Parnassos in the summer of 1922, Susan Glaspell and her husband received a visit from their friend Elias Scarmoush, a shepherd who tended his sheep on the mountain. They had met Scarmoush earlier, when they were living in the village of Delphi before taking up their summer residence in "the spruce," but now it was as if they were meeting him for the first time. Glaspell writes, "you do not know a shepherd until you know him on his mountain." She goes on to describe the shepherd and his mountain in her memoir *The Road to the Temple*:

> One evening we saw him leave his flock and start up to our camp. He came like a king; or like a high-priest – ritualistic as he stood under our spruce-tree and in his mighty voice said: "*Kalí Spéra, Kyrios Kouk, Kalí Spéra, Kyria.*" He was a violent-looking man, and simple. It was as if civilization, our world, had not been. We were afraid of not doing the right thing. He was so right. He had come to welcome us to the mountain. We would be all right there, for, "I," pounding his chest, "am here."... The sheep grazed below, alone with the dogs. If bells changed the shepherd would look, rise perhaps, give a cry which we did not understand. But the dogs understood. After a time, with

a certain fierce ceremony, "*Kalí Nichta!*" he said, in a voice for the mountains, and with perfect form returned to his sheep. (339)

All of the hallmarks of the noble savage are evident in Glaspell's description of Scarmoush, or in this case rather the noble peasant. "Civilization" melts away in the presence of this ancient man. He offers her contact with ancient life and ancient practices more in harmony with nature than anything she had known in the United States. He communicates with animals in ways that are incomprehensible to Glaspell. He is described as "violent-looking, and simple." The word "simple," a word she uses repeatedly in her descriptions of the people at Delphi, is tinged with the condescension of the educated classes for the "simple folk." But it is his simplicity, along with his violent appearance, that gives him power "like a king or a high-priest."

From the anti-foundationalist perspective, which often dominates critical discourse in the disciplines of the modern languages, Glaspell's encounter with people she deems primitive is *a priori* a false communication. This kind of primitivism is not only false, but it is disliked and dangerous because it stands on the same epistemological ground as any kind of colonialist and racist discourse. For the purpose of this paper, I regard these critiques as a point of departure. Beyond this, I seek to situate primitivism within Glaspell's life and work especially as this idea informs her residence at Delphi. Primitivism appears as a trend in which Glaspell seems increasingly aware of the shaky ground of her own assumptions about the primitive. The relation of primitivism to philhellenism offers crucial insights into the larger intellectual concerns of her oeuvre. Of particular interest is the way that Glaspell considers education and social class.

For Glaspell, the idea of the noble savage was, as it had been for Rousseau and for Herman Melville before her, a critique of "civilized" society, a way to question the values of the society in which she was raised and to which she felt her writing contributed. This is a critique that Glaspell takes up in the middle period of her career. Primitivism is found neither in Glaspell's early novels, nor in her late novels and plays. So, I suggest we might speak of a primitive period. Glaspell's primitive period, roughly confined to the 1920s, was a fairly tumultuous period in her life and work, as evidenced in the variety of genres into which she worked these ideas – *Inheritors*, "Dwellers on Parnassos," *The Road to the Temple*, and *Fugitive's Return*; that is, respectively, a play, a journalistic dispatch, a unique elegiac biography, and a novel – wide even for Glaspell and running the gamut of her broad compositional vocabulary.

In my view of Glaspell's career, I regard her body of work as instantiating larger changes in the history of ideas. Her early fiction may be said to share with literary naturalism a belief in progress and the epistemological certainty that language and narrative could offer an accurate transcription of the experiential world. Her middle works compare more with high modernism, for the way they register a realization that history may not move toward a brighter future, and for their self-conscious sense that the experiential world is only available to us through our own subjective perspectives. Glaspell's early work evinced a hope that scientific paradigms as well as metaphysical speculations would continue to codify social institutions, without the added problem of the sectarian conflicts associated with old doctrinal religions. Classical Greece seemed to inspire her that such an integration was possible. Her later work, on the other hand, almost completely abandons all kinds of scientism, often turning in its place to Christian rhetoric. Her work is still invested in metaphysical speculations, but it now regards such speculation as largely a private or intimate activity rather than an activity with the potential for public good. Of course, I do not have time to develop many of these arguments here.

My purpose in mentioning the broad directions of her career now is to explain the context in which I see the primitive period operating. Namely, Glaspell turns to primitivism in the middle of her career as a way of giving voice to her growing skepticism about ideas of progress and about the epistemological certainty that characterized late Victorian discourse.[1] It was, in some ways, these motives that inspired Cook and Glaspell to take up residence in Greece. If Glaspell came to Delphi expecting an experience of the primitive, it was, finally, her experience of Delphi that seemed to have cured her of her interest in primitivism. When she actually got to know the people here, she began to know individuals, not cultural archetypes. As such, we see her reasserting late Victorian paradigms about the civilized and the primitive, but each reassertion becomes more and more ghost-like, less and less convinced of the certainty of our understanding across cultural boundaries. For example, when she narrates a meeting with Elias Scarmoush subsequent to the one I began with, she repeats her own previous phrase but now as if it were a tired truism. She writes, "As always, Elias brought with him that feeling of 'civilization' never having been at all." The fact that she puts civilization in quotation marks indicates that the phrase has been evacuated of some of its earlier significance or authenticity.

Glaspell's interest in the primitive predates her residence at Delphi, but not by very much. Perhaps her most blatant invocation of the tradition of the noble savage occurs in *Inheritors*, her 1921 Provincetown Players play and her penultimate play prior to her move to Greece that would effect her break with the group. Although the primitive subject of *Inheritors* is not a personal acquaintance of Glaspell's, in the way that Elias Scarmoush is, neither is the noble savage in *Inheritors* a fictional person. She invokes the historical figure of Black Hawk, the Chief of the Sauk and Fox tribes, who led the armed resistance against the U.S. government that is now known as the War of 1832. One of the fictional characters in *Inheritors*, Silas Morton, a "pioneer" homesteader, had supposedly known Black Hawk prior to the War of 1832. Morton describes Black Hawk:

> He looked like the great of the earth. Noble. Noble like the forests – and the Mississippi – and the stars... Sometimes I feel as if the land itself has got a mind that the land would rather have had the Indians. (111)

Like her description of Scarmoush written some seven years later, Glaspell's depiction of Black Hawk as a type of noble savage endows the figure with nobility based on his seamlessness with nature. In each case, the nobility of the primitive subject means that he is a kind of heroic model for the rest of us; in each case, we look to some activity or practice – some work – that harmonizes him with nature. In the case of Scarmoush, it is his work of shepherding; Black Hawk, similarly, was "something many nights in his canoe had made him."

I bring up this example of an interest in the noble

savage prior to Glaspell's residence to Delphi in order to make two points.

The first is that in *Inheritors*, the noble savage not only signifies the Romantic notion of greater harmony with nature, but also this invocation, part of its critique of the civilized, is bound up in the need for better cross-cultural understanding — an ethic that motivates Glaspell's writing throughout her oeuvre. It is *because* Silas Morton regrets the consequences of the War of 1832, regrets the Native American dispossession, that he decides to give away his possessed Indian territory. Morton donates his land for the foundation of a college because he believes learning helps us to "better understand the other person." The belief in education and the belief in the nobility of the primitive are not mutually exclusive in *Inheritors*, at least not in Act I. Morton says, "'twould have done something for us to have been Indians a little more." If we had had more learning, he thinks, we would have had more empathy, and if we had had more empathy, we might not have warred with the Native Americans and usurped their lands but instead have learned from them. I note this in part to defend Glaspell from that common critique of the concept of the noble savage, articulated, for example, by John R. Cooley, in his study, *Savages and Naturals* (in which he indicts Eugene O'Neill among others):

> This mode of thought, in its sentimental regard for the land and the natural man, blatantly disregards the brutal circumstances under which red and black people have been forced to live in America. Writers in this mode characteristically fail to distinguish between their sentimentality for a particular way of life and the facts of white America's ... subjugation of Indians, its slavery and exploitation of blacks. (31)

In Glaspell's case, it is actually because of the "subjugation of the Indians" that Glaspell turns to primitivism as a way of critiquing a society that would so subjugate. Indeed, in *Road to the Temple*, Glaspell shows that Cook was quite disturbed by this subjugation as well, and that Delphi was the setting in which he felt that regret most acutely.

My second reason for bringing up primitivism in *Inheritors* is to demonstrate that Glaspell in fact came to Delphi in search of some sort of experience of authenticity that was lacking in the society she left behind in the United States. This point, which I find very persuasive, does suggest the applicability of another common critique of primitivism — to put it bluntly, that primitivism is prejudice. To adapt the words of Roy Harvey Pearce from his groundbreaking study, *Savagism and Civilization*: Glaspell, studying the savage, in the end only studied herself.[2] What I mean is, by regarding Black Hawk as "something that's never been caught... something many nights in his canoe had made him" Glaspell is not accessing Black Hawk's experience or Native American experience as much as seeking to fulfill her own wish for a model of closer contact with nature (111). When this need remained unfulfilled by imagining historical figures in her plays, the author herself would depart for a place where ancient history might still be on the surface. It is not surprising then that she finds Scarmoush "so right," as if he were exactly what she was looking for.

The earliest published evidence of her impression of the way of life at Delphi is probably "Dwellers on Parnassos," an article appearing in *The New Republic*, January 17, 1923. In this article, it is very clear that her impressions of the Greek way of life reflect inevitably upon Glaspell's own American upbringing, serving an already conceived agenda. She is drawn to the seasonal migration between "the Spruce" and the town, but she is particularly interested in the way the Greeks work. In expressing this interest, she is expressing doubts about ideas of progress. She writes:

> They pull wheat by hand on Parnassos, outraging one brought up in Iowa. If your eye has reached as far as eye can reach across the wheat fields of Minnesota and Dakota, you smile at a wheat field that wouldn't make a tennis court. But in the twilight of the September day as I helped pull the last wheat at Kylania ... —drinking and singing and dancing with the through the gay excitement of the last lap, I thought of our way and of their way, and wondered why all gain must hold so much of loss. (199)

It would be valid, I think, to view this critique of American farm practices as in line with movements in environmental ethics. But, more to the point, by "all gain must hold so much of loss," she probably is considering the efficiency of American industrial farming as progress, as a gain in production, but a loss in humanity, in the pleasure of working. Glaspell may also be thinking again about the dispossession of the Native Americans, to which she might refer only in this vague allusion to "loss," disguising what was probably too radical for the pages of *The New Republic*.

But we cannot make too much of the comparison between noble savage and noble peasant. Indeed, there are several ways in which both the *The New Republic* article and later the memoir reveal the exceptional context for Glaspell's regard of Greek peasants as primitives. Built into Glaspell's thinking on the primitive is a whole theory of history. In this idea of history, the assumption is that culture is a continuous progression. Ancient culture is not so much *different* from American culture as prior to it. Glaspell is interested in the way of life at Delphi, because, in her view it predates the civilization of Classical antiquity and has endured intact. In "Dwellers on Parnassos," she calls it "this way of life that was in Greece before Homer was in Greece." The question becomes to what extent civilization can coexist with primitive culture. In the traditional view of primitive society, such as America before colonization, "civilization" had yet to develop in the place. It took European settlement to civilize America, or such was the common view until perhaps the mid-twentieth century.

This cannot be said of Greece. In Lewis H. Morgan's 1877 study *Ancient Society, Or Research in the Lines of Human Progress from Savagery Through Barbarism to Civility*, which Glaspell had very likely come in contact with as an undergraduate at Drake, the Greeks are regarded, as was fairly standard at the time, as among the first of "civilized" peoples in the West. In addition, Morgan singles out the Greeks as the people most clearly evincing his six stages of progress, citing the *Iliad* in particular as "present[ing] our first comprehensive picture of Aryan society while still in barbarism" and as a work that itself narrates the progress of the Greeks from barbarism to civility (17, 32). It was this special place accorded to ancient Greece as a kind of lost father of the West by nineteenth-century scholars that made modern Greece a subject of study. The excavation of Delphi (which Glaspell mentions repeatedly in *Road*) was undertaken not by Greeks but by French archaeologists, and this is may be seen today in the light of the history of the colonization of the near East by countries in Western Europe (think: the Elgin Marbles). Classicism in the academic establishment during the days of Victorian archaeology was usually a separate discourse from discourses of primitivism, but the discourses were both inflected by similar assumptions about historical time.[3]

This similarity can be seen at times in Glaspell's memoir, as obviously it was not only the primitive that Glaspell and Cook had sought in coming to Greece, but also classical civilization. Soon after introducing the reader to Andreas Korylss (Korlyss owned a wine shop in Delphi and befriended Cook and Glaspell), Glaspell relates a moment in which Cook tries to pay the man a compliment by remarking on his resemblance to Aristophanes:

> Jig thought [Korlyss] was a good deal like Aristophanes. He spoke of this one day and Andreas replied—"Oh, yes, I know him, he is a doctor in Creso." When Jig laughed (and he hated himself for having laughed), Andreas said, with a simple humility, "You know I am not a learned man." "You are more like the contemporaries of Aristophanes," Jig told him, "than many a man who is learned about them." (326)

This moment must have been an uncomfortable one for those who experienced it, and it is certainly uncomfortable to read about. How exactly do Cook and Glaspell regard their friend at this moment? Cook's analogy indicates the extent to which their encounters with their Greek contemporaries were conditioned by the expectations raised by study of the classics, that is, by their educations. Perhaps there really was a striking resemblance — whether it was physical or behavioral or spiritual — between Korylss and Aristophanes, but, as likely, Cook was in search of classical analogies and Korlyss fulfilled this want.

Aristophanes, living in the Golden Age of classical drama, is not usually regarded as a primitive figure, even considering the harshest possible views of his sense of humor. But Cook's idea that Korlyss is "more like the contemporaries of Aristophanes than many a man who is learned about them" is in pattern with noble-peasant primitivism to the extent that it would seem to praise authenticity at the expense of cultivation. Primitivism is often regarded, correctly I think, as posing a challenge to classicism at this time. Glaspell and Cook may in fact have turned to primitivism as a way of questioning the assumptions with which they were educated, assumptions in which the Greeks are elevated as a paradigm of an achieved civilization. The structure is to supplant one assumption for another. In pattern with this, Cook's comparison between Korlyss and Aristophanes at first confers status on Korlyss by classical analogy and then redeems the analogy by inversion, allowing Korlyss's authenticity to dictate the meaning. Whatever conflicts were present in the ideas, this analogy shows that primitivism mixed with classicism with surprising ease in shaping Cook's and Glaspell's expectations and thus their experience with the country.

In *Inheritors* as well, both ideas are present without much exploration of their latent conflict. Primitivism in *Inheritors* is associated with anarchism. The figure of Black Hawk suggests to Silas Morton the social evil of the institution of private property, as he imagines saying to Black Hawk "not your hill, not my hill, but... hill of vision" (115). The fact of dispossession undermines the legitimacy of claims on the land, shaking the foundations of law. Blackhawk embodies a world prior to this order. Classicism in *Inheritors*, on the other hand, represents the harmony, order, and holism that society might achieve. Professor Holden explains what traveling to Greece had meant to him, recollecting it as part of his selection of a disciplinary field. He says, "I knew then that I wanted to teach something within sociology, and I didn't want anything I felt about beauty to be left out of what I formulated about society. The Greeks ... were able to let beauty flow into their lives – to create themselves in beauty" (133). Holden's view, I think, is one that Glaspell very likely shared – that Classical Greece, more than modern America, was integrated, proportional, and whole. When Glaspell depicts Greece both in the memoir *Road to the Temple* and in the novel *Fugitive's Return*, she often uses the word "form" in a very enigmatic way to represent the mystique of the place. She says that Scarmoush, "with perfect form returned to his sheep." Both primitivism and classicism represent philosophical alternatives to the dominant paradigms of what would come to be called "American civilization." They are two keys to fit the same lock.

I suggest that Glaspell's classicism be considered a kind of humanism. That is, the imagined continuity of Greece with its ancient and classical past granted access to the kind of authentic experience that took them out of the fractured climate of modernity in which science and religion and art and politics were all rapidly falling into their separate disciplinary corners. Hellenism was instructive of a more unified and harmonious society not only to Glaspell and Cook, but also to so many modern writers from Eliot to H.D. In order to emphasize the influence of this kind of thinking on the educational establishment, I must observe also the resemblance between Glaspell's ideas about Greece and those of Irving Babbitt. Babbitt writes, "Greece is the most humane of countries, because it ... formulated the law of measure" (24). Babbitt, of course, is a much more conservative thinker than Glaspell, and he, despising every form of "Rousseauism," could never have countenanced any critique of the cultivated learning that primitivism represents. Nonetheless, his humanist doctrine of general education with emphasis on the classics provides a significant context for understanding Glaspell's concern with "culture" and with an education that would integrate and make meaningful the various forms of human labor and pursuit. It may be correct to call this "neoclassicism" because the title of Glaspell's first novel borrows the image of a beaux-arts neoclassical sculpture, Merci's *Gloria Victis*. Still, I maintain that humanism more sufficiently describes a place for Glaspell within intellectual history. Whether like Babbitt — who worked diligently to advance Humanism as a movement — or, perhaps a more likeable comparison, like William James, who modeled his philosophy of pragmatism on Schiller's "humanism" — Glaspell was, especially in her early work, involved in an attempt to reconcile science and religion. Not surprisingly, her experience in Greece coincides with her reevaluation of these ideas.

I would like to conclude with three passages exemplifying her early, middle, and late work as a way of accessing what was at stake, and of showing how her experience in Greece would shape her reevaluation of these ideas.

A moment from *The Glory of the Conquered* (1909) is representative of the epistemology of Glaspell's early work. As I read it, this novel, about a marriage between a scientist and a painter, is Glaspell's most strident attempt at a humanist fiction — to create an art that would express the great unity of human culture, as she felt Greek drama had done. When scientist-husband Karl Hubers blinds himself in a laboratory accident, painter-wife Ernestine Stanley decides that she will become Karl's eyes for his research — both as a loving gift to him and so that his important work (curing cancer) can continue. There is a chapter in this novel called "eyes for two," in which the couple goes for a walk on a beautiful day. Karl, still unaware that his wife is training to be his eyes, expresses how connected he still feels to the beauty of the day: "there's no reason why I should be shut out from the world, Ernestine... when you have eyes for two." Here Glaspell has enormous faith in our ability to reach one another. Of course, where she places her faith is in education — education and progress. The novel is set at the University of Chicago, where Ernestine marvels at "all the ideas here in embryo," wondering "what things now slumbering here would step, robust and mighty, into the next generation." In Glaspell's early work, she seems to have faith that education will cultivate scientific and religious practices that will lift society to greater justice, equity, and beauty.

It is exactly this project that she begins to reevaluate just before she comes to Greece. Representing the middle of her career, I recall the hilarious scene in Act I of *The Verge* in which Tom Edgeworthy is locked out of the greenhouse and is trying to get in; inside, Dick Demming and Harry Archer are discussing this very issue. Harry says that Tom "might have some idea that we can't very well reach the other." Harry finds this notion preposterous: "Damn nonsense. What have we got intelligence for?" But Glaspell is writing *The Verge* to seriously interrogate that very idea. Tom Edgeworthy is "shut out from the world," and he must resort to violence, firing a revolver into the air, due to his inability to communicate. This stage image, conceived so soon after World War I, represents disappointment with a civilization — the product of intelligence — that has made better weapons but not better ways to communicate.

By the time Glaspell writes *The Road to the Temple*, she seems to have made a complete reversal of her earlier faith in cultivation. I think this is the sense of that curious remark of Cook's to Korlyss, that he "is more like the contemporaries of Aristophanes than many a man who is learned about them" — Aristophanes and his contemporaries here being a model for more genuine, less formalized communication. The way Glaspell frames this whole exchange shows an intense awareness and interest, as does the play *Inheritors*, in how education plays into social class. She seems painfully aware in this episode that Cook's learning does not help him to "reach" the other person, if the other person, missing references to classical literature, is not of the same coterie.

By the time we get to Glaspell's late work, well after her primitive period, her novel *The Morning is Near Us* contains a moment in which an exact echo of *The Verge* appears: "something was dying in her: a faith in which she had always lived; the faith that we could reach one another ... That was something given us in grace" (217-18). As with her primitivism, the structure of this form of Glaspell's humanism is one of repeated reassertion of a paradigm with a fading conviction.

Glaspell's primitive period coincides with an epistemological revolution. Her residence in Greece is the fulcrum of her belief in progress and the potential for universal understanding. She learned by experience at Delphi the limits of her own education.

Works Cited

Babbitt, Irving. *Literature and the American College*. Boston: Houghton, Mifflin, 1908. Print.

Calinescu, Matei. *The Five Faces of Modernity*. Durham, North Carolina: Duke University Press, 1987. Print.

Cooley, John R. *Savages and Naturals*. Newark, Delaware: University of Delaware Press, 1982. Print.

Glaspell, Susan. "Inheritors." 1921. "The Verge." 1921. C.W.E. Bigsby, ed. *Plays by Susan Glaspell*. Cambridge, Eng.: Cambridge University Press, 1987. Print.

_____. *The Glory of the Conquered*. New York: Frederick A. Stokes, 1909. Kessinger. Print.

_____. "Dwellers on Parnassos." *The New Republic*. 17 Jan. 1923. Print.

_____. *The Morning is Near Us*. New York: Frederick A. Stokes, 1939. Print.

_____. *The Road to the Temple*. New York: Frederick A. Stokes, 1927. Forward. 1941. Print.

Martin, Ronald E. *The Languages of Difference*. Newark, Delaware: University of Delaware Press, 2005. Print.

Morgan, Lewis Henry. *Ancient Society*. 1877. New York: Henry Holt, 1907. Print.

Pearce, Roy Harvey. *Savagism and Civilization*. Berkeley, California: University of California Press, 1988. Print.

Notes

1 There is precedent for regarding the high modern vogue for primitivism in light of this same intellectual history. Ronald E. Martin, in his book *Languages of Difference: American Writers and Anthropologists Reconfigure the Primitive*, looks at primitivism in the writings of a number of Glaspell's contemporaries including O'Neill as "attempting to avert ethnocentricity, to cancel the vagueness and sweepingly inclusive implications of absolutist language and opposite." Martin regards this form of primitivism as a kind of intermediary between the epistemological assumptions of nineteenth-century ethnocentrism and post-World War II antifoundationalism. He says of the modernist writers, "they didn't launch us into a sea of absolute relativism even as they loosed us from the tethers of primitiveness and its opposite" (13). Primitivist writing from this period is often involved in the project of shedding this prejudice even as it relies upon and recapitulates some the prejudiced assertions of the earlier conception of the primitive.

2 Pearce writes of the relation between Europeans and Native Americans: "Studying the savage, trying to civilize him, destroying him, in the the end they had only studied themselves, strengthened their own civilization" (xvii).

3 This notion of historical time is elaborated by Matei Calinescu in his book *The Five Faces of Modernity*. According to Calinescu, this sense of historical time is the philosophical basis for the cultural event of modernity (see especially, "The Idea of Modernity," 14-46).

"For you know that Greece is the chord I thrill to!": The Philhellenic Friendship of George Cram Cook and John Alden

Steven Wertzberger and Victoria Conover

In *The Road to the Temple,* Susan Glaspell quotes a letter that John Alden wrote to George Cram Cook from Greece in early 1894.
> Dear Cookie:
> Two months I stayed in Athens, with your name often in my memory, sometimes on my lips, for Hill is there and we recalled that inspired twelve hours when all of us were, in the truest sense, alive—alive as I have been but few times in my life. Athens is all that your fancy makes it—a glorious relic framed in the loveliest natural beauties. I have climbed the Parthenon and been silent. (69)

Alden, while conducting archaeological field work in Candia, Crete, "this quaint Venetian walled city of the Levant," wrote this letter about his experiences to Cook, his fellow classicist and former classmate:
> I am beginning to speak and understand [modern] Greek. My life over there in America seems part of a dream past. I am become a creature of the seasons, of horseback rides and encounters with wild dirty peasantry, of sweet tawny wine. One blue night in the Aegean, as our little ship rolled under the lee of Melos and the wise constellations shone from a pale violet

sky on a sea that was blue and was black—I wished for you then. (69)

The importance, for Cook, of Alden's friendship and kindred love of Greece when he was a student at Harvard is made clear by the title as well as the content of the chapter, "John Alden," in *The Road to the Temple*. Indeed, Glaspell gives an account, certainly related from Cook, of the night on which the two undergraduates were "in the truest sense, alive" (69). That night was filled with discussions on several topics including nature, God, and the meaning of life. This passage illustrates the bond shared between Alden and Cook. Glaspell explains more about the importance of that night: "These two young men—students, lovers of beauty, met and modified one another, what came into being between them was a thing in itself, and that thing their creation" (58). Between Alden and Cook was the feeling that the ancient world was superior to modern life. In fact, in his notes for an autobiographical novel, Cook admiringly describes Alden as "a classical monomaniac who talked Latin and looked at the rich-minded Greeks through eighteenth-century eyes" (60).

Cook, as we know from Glaspell's volume, had an opportunity to travel with Alden to Greece. Glaspell explains, "Jig [Cook] was eager to go with him [Alden], wanting this more than to come back to Harvard for another year and his M.A" (61). Cook appealed to his father for money for the venture. The letter he wrote to his father plumbs the depths of Cook's passion for Greece and explains how the spiritual richness of this experience could benefit Cook in practical ways:

> All this year Greek has been unfolding its beauty. The country is becoming for me, as for so many others, as a lost Fatherland. I could sail with John. Such an-

other chance may never come... And then, with the intimate knowledge of the most stirring life the world has known, to unfold what powers I have in the Homeric West—perhaps in Chicago, the center of it all, to leave what mark I can upon the life of the world where the world's life is to-day most active. This is perhaps the first impulse I have had to identify myself with the actual world. Mighty things from without would give my mind the objectivity it lacks. I could deal with things afterwards with unconsciousness of self. (61)

Cook's mother replied that it might be possible to fund his trip if Cook's father's investment in a gold mine was profitable. It was not. Cook's mother wrote back with the bad news. Cook was devastated: "I sit here and dream of Greece. I hear—see—the blue waves of the Aegean beating on the shore" (63). But Alden's voyage to Greece and the letter he sent back to his friend kept the dream of Greece burning in Cook's mind. What Glaspell doesn't tell us is what Alden was doing during the nearly nine months that he spent in Greece.

The 13th annual report of the American School of Classical Studies in Athens lists three 1893 graduates of Harvard among the 1893/94 class (63). In addition to John Alden, there is Otis Shepard Hill (the Hill mentioned in Alden's letter to Cook above), and Joseph Clark Hoppin (66). This suggests that Cook was not merely going to travel to Greece, but had also hoped to spend a year with his friends at the American School. The mission of the school, then as now, was to train American Classicists and archaeologists on the ancient sites. Hill and Hoppin followed the normal course for students. Alden also arrived in Athens in late September, but two months later he was on his way to Crete.

In May of 1893, the Council of the Archaeological

Institute of America decided to field an exploration of Crete with a sum of four thousand dollars. The Council said that "the island of Crete has long been a coveted field to archaeologists. Situated between Greece and the Orient, it lies in the natural track of commerce and civilization in their westward and eastward flow and it is believed that its soil hides the solution to many problems of early culture and art" ("Explorations in Crete" 78). The Council went on to note that others have tried to explore the antiquities in Crete, commenting that "Schliemann tried it and failed, and other European archaeologists and archaeological schools have been repulsed" (78). The reason that Crete was under-explored in 1893 was, in large part, because the island was still under Ottoman control, and the Ottoman authorities were well aware that many of the archaeologists and archaeological schools interested in excavations on Crete were based in Athens. Further, the local scholars interested in archaeology did not encourage exploration for fear that whatever artifacts were found might be taken to Istanbul. For this initial American excavation of Crete, the Americans turned to Italy for a director, noting that "the only person who has really achieved success" in working on Crete was "Professor Federico Halbherr of the University of Rome, who spent three or four years there about a decade since" (78). In the mid-1880s Halbherr had worked at Gortyna, and his major find was the famous code of laws, as well as other inscriptions. Halbherr accepted the assignment, and formed an ambitious plan for the coming year. He would return to dig at Gortyna, move on to the temple of Asclepios at Lebena, then go to Eleutherna in the center of the island, and finish at two sites in Eastern Crete, Itanos and Praisos. Halbherr notes that he has not included Knossos, because "the French have their eye on the site." Arthur Evans, who arrived on Crete some years later, was, as we know, less worried about annoying the French. Unfortunately, Halbherr did not fare any better with the Ottoman authorities than other archaeologists, and permit delays as well as illness forced him to change and pare down his activities to surveys in the center of the island. In his report on his activities in the American Journal of Archaeology in 1896, Halbherr says that "The Institute arranged that I should have, as a companion in my work of exploration, John Alden, a graduate of Harvard. He joined me at Candia, Dec. 22nd, 1893, and his arrival was the signal for the beginning of long excursions into the interior" (529). Alden's responsibilities were to copy inscriptions and to photograph remains, and he was awarded thirty dollars for expenses for camera equipment. The first aim, Halbherr tells us, was the epigraphical exploration of the province of Pediada, "which I confided almost entirely to Mr. Alden" (529). For two months Alden roamed over central Crete recording inscriptions, some of them on blocks of stone now part of the houses of a village. On March 6, 1894, Halbherr tells us that Alden, "who had come to Crete for the special purpose of assisting in the excavation of the agora of Gortyna, finding that part of the work had to be abandoned, left me and sailed for Athens" (531). Alden was fortunate to work with Halbherr, whom Arthur Evans would call the "patriarch of Cretan excavation." But he was very unlucky by seven years, for in 1900, the same year that Evans began digging at Knossos, Halbherr began excavations at the Minoan palace of Phaistos (and would later uncover the famous Phaestos disk). Halbherr ended his career working at the Minoan site of Aghia Triada, near Phaestos. But in the winter of 1893/94, Alden missed the Minoans entirely; what a letter that would have been to write to Cook.

Alden did get a chance to excavate before he left Greece. Upon his return to the American School of Classical Studies, he went on a trip with the school's director, Rufus Richardson, that covered Aetolia, Acarnania, and Phocis—which must have included Delphi. In late March, Richardson took most of the students from the school excavation at Eretria to Euboea. But Alden and Hoppin went with Charles Waldstein to the American excavation of the Argive Heraion (Waldstein 331).

It was his experience in Crete that led to Alden's article that was published in *The Nation* in February of 1896. Alden's strongly anti-Turk "The Eastern Question in Crete" gives a brief history of the island and describes the cultural and political difficulties of an island inhabited by both Turks and Greeks. The article is clearly colored by both Alden's prior affinity for Greece and his recent visits to Greece and Crete. He describes the Greek locals as a "select body, the best of the isle," university-educated European merchants, landowners, and physicians – the "real *citizens*" of Candia, as Alden terms them – but also politically powerless (136). He characterizes the Turks, on the other hand, as Eastern, lazy, intolerant, secretive, and polygamous. Alden does, however, compare the similarly restrictive lives of both Greek and Turkish women, and even claims that the wives of the Turks enjoy greater freedom than their Greek counterparts. Overall, Alden believed the Turks are responsible for the crude living conditions found in Cretan villages, such as those he likely stayed in during his work for the Classical School: "For centuries the people of Crete have lived under oppressive and despotic aliens. Masters not of their own choosing have been forced upon them, and, although the Venetians were hard drivers, the latest comer has been the worst. At no period has the tenure of life been secure" (137). He supported the *Megali Idea*: "'Manifest destiny,' to use a phrase of the politicians, points to the union of two peoples alike in race, religion, and speech, still more closely bound by a common experience of Turkish oppression; and to the revived glories of the Byzantine empire, the 'great idea' in which all good Greeks live, Crete as well as Constantinople will be indispensible" (137).

It is in a letter to George Cram Cook dated 1896 that we learn more about Alden's activities after he left Greece at the end of the term of the American School in June of 1894. He tutored for several months in South Carolina when, as he put it, "a chance came and behold launched me into literature!" That is, Alden collaborated with Elbridge Streeter Brooks on *The Long Walls: An American Boy's Adventures in Greece* (1896). Brooks had written a series of books for young people, but the descriptions of Greece and of archaeology certainly come from Alden. Alden was also the literary editor of a pamphlet called *The Shadow*. He even asked Cook for some content for his new journal: "Send us some verses—not shorter than a sonnet." This journal includes a variety of works: short fiction, essays, poems, and even sheet music are published in it. Alden himself writes a variety of articles. In "Literary Value of Landscape," Alden discusses the beauty of nature in places such as Italy, Greece, and New England (*Shadow* 3-5). It seems that *The Shadow* had a fairly short run (four issues ranging from February to June of 1896) and Cook never had any articles published in it.

Alden also seemed to be responding to a suggestion by Cook that they travel to Greece: "And now you come with your stirring and subtle proposition – for you know that Greece is the chord I thrill to!" Though Alden declined Cook's invitation due to his engagement to be married, he vividly remembered his time in Greece: he recalled being taught Modern Greek by a Cretan Greek in a Turkish *camii* (mosque), stating "remember it's the SAME LANGUAGE – the noblest speech ever devised by man spoken now." Alden's eagerness to learn Modern Greek and his belief in the continuity of the language mirror Cook's own determination to master Greek when he first arrived in Greece. Glaspell relates Cook's jubilance at purchasing a Liddell-Scott Greek-English Lexicon, his indecision over whether to learn *Katharevousa* or *Demotiki*, and his exasperation with Americanized Greeks who insisted on addressing him exclusively in English or French. Like Alden, "[w]henever he [Cook] acquired a present-day word which was also the old word it was to him an electric shock from the far past, a nerve through the centuries of life between" (*The Road to the Temple* 318). Glaspell writes that Cook came to Delphi because, he claimed, "I love the Greek words so much that I wanted for my friends men who have never spoken any other. I wanted to say all the common things, 'Good night' and 'Good morning': 'Give me some bread' and 'Let us sit down under the tree,' in words that said those things long ago" (325).

Cook and Alden seem to have lost contact after the receipt of this letter. But at his death in 1914, Kenneth C. M. Sills of Bowdoin College wrote a letter memorializing Alden to the editor of *The Nation*. Sills described, in broad strokes, what Alden had been doing for the fifteen years prior to his death:

> That personality and scholarship are still the qualities most prized in the public-school teacher is the fact shown by the striking tributes paid to the memory of Mr. John Alden, whose death, in the early forties, was recently reported. For the past fifteen years he had been a teacher of Greek in the Portland High School... Mr. Alden was by temperament and training entirely competent to fill a university post. To some of his acquaintances, indeed, it seemed strange that he should have chosen school work; yet so abundant was the fruit of his labors at the Portland High School that he did more for sound learning and the classics, at least in his native state, than any other man has done in the last twenty years...That high school teaching does not necessarily interfere with the career of the scholar, his life abundantly proved...Mr. Alden showed what one man can do to uphold the best traditions of scholarship and culture in a public high school. (431-432)

The most striking idea to note in the letter Mr. Sills sent to *The Nation* is that Alden never lost his love of the Greek language; Alden's passion for Greece burned just as brightly at his death as it did as when he was an undergraduate at Harvard in 1893.

In her book, *The Road to the Temple*, Glaspell tells of finding an unsent letter from Cook to Alden in December, 1900. But she only found it after she returned from Greece after Cook's death:

> "I will send it now," I thought, and only remembered then that John Alden, too, is dead. I could only sit holding it, thinking of those friends who in their youth loved beauty together, drawn to each other by love of the life long gone. They wanted to go to Greece together. John went first. Jig went after. I wanted to tell that his old friend wanted him in Delphi: that he

wished he could study Greek with him once more....
Each strong with the strength of two ... But why was
this letter "unsent"? I do not exactly know, and it
makes life lonely as distant graves. (109)

Glaspell asks an interesting question. Cook and Alden do not seem to have kept in touch: "It occurs to me that you have faded more than need be from my life," Cook wrote (106). But from Alden's endeavors in 1893 we get an impression of the kind of experience Cook would have had if money had not kept him home. When Cook eventually did make it to Greece, his experience was much like Alden's experience: both were overwhelmed by Greece's natural beauty and the links the modern language maintains with the ancient. Is the similarity in their reactions a result of their shared experiences at Harvard? Did Alden's views from Greece influence Cook? These are intriguing questions. What is clear is that Cook's dream of Greece was still alive thirty years after his first attempt to travel to Athens with Alden failed. Would there have been a Provincetown Players if Cook had realized his Greek dream in 1893 and gone to the American School of Classical Studies? What seems clear is the road not taken some thirty years before led to the road to the temple and Delphi with Susan Glaspell in 1922.

Works Cited

Alden, John. Letter to George Cram Cook. 1896. Cook and Glaspell Papers. Berg Collection, New York Public Library.

Alden, John, Arthur Russell, and R.H. Loines. *The Shadow: The best in this kind are but shadows* 1.1-4 1896: 1-101. Print.

Brooks, Elbridge S. and John Alden. *The Long Walls: An American Boy's Adventures in Greece; A Story of Digging and Discovery, Temples and Adventure.* New York: GP Putman's Sons, 1896. Print.

"Bulletin 2: Appendix to Annual Reports (1896-1897)." *American Journal of Archaeology* 1.6 (1897): 25-156.

"Explorations in Crete." *American Architect and Architecture* 44 (1894): 78. Print.

Glaspell, Susan. *The Road to the Temple.* New York: Frederick A. Stokes Company, 1927. Print.

Halbherr, Federico. "Report on the Expedition of the Institute to Crete." *The American Journal of Archaeology and of the History of the Fine Arts* 11.4 (1896): 525-538. Print.

_____. "Cretan Expedition XVII. Ruins of Unknown Cities at Hagios Ilias and Prinià." *American Journal of Archaeology* 5.4 (1901): 393-403. Print.

Sills, Kenneth C.M. Letter. *The Nation* 16 April 1914: 431-432. Print.

Waldstein, Charles. "A Head of Polycletan Style from the Metopes of the Agrive Heraeum." *The American Journal of Archaeology and of the History of the Fine Arts* 9.3 (1894): 331-339. Print.

Introduction to Essay by Neith Boyce

Stephanie Allen and David Roessel

The typescript of "Iowa to Delphi" is in the boxes of the writer Neith Boyce in the Hapgood Family Papers in the Beinecke Library at Yale University (box 7; folder 97). Although the piece is clearly intended as a review—or a draft of a review—of her friend Susan Glaspell's book about the life of her deceased husband George Cram Cook, along with two works of Cook that Glaspell had posthumously published, *Greek Coins* and *Athenian Women*. Since Boyce was friends with both Cook and Glaspell, her essay stands as a touching tribute to both the subject and the author of *The Road to the Temple*. Indeed, the fact that the piece is more of a tribute than the usual periodical review may be the reason that it was never published.

Part of the review, as is often the case in the genre, relies heavily on Glaspell's text. "In his memory," Boyce writes, "there in the old stadium of Delphi, the Pythian games are to be revived. And on Parnassos his life among the villagers and shepherds is passing into legend and song." This quotation from "Iowa to Delphi" has remarkable similarities to a passage from Glaspell's book:

> And in the stadium of Delphi, in memory of George Cram Cook, Greeks have revived the Pythian games… Already he has become legend on Parnassos. When they sit now at Andreas's, or on the mountain before

> the lamb, they tell stories of Kyrios Kouk. From story
> he is even now going into their songs. (444)

Boyce inserts some of her own personal recollections of Cook, such as the following comment: "to all his friends and acquaintances here he was Jig—impossible to speak of him otherwise than by that rather ridiculous nickname, ridiculous for the big handsome man with thick tossing mane of gray hair and vivid eyes." And the following passage seems more in tune with a reminiscence of Cook than a review:

> But he never acquired a tag—sculptor, poet, playwright, novelist... I remember at Provincetown finding him one day in a fine frenzy rolling on his tongue a newly discovered Sapphic fragment...No, you couldn't say what Jig was, he didn't fit any pigeonhole. His friends thought him a dilettante, a playboy, frittering away his time, though no one could work as hard as he did at what interested him for the time being.

Boyce depicts Cook as something like an overgrown child, who would throw himself enthusiastically into things and then soon get bored. Left unstated, but understood, was that Glaspell was the anchor that added weight and ballast to Cook's whimsy. This mirrored Glaspell's own view of their marital roles in *The Road to the Temple*, in which, as Ozieblo observes, "she transformed herself into his handmaiden" (3).

One criticism of Glaspell's volume has been that it is largely hagiographic and offers a romanticized version of George Cram Cook's life. As Ozieblo notes, Glaspell knew that Cook "was a genius and saint only in her eyes" (3), and his drinking and histrionics were legendary in Greenwich Village (see 192). Boyce was aware that Cook's death weighed heavily on Glaspell, even after the three years that it took her to write the book, and added nothing that challenged the view of Cook presented in *The Road to the Temple*. This included Cook's reason for leaving the Provincetown Players in 1922 and moving to Greece. Glaspell portrays the move as the next logical step in his life as well as the culmination of a dream of Greece that Cook had had since his early years—in planning Cook's life, Glaspell wrote to a friend that "Greece begins in Iowa" (quoted in Ozieblo 231). Others thought that the Provincetown theatre had outgrown Cook; Charles Kennedy thought of Cook as "a poseur, that he pontificated too much," an amateur in a theatre that had become increasingly more professional (quoted in Ben-Zvi 255). Boyce follows Glaspell's viewpoint, noting that once Cook's ideas for Provincetown "failed him, his energy turned to the fulfillment of a lifetime's desire."

In his autobiography, *A Victorian in the Modern World*, Boyce's husband, Hutchins Hapgood, suggested that Glaspell's attitude toward Cook underwent a "subtle change" when she began a relationship with the younger Norman Matson, in Provincetown in late 1924. "The book remained a monument to her departed husband but, in my imagination at least, while all the things possible were said about Jig [Cook], something of his spirit, and that the first part of it, did not reappear" (499). After the book was published, Hapgood related that he told Glaspell this at a party. "Susan, you left out of the book the finest thing about Jig's spirit. Jig cared most intensely about the light that was never on sea or land, but much as you loved him, you didn't love that part of him. You perhaps, like most women, wanted him to be practical. He felt that before he left New York in despair." Hapgood concluded this story by saying that the next day he received a note from Susan asking, "What would you feel if Neith had just died and I had said to you that you neglected the best part of the woman you had been living with so many years, and perhaps caused the death of her spirit?" (500). Hapgood apologized, and, by his account, Glaspell generously forgave him. But he does not seem to think that he was wrong since years later, while Glaspell is still alive, he included the passage in his autobiography. For Hapgood, Cook's departure from Provincetown was more than the rejection of his ideas by the Provincetown group, but also the lack of support and encouragement for those ideas from Glaspell herself. Cook could not soar and find his true self because Glaspell was tying him down by wanting him to be practical.

This is typical of the way that Hapgood viewed the relations between the modern men and women of the Greenwich Village set. Further, it seems clear that Hapgood saw the Cook/Glaspell marriage through the prism of his own relationship with Boyce. As Deboer-Langworthy notes, Boyce and Hapgood are "remembered not for their writing but for their marriage" because they both wrote about it so openly and honestly (1). It was, in many ways, a classic Greenwich Village relationship. (Some of those texts are available in the Trimberger volume.) While theoretically a meeting between equals which was not bound by convention, as an "open marriage" it was "more open for Hapgood than for Boyce" (Deboer-Langworthy 14). Indeed, the women of bohemia were supposed to offer not only maternal moral aid but also financial support to wandering, feckless intellectual companions who wanted freedom to find themselves. It is telling that in the play "Enemies," written by Hapgood and Boyce, "She" says to "He" that "I have always hoped that you would settle down," which "He" considers a trap (quoted in Trimberger 187). This sounds eerily similar to what Hapgood had said to Glaspell about her relationship with Cook.

In Provincetown, Boyce and Glaspell were among a group of women of whom "each was a serious, disciplined professional, happiest when she could be left alone to write fiction and prose." They "kept their own names and wrote under them. They were also early champions of suffrage and women's rights. They were highly ambitious; their independence and personal space vital. ...None relished traditional female roles or duties ... In fact, each woman was the central financial support of her household, since none of the husbands held any sustained paying jobs for long" (Ben-Zvi 141). Boyce and Glaspell were both married to kindred spirits with similar sentiments about marriage, and as Ozieblo notes, "Glaspell frequently turned to Boyce for solace and advice" during difficult times with Cook (39, 59). It is no surprise that the works of both Boyce and Glaspell explore the problems of modern marriage for the modern woman.

So it is instructive to place Boyce's comments about *The Road to the Temple* beside what her husband later said in his autobiography. Hapgood suggested that Cook's marriage resembled to a degree the plot of Trifles, Glaspell's play in which a wife kills her husband; though, in Hapgood's estimation, the murder is not of the body but of the spirit. If we can posit that Boyce knew her husband's opinion of *The Road to the Temple*, then her review is about something more than a book. Through many of her other works, Glaspell wanted to show the importance of female solidarity and the tragedy of how women sometimes uphold the male hegemony. Boyce understood Glaspell and her ideas intimately and "Iowa to Delphi" reflects that sentiment. She both stands with and reinforces Glaspell's depiction of Cook and her role in Cook's life, even as Hapgood, her own husband, said that Glaspell had somehow gotten it all wrong.

We are grateful to David Hapgood and the Hapgood Estate for permission to allow Boyce's essay to be published here so that Boyce and Hapgood can once again be put in conversation.

Works Cited

Ben-Zvi, Linda. *Susan Glaspell: Her Life and Times*. Oxford: Oxford University Press, 2005. Print.

Black, Carol. *The Women of Provincetown, 1915-1922*. Tuscaloosa: University of Alabama Press, 2002. Print.

DeBoer-Langworthy, Carol. *The Modern World of Neith Boyce*. Albuquerque: University of New Mexico Press, 2003. Print.

Glaspell, Susan. *The Road to the Temple*. New York: Frederick A. Stokes Company, 1927. Print.

Hapgood, Hutchins. *A Victorian in the Modern World*. New York: Harcourt Brace, 1939. Print.

Ozieblo, Barbara. *Susan Glaspell: A Biography*. Chapel Hill: University of North Carolina Press, 2000. Print.

Trimberger, Ellen Kay, editor. *Intimate Strangers: Portraits of a Modern Marriage, 1899-1944.*

Selected Works of Neith Boyce and Hutchins Hapgood. New York: Feminist Press of the City University of New York, 1991. Print.

Iowa to Delphi

Neith Boyce

A man born and bred in Iowa, of people who came in covered wagons, crossing the Mississippi, from New England, lies buried by the ancient wall in Delphi. His body washed in the wine of Parnassos, dressed in the Greek shepherd costume of black and white, borne on an open bier by his friends of the mountain village, was given their rites of the Greek church, though he was of no church. To mark his grave the Greek government, at the request of Greek poets, decreed a thing without precedent, that one of the great fallen stones from the Temple of Apollo be moved from its place. In his memory, there in this old stadium of Delphi, the Pythian games are the be revived. And on Parnassos his life among the villagers and shepherds is passing into legend and song.

Known on Parnassos as Kyrios Kouk, formally he was George Cram Cook, but to all his friends and acquaintance here he was Jig—impossible to speak of him otherwise than by that rather ridiculous nickname, ridiculous for the big handsome man with thick tossing mane of gray hair and vivid eyes. But Jig never bothered about personal dignity or personal anything, very much. He took no trouble to impress his personality on people about him. He never gathered it up into a hard mass and fired it at a mark in the limelight. He didn't concentrate on some one form of work and keep on year by year adding to its output until by that mass he could be identified and tagged with a reputation. People interested in him would try to get him to do this; he would listen and ponder, twisting his gray forelock, and smile wistfully and whimsically.

In his "long life—not faithless," a phrase of his own about himself at fifty, he wrote a great deal, novels, verse, articles, but he made no definite mark as a writer. He was a farmer for some years in Iowa,

> Pretending to raise vegetables,
> But really being architect
> In lines of green life and black soil.

He was always building, remodeling with his own hands his house at Provincetown and little house at Truro, modeling and casting the sundial in his yard, the busts and statues in his house, as later he built a wall at Delphi. He wrote and produced with the Provincetown Players two interesting plays, *The Spring* and *The Athenian Women*. But he never acquired a tag—sculptor, poet, play-wright, novelist. Nor was he known as a revolutionist, though he worked for advanced social movements, not as a scholar, in spite of his early and lasting passion for the Greek language and culture—I remember at Provincetown finding him one day in a fine frenzy rolling his tongue on a newly discovered Sapphic fragment...No, you couldn't say what Jig was, he didn't fit any pigeon-hole. His friends thought him a dilettante, a playboy, frittering away his time, though no one could work as hard as he did at what interested him for the time being. And something always did interest him, something he was doing himself or that someone else had done or was doing. Jig could be more enthusiastic about the personality, the work of someone else than about his own; he would pour out a rich flood of praise, his generous warmth would exalt and magnify a talent he admired. He was a wonderful press-agent for other people, not for himself. Once he asked his wife, "Susan, why do people undervalue me?" She replied, "Because you are so generous." But that was not it exactly. How are you going to estimate a person justly if you cannot put limits around him, define him?

What then did Jig leave to be his record, besides the stones and songs of Parnassos? There are two fine children, born of his second marriage—for Jig was married three times—in whom lives much of him. There is the work Susan Glaspell has done for his memory. In *The Road to the Temple*, just published, she has most ably combined a careless wealth of material of Jig's own—scattered pages of reminiscence, casual jottings, letters, old diaries—with her own fine clear warm telling of the moving story, to make a living portrait of the man, a deeply, typically American picture. Miss Glaspell also arranged the publication of *The Spring* in London, and of *The Athenian Women*, in Greek and English, in Athens; and of *Greek Coins*, her selection from Jig's verse, with memorabilia, and in these verses Jig is speaking as he used to speak across his table with the jug of red wine named Sappho and the brimming glasses. And then there is Jig's work with the Provincetown Players. Without him they would never have been a continuing force, and the American theatre might have lost the work of Eugene O'Neill and of Susan Glaspell—would at any rate have waited long and halted on one foot for years.

I remember the warmth with which Jig took up the first light suggestion of doing our own plays at Provincetown and how he instantly mobilized his forces for a performance: the first—and probably best—production of *Suppressed Desires*, acted by himself, Susan and Lucy Huffaker. A playlet, *Constancy*, opening the program, was set by Robert Edmond Jones—on the porch of our house with the sea plashing below and the night-sky as background; then the audience turned their chairs around and *Suppressed Desires* was played in the back of the room, to loud applause.

I remember the night we read *Bound East for Cardiff*, and the young O'Neill, slim and blackhaired with big tragic eyes, nervously heard out acclamation. Jig said he didn't see how we could produce it, how could we make that set, a ship's foc'sle? But by next day he had seen how to do it and was hard at work with saw and hammer in the fish-shed at the end of Mary Vorse's wharf, which had become our theatre. I remember Jig as Yank the sailor in his rough bunk—waves splashing under the wharf all through his dying words. Many a time that summer I heard Jig's deep voice mixed with sounds of the sea, for he would come to our house to play chess with Hutchins Hapgood, there would be the long session they both loved with a jug of wine named Bacchus and talk about the things Jig is speaking of in *Greek Coins*; and Jig would go home at dawn along the beach.

The second summer of the theatre at Provincetown there was John Reed, writing and producing playful skits, acting comic parts in them, between his revolutionary adventures in Mexico and the Paterson strike, and his final adventure in Russia, where his grave is now by the wall of the Kremlin. John Reed seeking the ideal society in Communist Russia—Jig Cook seeking the revival <survival> of ancient Greek culture in modern Greece: knights-errant, poets in action, incorrigible dreamers both of them, their dreams perhaps going out by the gate of ivory.

Jig had his strict ideal for the theatre when that winter the life in it took it to New York, to the old bottling-works in Macdougal Street. He gave himself hand and brain to that work <ideal>. He held together a changing group of uncertain people, many of them gifted but all more or less bent on projecting themselves and their work, none devoted as he. He worked fanatically as men work only for an idea, molding and using that group as he work rebellious clay. Then when success came in money and public notice, talk of a bigger theatre and of going uptown, Jig said this: "What we need is a smaller theatre."

Edna Kenton's story of the Players in *Greek Coins* gives this picture of Jig, after the success of Emperor Jones, when the theatre-group was flushed with triumph:

> He had done an unprecedented thing—had chosen to call us all together—to do no more than read to us some pages written for another group—Plato's if I am not mistaken—words not his own that might perhaps call back the old spirit, already poising its wings for flight, of experiment for play, let the result be what it might. The dangers then were so hidden, so vague, that only a few of us sensed them, and the words had fallen mostly on ears vibrating to uptown applause. He had tried, and he had failed, and he closed the book.

When he knew this material had failed him, his energy turned to the fulfillment of a lifetime's desire. In *The Road to the Temple*, Miss Glaspell records this change:

> One day I went over and found him sitting alone in the theatre. The curtain was up, the blue light he loved was on the dome—which is nothing, which is infinity. We sat there together in that place to which he had given so much of himself, and through which so much of him was realized. At last he spoke. "It is time to go to Greece," he said.

He was to sail on a Greek ship, four weeks at sea, during which time he began to speak modern Greek; <he was> to live in Athens, then on Parnassos in a hut of boughs, made with his own hands; there, drinking the bitter Greek wine, to talk to shepherds and village people of the glories of their own past, the secrets of the old temple of Apollo, to plan with them plays of their own lives to be acted in the stadium, striving always to link these Greeks of today to that old Greece he loved. In less than two years he had so mastered modern Greek that he was translating into it his play *The Athenian Women*. He had become part of the life of Parnassos, so much so that he was proposed for president of the commune, and—a truly Jiggish touch this—applied for admission to a Greek monastery. Thus he wrote to Susan during her absence in America:

Write or telegraph whether you wish to become co-proprietress of a hotel at the Castalian spring, director of the theatre at Delphi and mayoress of the village, or whether you prefer to be the grass-widow of monk in the monastery of Prophet Elijah.

Works Cited

The Spring. A Play by George Cram Cook. London: Ernest Benn.
The Athenian Women. A Play by George Cram Cook. Original text with a modern Greek translation. Athens: H.F.Kaufman.
Greek Coins. George Cram Cook. Poems and Memorabilia. New York: George H. Doran Company.
The Road to the Temple. Susan Glaspell. New York: Frederick A. Stokes Company.

Neith Boyce's "Iowa to Delphi," courtesy of David Hapgood and the Beinecke Rare Book and Manuscript Library, Yale University. Copyright 2013 by the Estate of Neith Boyce. Transcription published by permission of the Estate of Neith Boyce.

A Journey Toward Gnosis:
The Place of Delphi in H.D.'s *Majic Ring*

Demetres Tryphonopoulos

Remembering in the mid-1940s her failure to reach Delphi during her 1920 trip to Greece, the first of two such trips, H.D. affirms that this sacred site had been the chief goal of that journey, with Athens being a close second.[1] During her second trip to Greece in the spring of 1932, H.D. did manage to get to Delphi, a site that, all along, looms large in her imagination and poetry. Interestingly, in describing in *Majic Ring* (the recently published novel she wrote in 1943-44 in London) one of her most significant visionary sequences experienced aboard the *Borodino* during the first leg of her three-week voyage from London to Piraeus, Greece, H.D. chooses from among the experiences she had during the first, unsuccessful approach to Delphi in 1920 rather than from the second, successful one during her 1932 trip. Convinced that a group of dolphins is accompanying the *Borodino*, she spots three of them leaping together in perfect unison, and spies into the distance an island she comes to think of as the lost Atlantis. This vision develops into a key moment in H.D.'s personal reconstruction of a wisdom tradition: the school of mythological dolphins leads a ship of Cretan priests to the shores of the Gulf of Corinth, a journey whose *telos* is the founding on the site of Delphi of the celebrated

Apollonian oracle, an event that in H.D.'s syncretic narrative and imagination signals the end of an old dispensation and the dawn of a new one.[2]

It was not until her second trip to Greece in April 1932, then, that H.D. managed to reach Delphi, the site she had long considered the ancient center of prophecy and poetry and one that had served as a potent symbol and as psychic wellspring of the inspiration she required for her creative work.[3] As already suggested, in her writings of the 1940s, H.D. chooses to deal not with the actual site she had visited in 1932 but with the sacred place she had constructed in her imagination through her reading and psychic questing before and after she had been prevented from reaching Delphi in 1920. Suffering from writer's block in the late 1920s and early 1930s, H.D. had been restored to creative health by no less a figure than Sigmund Freud by whom she had been analyzed in Vienna in 1933 and 1934.[4] Indeed, it is Freud whom H.D. remembers in her poem "The Master" as the one "who set me free / to prophesy"[5]; and it was Freud who had encouraged her to pursue her questing and mythmaking – in other words, her *mythopoeia* – which were rooted in her version of the legend and meaning of Delphi.

In "Writing on the Wall," her 1944-45 record of her time with Freud in Vienna, H.D. refers to her "feelings for the shrine at Delphi" and goes on to muse about her 1920 experience of approaching and glimpsing at the ancient site without being able to reach it:

.... Actually, we had intended stopping off at Itea;[6] we had come from Athens, by boat through the Corinthian canal and up the Gulf of Corinth. Delphi and the shrine of Helios (Hellas, Helen) had been really the main objective of my journey. Athens came a very close second in affection; however, having left Athens, we were informed when the boat stopped at Itea that it was absolutely impossible for two ladies alone, at that time, to make the then dangerous trip on the winding road to Delphi, that in imagination I saw so clearly tucked away under Parnassus. Bryher[7] and I were forced to content ourselves with a somewhat longer stay than was first planned in the beautiful island of Corfu.

But the idea of Delphi had always touched me very deeply and Bryher and I, back in that winter London of the previous spring – it was a winter London that spring – had talked of the famous sacred way. She herself had visited these places with her father before the 1914 war and I had once said to her, while convalescing from the 1919 illness, "If I could only feel that I could walk the sacred way to Delphi, I know I would get well." We were going in another direction, Brindisi, Rome, Paris, London.... Travel was difficult, the country itself in a state of political upheaval; chance hotel acquaintances expressed surprise that two women alone had been allowed to come at all at that time. (49-50)

In "Writing on the Wall" and *Majic Ring*, both written in 1943-1944 London, H.D. recalls her imagined, recovered site of Delphi and its meanings, which are at the very heart of her creative process but also behind the shape of H.D.'s fiction and poetry of the 1940s. *Majic Ring* is based largely on séance notes H.D. kept in late 1943 and early 1944 and provides conclusive evidence of her construction of a unique occult tradition at the heart of what emerged as visionary politics.[8] Like several of her prose works and like *Trilogy*, *Majic Ring* is the story H.D. herself seems to have written and rewritten since her trip in 1920 to Greece aboard the

Borodino. According to H.D. herself, this is "an occult or supernatural experience that I had had in Greece, when Bryher took me there after [World] War I .... [it involves] the projection of a series of picture-symbols on the wall of the hotel bed-room, just as we were about to leave Corfu."[9] One of these "picture-symbols" was the Delphic tripod, which H.D. refers to as "the symbol of prophecy, prophetic utterance or occult or hidden knowledge; the Priestess or Pythoness of Delphi sat on the tripod while she pronounced her verse couplets, the famous Delphic utterances, which it was said could be read two ways" ("Writing on the Wall" 51).

Both *Majic Ring* and *Trilogy*, I claim, constitute "an occult or supernatural experience" H.D. underwent during her trip in Greece and suffered through again during World War II in London. The aim of the occult enterprise H.D. has in mind here is to occasion *palingenesis* or soul-making or *gnosis*.[10] H.D.'s *Trilogy* is meant to be read as Hermetic *palingenetic* literature; that is, the poem does not so much describe or report initiation as enact one for the reader. With its incantations and liturgical or ritualistic rhythms, *Trilogy* comprises a *palingenetic* text; *Majic Ring* offers the raw material and exegesis leading to such a reading of *Trilogy*.[11] Borrowed from the Eleusinian mysteries, the ritual of *palingenesis* involves the following progression: *katabasis / dromena / epopteia* – that is, descent, wandering, and revelation or *gnosis*.[12]

Majic Ring has its roots in, and arguably constitutes, the most lucid, systematic expression of H.D.'s heterodox tradition. This unpublished text provides insight into the making of this tradition and constitutes what H.D. calls her "work," her "means of contributing a few psychic-scientific facts or of throwing a little light on the great darkness of the mysteries [that] surround us" (*Majic Ring* 22).[13]

The first third of the *Majic Ring* presents a series of five letters, dated November 5 through December 12, 1943, addressed to Lord Howell, Delia Alton's name for Hugh Caswall Tremenhere, Lord Dowding (1882-1970), retired Chief Air Marshal of the Royal Air Force (R.A.F.) and renowned victor of the Battle of Britain that preceded the Night Blitz.[14] The journal entries dated December 17, 1943 through January 26, 1944 that come next deal, for the most part, with H.D.'s revelatory experiences during her 1920 voyage, first aboard the *Borodino* and later on the Acropolis and in a Corfu hotel room. The closing brief addendum, dated April 10-15, 1944, offers an account of what I suggest is the narrative's *palingenetic epopteia* and *telos*. In this reading, the entire text is a kind of *proleptic epanodos* or forward return, with H.D. seeing herself in the role of explorer or path-finder who "come[s] back again, re-trace[s her] steps, re-invoke[s] the story" in an attempt to deal with and make sense of an unfinished chapter of her life, what she calls "the Greek scene" (52). Importantly, although the visionary experiences described here and elsewhere happened in 1920, H.D. could not come to terms with them until she had made sense of them in *Majic Ring*. And in any event, H.D. was unwilling to speak openly, afraid that her experience and "philosophy" would not stand up to inexpert examination.

As appreciated when one studies work composed two decades later, H.D.'s "Greek scene" was comprised of four visionary or occult experiences that allowed her to come to terms with her creative and spiritual self; of these, two (the second and fourth) are discussed in detail in *Majic Ring*: the second is the "dolphin" vision of 1920 aboard the *Borodino*; and the fourth and final vision involves a series of dance scenes experienced in her Corfu hotel with Bryher acting as audience.[15]

Perhaps the most significant of these visions is that of the dolphins, which H.D. has aboard the *Borodino* during the first leg of her "three weeks trip out" (71) to Greece. The February 1920 vision occurs as H.D.'s boat nears "the Pillars of Hercules, the straits of Gibraltar" (87), before sailing into the Mediterranean. H.D. finds herself standing on the deck besides the English-born, New Delhi-bound architect Pieter Rodeck (Peter van Eck in the novel), who speaks the ancient wisdom tongues (Arabic and Greek), has been to Athens, Egypt, and Jerusalem, and possesses "some power, or mystery knowledge" (87). However, it is not Rodeck standing beside her during her vision but, rather, "Anax Apollo, Helios, Lord of Magic and Prophecy and Music" (88).[16]

Convinced that a group of dolphins is accompanying the boat, H.D. "sees" three of them leaping together in perfect unison. She spies an island, only to discover later that neither her vision nor the presence of Rodeck, the dolphins, or the island was real.[17] What is real, nonetheless, is the "light that never was on sea or land" (88) — and the opportunity to employ the dolphins in her personal reconstruction of a wisdom tradition that includes mythological "dolphins who led, ... the ship of the Cretan priests to the shores of the Gulf of Corinth," thereby reviving a pre-historic Cretan cult and giving a god's name forever to "the most famous shrine of antiquity, ... called Delphi" (88).[18] H.D.'s etymological game connects "δέλφις" (dolphin) and "Δελφίνιος" (Delphian), an epithet of Apollo, with "Δελφοί" or Delphi.[19] Inasmuch as one "once carried a poet [Arion] on his back" (90), the dolphin becomes

H.D.'s prophet, guide and inspiration, as well as "the instrument of the new dispensation" (90). In her reading, the dolphins accompanying the ship symbolize "the end of the journey... the end of an old dispensation and the beginning of a new" (88).

Symbols of regeneration in Greek myth and sacred to Apollo, dolphins are legendary for rescuing mortals at sea and ferrying the dead to land.[20] When Rodeck holds up "a square-palm ... turned flat downward, above the water" and apparently draws a single dolphin "above the level of the deck" and says, "That one, ... nearly landed" (89), H.D., who has more than two decades (1920-1943) to ponder his cryptic utterance, is "still at a loss to know exactly what he did mean" (89). Rodeck does explain or H.D. imagines him to have explained:

> If it had landed, I would have constructed the bit and bridle for you, and he would have been your guide and inspiration. He didn't land. He almost landed but he fell back into the waters of Atlantis, or rather of the Atlantic. I might have made you an instrument of this new dispensation—for you know we are at the turn of the age—my dolphin planted my oracle at Delphi ...
>
> ... for you do know that I am not Mr. van Eck. You might mix the dimensions, before a lot of people, and make a fool of yourself... But you will later remember one or two apparently disconnected incidents, chiefly of your life in London, and you will say ... that I have loved thee. (90)

The near landing at Delphi, the ὀμφαλός or center of the earth, hints at a promise[21] to be fulfilled later on in the text when H.D. is absorbed into the light by a welcoming androgynous figure. Aboard the *Borodino*, H.D. is evidently initiated into the ancient mysteries of Apollo, who becomes her *angelos* or guide; she has "had a glimpse of perfection" of the Platonic "'absolute' of beauty—the lost Atlantis" (116). H.D. may have been unsure of the external reality of her experience, but she was certain of both its import and her own objectives.[22]

The dolphins and Rodeck, in H.D.'s view, have blessed her "unaware," and the burden of mortality, the Albatross, has fallen into the sea (91).[23] H.D.'s vision reveals "the promised land, the islands of the blest, the islands of Atlantis or of the Hesperides" (91). "We were on a mythical ship, on a mythical voyage of high purpose," she relates. "We were nearing land, we were in sight of the kingdom of heaven" (91-92). It is this mythical kingdom, this "new dimension," which H.D., who throughout situates herself as "one of the guardians of the Propylaea ... or Gateway or Porch" (101-02), is able, at the end of *Majic Ring*, to step into the light of illumination. In *Majic Ring*, H.D. often finds herself in the role of "initiate" waiting in an outer room, the "propylaea" or "pronaos," before passing through a door or over a threshold into the inner chamber or sanctum. The narrative ends with a vision of H.D.'s entry into the "holy of holies" (249), her return to the source of light. H.D.'s union with the light, a *hierogamia* or marriage of the human with the divine, proved necessary, it seems, for H.D.'s future work.

Majic Ring concludes with three entries written on April 11, 13, and 15, 1944, which deal with a "significant [but incomplete] dream" (136) during Holy Week 1944, and one she has on Easter Sunday. In the first, a voice announces, "You are dead" and instructs her to walk from her bedroom to her living room, cross the threshold that the neophytes in the old temple ceremonies passed through, and enter an inner chamber where she will find herself lying in a coffin (163). The coffin is empty, however, and the dream ends without resolution.[24] When told of it, Bryher responds, "that sort of dream is always supposed to be lucky, to predict a new life or an awakening" (164). On Easter Sunday night there is "another dream, very real this one, and not *in part* but a complete whole" (165; H.D.'s italics). Standing in the foot of her bed H.D. perceives, "with a completely un-dimmed, uncomplicated ego," an impressive figure whose countenance is the "white of old ivory" and who is wearing a "high white crown-cap" and white robes but not carrying any sign denoting a specific denomination. "This person is Love itself, he is mother, he is father [and] draws me to him, I am as it were, simply melted into him. ... absorbed back into him" (165).[25] This is an experience H.D. expresses in a cautious yet remarkable claim: "Perhaps the woman on the boat going to Greece, in the early spring of 1920, did see God ... Possibly, the girl and the woman did see projections of that white light that is final illumination" (168). I suggest that H.D. in her dreams "suffers" through the tripartite ritual of *palingenesis*: *katabasis / dromena / epopteia*. The last section of *Majic Ring* presents therefore a *katabasis*, the speaker's death. The rest of the story represents the *dromena*, or wandering through, experiences of an initiate fragmented emotionally by "a still-born child and a baby, four years later, whose birth was a miracle and whose living was a wonder but who had all but taken my life ... a husband's subtle deflection and a friend's desertion and the falling away of an entire set of acquaintances" (71). Finally, H.D.'s absorption into "[t]his person [who] is Love itself," or the "see[ing] of God, "that white light that is final illumination," represents the stage of *epop-*

teia or *gnosis*.

H.D.'s project, which she did not necessarily understand but pursued relentlessly "for twenty years," is a matter of collecting fragments of a faith forgotten – reconstituting or making sense of the *gnosis* or *sophia* of mystery religions. "We of the esoteric wisdom," H.D. writes, are after "the new dimension," which she then deciphers:

> The new dimension is the very old occult dimension which fell into disrepute in the East and became a byword for charlatanism in the West. But the alchemists and the astrologers of the middle-ages were fostering this spirit, were cherishing a germ or seed of the Great Mother's store of wisdom, and we are told there were "initiates", hidden from time to time in the most discreet worldly circles, knights and crusaders. And there were individuals, high in power, who it has been hinted, managed to direct a thread or rivulet of this Ancient Wisdom into a ceremony and some of the ritual of the Church of Rome. (154-55)

Majic Ring is the story of a woman on a boat to Greece, in early spring of 1920 who, according to her own testimony, "did see God"; it is also the clearest extant account of H.D.'s heterodox tradition, and reveals an artist in whose alchemical crucible Greek (including Delphic), Egyptian, Eastern, and Aboriginal mythologies and literatures, traditional and contemporary Christianity, Hermeticism, Gnosticism, the Albigensians, Spiritualism, the Cabbala, Theosophy, the Moravian Church, and Freud combine in a quest for truth and a new dimension. Most especially, with *Majic Ring*, "*the story of Greece has been written*" (159; H.D.s' italics).

Majic Ring represents, then, a vibrant occultism that fed H.D.'s other writing of the period: it is made up of the notes she wrote while, during the final years of World War II, she found herself in the process of determining her role as a visionary artist capable of bringing good into the world. Notably, H.D.'s personal reconstruction of a wisdom tradition is inspired by her understanding of, and reverence for, Delphi and the story of the founding on the site of this celebrated Apollonian oracle.

Works Cited

Friedman, Susan Stanford. *Psyche Reborn: The Emergence of H.D.* Bloomington: Indiana University Press. Print.

H.D. *Tribute to Freud* 1956; New York: New Directions, 1974. Print.

———. *Majic Ring by H.D. (writing as Delia Alton)*, ed. Demetres P. Tryphonopoulos. Gainesville: University Press of Florida, 2010. Print.

———. *H.D.: Collected Poems, 1912-1944*. Ed. Louis L. Martz. New York: New Directions, 1983. Print.

Tryphonopoulos, Demetres. *The Celestial Tradition: A Study of Ezra Pound's The Cantos*. Waterloo, Ontario: Wilfrid Laurier University Press, 1992. Print.

Notes

1 See H.D., *Tribute to Freud* (1956; New York: New Directions, 1974): 49. This 1974 edition, with a foreword by Norman Holmes Pearson, includes "Writing on the Wall" (written in the fall of 1944 and first having appeared in *Life & Letters Today*, London, 1945-46); "Advent" (a continuation of "Writing on the Wall" assembled in December 1948 and based on her so-called Vienna note-books of the spring of 1933); and "Appendix: Freud's Letters to H.D." (a selection

of nine letters, five of them written in German and the others in English, written between December 18, 1932 and February 26, 1937).

2 For more information on the original myth (as presented, for instance, in Herodotus and Pausanias) and H.D.'s syncretic vision based on it, see *Majic Ring by H.D. (writing as Delia Alton)*, ed. Demetres P. Tryphonopoulos (Gainesville: University Press of Florida, 2010): xxii, xxxv, 81, 83-84, 110-13, 190n41, 190-91n42, 197n22, and 228n152.

3 In a chapter entitled "Delphi of the Mind: The Unconscious as Muse and Prophet," Susan Stanford Friedman explains that "With Freud, H.D. developed her own theory that the unconscious is the Delphi of the mind, the wellspring of art and religion" (70). Friedman goes on to quote from section 55 of "Writing on the Wall":

Know thyself, said the ironic Delphic oracle, and the sage or priest who framed the utterance knew that to know yourself in the full sense of the words was to know everybody. *Know thyself*, said the Professor, and plunging time and again, he amassed that store of intimate revelation contained in his impressive volumes. (*Tribute to Freud* 72-73).

"Delphi of the Mind" comprises chapter 3 of Friedman's brilliant *Psyche Reborn: The Emergence of H.D.* (Bloomington: Indiana University Press, 1981): 70-86.

4 The dates of H.D.'s sessions with Freud, the "blameless physician" (see dedication of "Writing on the Wall," *Tribute to Freud* 1) were May 1-June 12, 1933 and October 31-December 2, 1934. H.D. provides detailed accounts of these sessions in *Tribute to Freud*.

5 And it was he himself, he who set me free
    To prophesy,

    He did not say
    "stay,
    My disciple,"
    he did not say,
    "write,

each word I say is sacred,"
he did not say, "teach"
he did not say,
"heal
or seal
documents in my name,"

no,
he was rather casual,
"we won't argue about that"
(he said)
"you are a poet."

(See *H.D.: Collected Poems, 1912-1944*. Ed. Louis L. Martz. [New York: New Directions, 1983]: 495; the entire poem is printed on pages 451-61 of this volume.)

6 The commercial port of Itea on the Gulf of Corinth is situated on a plain below Delphi. In the 1920s and 1930s, the eighteen kilometer trip from Itea up the rugged and mountainous side of Mount Parnassus to Delphi would have been both arduous and tricky. To the east of Itea is Kirra, the ancient port of Delphi.

7 Bryher (1894-1983), H.D.'s companion, was born in London as Annie Winifred Ellerman; the two met in 1918 and remained companions until H.D.'s death in 1961. They traveled together to Greece from February to May 1920, sailing from London on February 7 aboard *Borodino*, owned by Bryher's father, shipping magnate Sir John Ellerman; in fact, the ship had been recalled from duty as ice-breaker in the North Sea and commissioned especially for transporting Bryher and H.D. from London to Piraeus. The *Borodino* docked at Piraeus, Greece on February 27, 1920.

In the final draft of *Majic Ring*, Bryher is called Gareth while H.D. refers to herself as Delia Alton. Pieter Rodeck and Havelock Ellis (not mentioned in *Majic Ring*), were also present aboard *Borodino* and at the Propylaea in Athens, as revealed in various autobiographical notes and "Advent," *Tribute to Freud* 153-68).

8 *Majic Ring* also offers a road map for, and a prose record of, the writing process and substance of *Trilogy*, H.D.'s masterpiece about, among other things, World War II London. For a fuller discussion of *Majic Ring* as sourcebook for *Trilogy* see my Introduction (especially xxv-xxvi) and Notes (especially 183-84, note 20) to *Majic Ring*.

9 For a fuller definition of occultism see my *The Celestial Tradition: A Study of Ezra Pound's The Cantos* (Waterloo, Ontario: Wilfrid Laurier University Press, 1992): 23-58 and the Introduction to *Majic Ring* (21-39) of which this essay is an abbreviated, revised version.

Here it may suffice to say that occultism is an exclusively Western phenomenon (though it often turns to Eastern religions for inspiration and guidance) characterized by radical syncretism, eclecticism, monism, and non-theism; occultism claims to offer the possibility of direct contact with a spirit world. Perhaps the touchstone for the occult is a belief that throughout time certain individuals have experienced communion with the divine, thereby gaining special *gnosis* or wisdom. Occult believers view themselves as the heirs of ancient wisdom preserved in written texts and in oral traditions of secret groups of initiates, passed on from adept to adept or rediscovered from time to time by mystical illumination. Occultists claim the existence of a single, uninterrupted thread of knowledge reaching back to antiquity.

10 Perhaps the most distinctive feature of occult writing is its radical syncretism. I consider H.D. an "occult" writer primarily because in her prose and poetry radical syncretism constitutes the very fabric of her thought.

11 I read both Ezra Pound's *The Cantos* and H.D.'s *Trilogy* as *palingenetic* texts. For a detailed discussion of Pound's epic as *palingenesis* see *The Celestial Tradition* and for *Trilogy* see the Introduction and notes to *Majic Ring*.

In the unpublished *Compassionate Friendship* (written 1955), H.D. clearly refers to the "action" of this work, and to the Delia Alton novels of which *Majic Ring* is one, as initiation which, moreover, would have been impossible were it not

for her sessions with Freud:
I had my questions and my answers in that period of [World] War II London, but without my preliminary work with the Professor [Freud], I could never have faced this final stage of the initiation. *The Sword, The Rose, The Mystery* (and the earlier *Magic Ring* [sic]) outline the process or processus [sic].(Yale Collections of American Literature, Beinecke Rare Book and Manuscript Library, Yale University, Series II. Writings, 38, 1012, page 31).

All of these texts have now been published: *The Sword Went Out to Sea (Synthesis of a Dream) by Delia Alton*, ed. Cynthia Hogue and Julie Vandivere (Gainesville: University Press of Florida, 2007); H.D. (Writing as Delia Alton), *White Rose and the Red*, ed. Alison Halsall (Gainesville: University Press of Florida, 2009); H.D., *The Mystery*, ed. Jane Augustine (Gainesville: University Press of Florida, 2009); and *Majic Ring by H.D. (writing as Delia Alton)* (2009).

12 For a fuller account of this tripartite, initiatory process, see *The Celestial Tradition* (101-08). *Katabasis* constitutes the initial stage of the *palingenetic* process, often represented as a literal descent to the otherworld or death; *dromena* signifies the stage of wandering or confusion suffered by initiates; *epopteia*, the state of "having seen" or revelation, is often expressed by light imagery and has a soteriological or revelatory dimension.

Palingenetic transmutation is perhaps nowhere clearer than in Section 8 of *Tribute to the Angels*, where the alchemical purification and redemption of a goddess takes place and a new woman is revealed (see H.D., *Trilogy* [1944-46; New York: New Directions, 1998]: 71). Here occult archetypes are tossed into an alchemical/etymological crucible, melted, fused, and altered, so that the bitterness intimated by the Hebrew *marah-mar* is slowly distilled, transformed into the "Star of the Sea," Mary, Mother of Christ, and sea-born Aphrodite.

13 In "H.D. by *Delia Alton* ['Notes on Recent Writing']," ed. Adelaide Morris, *The Iowa Review* 16.3 (1986): 180-221, H.D.

defines her psychic-research or "the 'work,' as they [that is, theosophists and other practitioners of occult activities] came to call it," uncharacteristically expressing her suspicion of its "siren-voices" (198). The noun "work" is also used several times in *Majic Ring*.

14 Upon his retirement in 1941, Lord Dowding became a public proponent of Spiritualism, delivering lectures and writing extensively on the subject. His publications include the spiritualist treatises *Many Mansions* (1943) and *Lychgate* (1945), both of which H.D. read. H.D. first saw him when she attended one of his lectures at Wigmore Hall on October 20, 1943; they corresponded and met several times, with Dowding becoming one of her guides but also one of those men in her life who, like Pound, D.H. Lawrence, and Freud, she felt had betrayed her.

15 The first of the four visions, accounts of which are found in *Notes on Thought and Vision* (18-21), "Advent" (*Tribute to Freud* 130, 147-48), "Pontikonisi (Mouse Island)" (published in *Pagany* 3.3 [1932]: 1-9), and letters H.D. wrote to Bryher from Vienna in early 1933 (*Analyzing Freud: The Letters of H.D., Bryher and Their Circle*, ed. Susan Stanford Friedman [New York: New Directions, 2002] 50, 60), occurred in the Scilly Isles in 1919. It involved what H.D. has described as a "jelly-fish state" or "vision of the womb," a sense of *epopteia* or ecstatic "seeing." The second, the "dolphin" vision of 1920 aboard *Borodino* with Pieter Rodeck (Peter van Eck in *Majic Ring*), is discussed in "Advent" (*Tribute to Freud* 154-62, 182-87), H.D.'s letter to George Plank in *Collected Poems* (xxvi), as well as in *Majic Ring*. The third, H.D.'s 1920 "Delphic" vision at the *Hôtel Angleterre et Belle Venese* on the Ionian island of Corfu, manifested as a series of images on the hotel wall: the head and shoulders of an airman or soldier, a goblet or mystic chalice, a lamp, a tripod like that used by Pythia at Delphi, a ladder spanning heaven and earth, and Niké or Winged Victory triumphant and climbing a ladder. This sequence is described in "Writing on the Wall" (*Tribute to Freud* 44-56) and "H.D. by Delia Alton" (198-99). The fourth

and final vision, a series of dance scenes experienced in her Corfu hotel with Bryher acting as audience is recorded in "Advent" (*Tribute to Freud* 172-73) and *Majic Ring* (120-42). In this sequence of dance movements, Delia variously presents or represents a tree; an Indian medicine man; an Indian girl named "Minne-ha-ha" (whose hieratic costume "is an exquisite outward sign of an inward perfection"); a female mountain-spirit; a California woman singing in Spanish; a lisping island maiden; a Japanese girl; a Greek mountain boy; a Tibetan "priest of some high mystery"; and, finally, a Lady in a tower, wearing rich jewels "full of traditional occult power" and named, like the earth-mother, Rhea.

The best discussion of these four episodes in the context of H.D.'s visionary poetics remains one by Adelaide Morris: "The Concept of Projection: H.D.'s Visionary Powers," *Contemporary Literature* 25.4 (1984): 411-36.

16 For the Rodeck/Cecil Grey and Bryher/Helios (Apollo) parallels, see Morris's "A Relay of Power and Peace: H.D. and the Spirit of the Gift," *Contemporary Literature* 27.4 (1986): 493-524; esp. 81n.65. It may well be that H.D. and Pieter Rodeck were romantically attracted: Rodeck suggested H.D. abandon her companions and travel on with him, an invitation she refused. Later he sent her (presumably from Alexandria) a crystal ball; and ten years later, they again saw each other socially in London – but when prompted by H.D., Rodeck seems to have had no recollection whatsoever of the dolphin episode.

17 The person whom H.D. presents as having "witnesse[d]" Delia's vision is Rodeck's "perfected" double, having neither a deep scar over his left eyebrow or the thick-rimmed eyeglasses of the actual man.

18 H.D.'s "Delphic" vision aboard the *Borodino* (told here and elsewhere retrospectively) nonetheless points to the fact that visiting Delphi was the principal objective of the trip to Greece. For an articulation of both the meaning of Delphi and her disappointment at having been prevented by circumstances to visit the oracle in 1920 see above. H.D. was

able (and ecstatic) to visit Delphi during her April 1932 Greek cruise; Louis Silverstein conjectures 13 April 1932 as the date of her visit (see "H.D. Chronology: Part Four (1929-April 1946; http://www.imagists.org/had/hdchron.html)).

19 Apollo is said to have seized Delphi after slaying the dragon, Python–symbolic of dark, underworld forces–and to have established a temple of his oracle. The epithets Pythian and Pythia, given to Delphi's prophetess, are derived from this Pytho.

While searching for attendants for his new sanctuary, according to myth, Apollo, in the guise of a dolphin, sprang aboard a ship sailing from Crete; the bewildered crew was directed to Crisa on Mt. Parnassus as the site for his oracle where, upon arrival, he revealed himself to the men and initiated them into service. Thus, Cretan sailors become his first priests. According to the *Homeric Hymn to Apollo* ("To Pythian Apollo," Part II), they called the place Delphi for the god who told them that since he had sprang upon their ship in the form of a dolphin, to pray to him as Apollo Delphinios and call his altar itself Delphinios (dolphin-like) ($\Delta\varepsilon\lambda\phi\iota\nu\iota o\varsigma$, ll. 493-97).

20 Dolphins appear in a number of Greek myths, invariably as helpers of humankind. Judging by artistic evidence from their ruined palace at Knossos, they seem to have been important to the Minoans. According to myth, a dolphin rescued the poet Arion from drowning and carried him safely to land – at Cape Taenarum, now Cape Matapan, a promontory forming the southernmost point of the Peloponnese. There was once a temple to Poseidon with a statue of Arion riding a dolphin located there (see Herodotus I.23 and Pausanias III.25).

Donna Krolik Hollenberg provides an insightful reading of this Coleridgean moment: "when her mysterious companion held his palm above the water, drew one dolphin up, and assured her that he loved her despite her earlier losses, his approval absolved her of the survivor guilt that had become connected with artistic achievement" (*H.D.: The Poet-*

ics of Childbirth and Creativity [Boston: Northeastern University Press, 1991]: 105-06).

21 *Majic Ring*, like *Trilogy*, is manifestly optimistic.

22 Later, H.D. conflates Apollo with Neoplatonism's "Thrice Great" deity (see *Majic Ring* 134).

23 The opening phrase is a variation on Coleridge's lines from *The Rime of the Ancient Mariner*: "O happy living things! no tongue / Their beauty might declare: / A spring of love gushed from my heart, / And I blessed them unaware: / Sure my kind saint took pity on me, / And I blessed them unaware."

24 H.D. discovers "just one fourth of the coffin," which should have contained her head, in the living room, but it is empty. She senses, first, a "presence ... standing back of Gareth," thinking of it as "very tall and clothed or draped in grey garments that covered the head and fell to the feet"; and, second, "another presence," that of "a small woman or a grown girl" who addresses her "quite clearly," inviting Delia to sit beside her on the couch so that they "could at last 'really talk to one another'" (164). The dream ends, however, before the conversation can take place.

25 It is an experience that H.D. presents through a trinity of images: first, in terms of alchemical white light of apocalyptic revelation ("the flowering of white, the white of flowers that are conditioned, are perfected by the perfect merging of fire and water, of sun and rain"); second, by a cautious yet remarkable claim to having seen God ("Perhaps the woman..., did see God"); and, finally, by returning to the imagery of white light of illumination ("Possibly, the girl and the woman did see projections of that white light that is final illumination") (162-69).

H.D.'s *Ion*: The Door Swings Both Ways

Matte Robinson

Nearly twenty years ago Diane Chisholm wrote a paper, true to the times, re-envisioning H.D.'s writing as "autoheterography," an ungainly coinage that nevertheless aptly conveys the strangeness of H.D.'s many masks, feints, and re-writings. Writing is, for Chisholm, not epiphenomenal to anything, and this stance resonates well with a writer whose pseudonym writes literary reviews of her own works. Unlike her male modernist peers, whose critical works were directed outward toward literature and culture, H.D. addressed the wide world by looking inward, through Delia Alton, through occult research, and through the writing and editing of the text of her own life—a life that included writing as autobiography, literary experiment, occult work, and dream-analysis. With such an inward-gazing oeuvre, works of translation stand out, if only for the fact that they are someone else's writing, filtered through H.D.

If this were science and not literary criticism, the reasons for doing extensive tests on the translations would be obvious. While it is still possible to provide a host of theoretical reasons why a work of translation such as *Ion* is important in the context of an entire writing career, I will instead focus on a few points in the play that intersect with her later writing, and with the notion (fostered by H.D. herself, among other people) that it comes at the cusp of a new phase or explosion in H.D.'s writing.

H.D. puts some of herself into the *deus ex machina* at the conclusion of *Ion*, a fact that is perhaps not fully realized until *Majic Ring* is taken into account. *Majic Ring* is another exceptional text in the corpus, because it comes very close to expressing clearly H.D.'s own occult philosophy—and an occult philosophy is at least analogous to a religious belief. That it was so uncharacteristically blunt is unusual, and even more unusual is the fact that H.D. buried it to the extent that she claims she forgot about it. Much of the material in it is replaced by another text that hints instead of telling, gestures instead of explaining. The two texts, interesting because of their uniqueness, have largely been overlooked by scholars: there exist few articles on either, and certainly no books. I suggest one reason for this here: that H.D.'s narrative layers and masks-within-masks paradoxically create the temptation to *believe* her rewritings, to be led on to read her work the way she decides it should be read. On the whole this strategy bears fruitful results, but there are exceptional cases in which she leads us away from information that is vital, but was perhaps too direct. To examine and test these exceptional cases is not really to read against the grain of H.D.—as if she had a grain—but to trust the instinct that this occult writer might have left a few mysteries behind. These are not the sort of mysteries that are there to be solved: they are there to deepen and complicate a discussion, to help it mature, to help glimpse the pattern in H.D.'s writing that she herself sought, through her many masks, to grasp hold of.

H.D.'s most voluminous work on her own writing,

"H.D. by Delia Alton," maps out a reading programme for scholars of H.D., one that will soon be easier to follow, now that most of the works mentioned are finally being published. It does not mention *Majic Ring*, probably because Bryher had not yet recovered the text and sent it to her. "H.D. by Delia Alton," because of this absence, encourages the impression upon picking up *Majic Ring* that it is a discarded draft of *The Sword Went Out To Sea*, the relationship of one to the other much like that of James Joyce's *Stephen Hero* to *A Portrait of the Artist as a Young Man*. But H.D. did not burn *Majic Ring*, she only hid it from herself. She returned to it years later,[1] revised it, and sent it to a typist.

In "H.D. by Delia Alton" she makes a distinction between the "early H.D." and "the H.D. of the later *Trilogy*." The casual and serious reader alike can discern that there is a major change in her writing around the time of *Trilogy*, that *Trilogy* is one of her masterworks, that the World War II-era writing that came at the same time as *Trilogy* is highly intertextual, and most exquisitely crafted in the long poem. Of all the works of the time, *Majic Ring*—which is written so closely with *Trilogy* that the poem is mentioned in the novel and the two works share several common images—is the least known, unglossed.

The poetry of *Trilogy* "seemed to project itself in time and out-of-time together ... and with no effort" ("H.D. by Delia Alton" 186), which means that it works within a four-dimensional matrix, one that cannot be adequately explained by using hackneyed words such as "timeless." The "out-of-time" is not Freud's or Jung's unconscious, nor is it the spiritualists' "akashic records,"[2] though it has affinity with these things. It can be contrasted with the mundane, the everyday, but the two are not opposites or mutually exclusive. They are probably interdependent, but they are difficult to evoke in writing at the same time. One of the reasons H.D. favored the later Delia Alton novels and ignored *Majic Ring* was that they have separate visions of how the two realms come together within the matrix: the later novels focus on H.D.'s spiritualist endeavors, specifically on her having contacted a group of dead RAF pilots who brought grim warnings about the dangers of nuclear conflict. Those who read H.D.'s assessment of her own writing see her as a spiritualist writer because of this, though Helen Sword has suggested in "H.D.'s *Majic Ring*" that the shift of emphasis in the later novels marks a transition as important as the one H.D. identifies with the war. The wartime novels, according to Sword, are quite different in character from the later Delia Alton works. Furthermore, Sword places *Majic Ring* squarely within the wartime period, separate from the other novels. Its flavor is distinctly occult, not spiritualist, and its trajectory is even more startling than toward a flock of dead pilots with an obvious message: it is about the turning of an astrological age and the coming of a new consciousness, heralded in by a world teacher, who is seen to be in direct contact with the author.

H.D. named *The Sword Went Out to Sea* "reality or truth," and "the synthesis of the dream" (205), while the translations were "studies" (221). At the time of her writing this, her vision of her development had its *telos* in the RAF messages. She admits, though, that "it would be difficult for a critic to assess the matrix" as well as "difficult for myself to assess it" (221). The matrix, she suggests, is best visualized as a harmonizing of the time-element and the out-of-time-element, as "two streams of consciousness, running along together (the time-element and the dream or ideal element) but in separate channels." H.D. does not recognize the distinction that Helen Sword makes, for she does not distinguish between the World War II and the period afterwards: the streams, according to her writing of this time, "came together in the end, in the War II and post-War II novels that I sign Delia Alton" (221). The late H.D. phase, for Delia Alton at least, is "the end"; perhaps, as in the distinction between modernism and postmodernism, this is the case and the end has come, and only the context in which the end is understood continues to shift.

At any rate, *Ion* is the final "study" or exercise that leads to the end or *telos*, and together these studies "are in a sense, the projection of the jewel or the crystallization of the jewel or jewels in the matrix" (221). Jewels, pearls: these images pop up again and again in "the end" period, but are perhaps most concentrated in the World War II period, if we accept it as a separate phase. It is the flaw in the jewel[3] in *Trilogy* that allows Kaspar the vision of the eternal. The pearl-of-great-price is a leitmotif linking all her texts of the period into a visionary net. H.D. is flexible enough with her metaphors that the matrix could contain one jewel or many, so these are images really, less fixed than symbol. All, like Wittgenstein's ladder, may be discarded once they have served their purpose.

The jewel or pearl, and the web or net or matrix, are important not only to H.D., but also to Robert Duncan, the author of the *H.D. Book*. Scattered like Osiris among long out-of-print journals, the book has never officially been collected into the unfinished whole that it is, except unofficially in a pdf document, made semi-respectable because of its usefulness and imagists.org's link to it. Duncan and H.D. corresponded late in her life, and his insight into her was as important as Delia Alton's: he was a fellow poet, a fellow critic, a fellow hermeticist. It may even have been he who introduced her to a particular usage of the word "hermeticist," as he was one, raised in the hermetic traditions. Though H.D. and William Butler Yeats are often compared because of their strong occult streaks, it was Duncan who informed H.D. of Yeats's occultism and spiritualist activities. Unhampered by academic conventions and blessed with his unique tripartite understanding of H.D.'s work, he produced a work that ferreted out many of H.D.'s secrets, though had he had access to a copy of *Majic Ring* he would have had an easier job, being able to confirm many suspicions. Even without this, he was able to access her work in a way that any non-occultist would find difficult, and he singles out *Ion*, in a way that H.D. as Delia Alton had:

> The transitions or notes which H.D. adds in her translation of the *Ion* of Euripides are initial to the major phase of her work that lasts from the inception of the War Trilogy with *The Walls Do Not Fall* in 1942 to the end of her life with *Hermetic Definitions* in 1960. (132)

Significantly, though, Duncan seems to be more interested in H.D.'s notes and transitional material than he is in the actual translation—the knowledge of the language, the history, the difficulties of rendering meter, rhyme, and versification in another language, the balancing of the old and the new, the now and the then, the temporal and the dream. The notes, according to Duncan, are the key to the nature of the work. They are studies, and the key is in their evaluation:

> What is involved is the change, from knowing how

> to do something that might be prescribed into knowing what must be done; from the mastery the craftsman has with his language to the obedience that the initiate must have who has come under the orders of meanings and inner structures he must follow. It is no longer her art but The Art. (132)

This is occult language. From craftsman to initiate, from her art to The Art, from literal language to inner structures, and it is encoded in the initiatory passage of consciousness in *Trilogy* from the master craftsman, the shellfish capable of generating the pearl-of-great-price, to the illumination of the trained magus and his initiation into the genuine vision of eternity. If H.D. and Duncan are correct, *Ion*, the third major translation work, represents the initiation of the initiation, "initial," as Duncan says, to the real work to come: "a turning point—the crowning achievement of her first phase, but also the declaration of her later work" (131). The World War II phase of her writing is about a new spirit being born, a new consciousness in a new age; *Ion* is the jewel that announces the beginning of this process in her writing, understood "as initiating a new spirit in Athens" in the text, but in her writing "as initiating a new spirit in her work to come" (Duncan 132).

"And last but not least," writes H.D. in a transition in *Ion*, "*deus ex machina* steps forth; intellect, mind" (254), and it is Athené, the figure with whom H.D. will identify herself in *Majic Ring*, where Athené symbolizes not only the brain as intellect, "but the brain as well, as the instrument through which the inner soul or the occult can also filter" (104). Here Athené and Niké A-pteros, the wingless Victory, are seen as one figure, and the narrator becomes one with the entity as well:

> I do not speak or my little Wingless Image does not

speak to the altogether unenlightened mind. She stands just within the Gate, she stands on the rock itself, of that city set on a hill, the Acropolis of Athens.

Hers is a special Gift and hers is a special Secret. (102)

H.D.'s use of the coordinating conjunction *or* often reflects her willingness to let metaphors be flexible; her conception of "spiritual realism" requires this flexibility because mere symbol always crystallizes, breaks away from its referent, which can only be spoken of in ever-shifting metaphor. The *or* in "I do not speak or my little Wingless Image does not speak" is the same as the *ors* found in "the projection of the jewel or the crystallization of the jewel or jewels in the matrix;" the series of rough equivalents are fanned out in order to provide a more accurate picture of something out-of-time and so not easily describable.

The Athené of *Ion* is a prototype or avatar of the goddess in *Majic Ring* that will also be an avatar of the narrator. Though she is an "abstraction" here "of antiquity and of all time," she urges mortals to develop and evolve by working in both channels: "in the end, if we have patience to wait, she says, if we have penetration and faith and the desire actually to follow all those hidden subterranean forces, how great is our reward" (*Ion* 254). Kreousa, then, becomes an extension of H.D. as well; united with Athené, this Athené whose Gift and Secret[4] are special and have as much to do with the inner soul as the dry intellect, Kreousa becomes herself "almost goddess." Kreousa's consciousness is H.D.'s consciousness as she prepares herself to receive the teachings of a new age and a new consciousness; like the evolving consciousness in *Trilogy*, it must develop from the shell-fish to the group mind of the flock:

The human mind dehumanized itself, in much the

same way (if we may imagine group-consciousness so at work) in which shell-fish may work outward to patterns of exquisite variety and unity. The conscious mind of man had achieved kinship with unconscious forces of most subtle definition. (254)

H.D.'s occult conception of Delphi at this time is that it is "the high-water mark of human achievement ... faintly to be imitated, at its highest, in the Italian *quattrocento*, that thing and that thing alone that we mean, when we say, Ionian" (254).

Ezra Pound and other occult modernists also believed that the golden age had passed by, though some of its traditions had been preserved in the verse and other artistic output of a few periods, including the troubadour poetry and the quattrocento;[5] but H.D. is unique in considering the Ionian period to be the acme of spiritual and civil achievement. That *The Sword Went Out to Sea* abruptly shifts perspective from wartime London to Ionian Greece is not a coincidence: cyclical time, or the repeat in history, is for her both an ancient Greek conception and a modern occult truth. Her positioning at the cusp of the dawning Age of Aquarius may allow her to witness the dawn of an age that will itself reach the heights the ancients once knew, and her contact with certain spirit entities seems to indicate that she will be participating in, helping along, the process of birthing the new age. *Ion* is a study in this process indeed, for Kreousa is re-envisioned in the transition notes as:

the mother, if she but knew it, of a new culture, of an aesthetic drive and concentrated spiritual force, not to be reckoned with, in terms of any then known values; hardly, even today, to be estimated at its true worth. For this new culture was content, as no culture had been before, or has since been, frankly with one and but one supreme quality, perfection. (254)

One cannot simply say that all the characters in H.D.'s writings (including her translations) are somehow her, because all of her literary facades are partly fiction as well—H.D., Delia Alton, Kat, Her Gart, Mrs. Aldington are all coordinating conjunctions, *ands* and *ors* that help describe something or someone who shares qualities with Athena or Niké, Kreousa or Mary Magdalene, who play a host of roles in the expansion of human consciousness. *Majic Ring* contains a catalogue of figures H.D. had encountered in waking and dreaming visions, all of whom are an aspect of this puzzle; one of them bears a striking resemblance to the figure of *Ion* the boy, son of Kreousa, in the only passage outside of her translation of Euripides's work that features the character. The scene is set up the way a scene in a play or screenplay would be:

> With no intermediate characters, with no odd shadowy figures as background or as chorus, we swing right across another stretch of water. Our minute-hand moves swiftly toward the end. We are in high mountains. The air is rarefied and the whole character of the sequence changes. (125)

The boy is not *Ion* but bears a close resemblance to him, to not only the physical but the spiritual eye:

> This boy is like the boy Ion of the Greek play – he is a novice or young priest of some high mystery. He is clothed in a white tunic, his feet are bare, his head is the normal close-cropped head of a young Greek from the Parthenon frieze – he is in that sense Greek, but he is here in the mountains as – well, a white Indian, I would say. He is of some Indian tribe, perhaps a lost tribe, perhaps of that "Vedic India" of which Ben Manisi spoke. (125)

This boy, an image not crystallized into symbol, a

piece of out-of-time reality, is in some sense Greek and in some sense Vedic, according to the dream-logic that merges people, places, and times. Though she channels him, speaks his words, she is also a listener, both part of him and separate from him, as a dreamer encounters a dream-figure. He seems to be possessed of the same high spiritual development as the Ion of the play, the product of the mother of a new consciousness. Ion in the play, and this Ion-like figure, are equivalent (but not identical) to Horus, the child of Isis and Osiris. "H.D. by Delia Alton" ends with a statement that lacks a clear antecedent, causing it to float there, isolated from the rest of the text: "This Isis takes many forms as does Osiris" (221). The boy, the fruit of the union of divine forces, seems to be eternally present in mountains, whether in ancient India or Greece, or unborn at the cusp of the aeon, contacting H.D. through dreams. Does this make H.D. a sort of mother?

She is a creator, and her poetry is the height of her creation. Her prose, difficult to look at directly with its layers and layers of truth, is offset by the clarity of her poetry; the notes to *Ion* buzz and swirl in comparison to the sparse, controlled lines of the play itself. *Majic Ring* churns and roils when compared to the ecstatic, directional couplets of *Trilogy*. "H.D. by Delia Alton" informs us that the "fire has raged round the crystal. The crystalline poetry to be projected, must of necessity, have that fire in it. You will find fire in [*Trilogy*]." The fire that her creation contains is a mark of her maturity as an artist, of having moved past the early phase to the maturing of her writing, her spiritual vision, and her dream. The Ion-like boy in *Majic Ring* becomes the symbol of or embodies the essence of fire, the fire that is found in the projected poetry:

> He is more "fiery" than anything that can be imagined, but it is the fire in rock-crystal, the fire in the north-star, the fire in the heart of a snow-flake. And by fire, I mean fire. There is no word but fire with which to describe his ecstasy, his intellectual cerebral intensity. For his mind is fire, this white-fire; it has been utterly purged of all dross, he has been as silver tried in a furnace of time, Purified seven times. (126)
>
> He has reached perfection of a very old tradition, he is born or twice-born or seven-times born, different colours of fire, until all merge in the dazzling white or final illumination. He is light and if the opposite of light is darkness, then I, as listener, was composite of all the "earth," in the furnace of which, he had been purified seven times. (126-27)

H.D. knows that this is an echo of the consciousness that is to be born anew in the new age, and that her poetry, "crystalline," is "to be projected" along both channels simultaneously, as a way of making that fire actual. She knows this dream-figure and can understand his discourse even though she cannot recognize a single word he speaks, because he is speaking a truth whose relative value has not changed, though it appears in various guises in various places and ages. H.D. has provided some of her energy to the *deus ex machina* in Euripides' *Ion* only to have the son of Kreousa return the favor here. He appears as fire, and as the living flame,[6] he is also the spirit of that which first burned in *Ion* at the dawn of the age that Kreousa mothered:

> Athens died long ago and Delphi has been a desecrated shrine for centuries. And yet something of all these is alive. It is singing or rather talking in such a profound intense way – what does he want? What can we do for him? What can we do for this white swan of

Phoebos, of Apollo, of the light that never was, of the light that is always? (232)

What they must do—what she must do—is piece together the puzzle, work out the mystery and uncover the secret that keeps the time-paths separate: that spiritual reality is eternal, but it has a particular face at any particular clock-time. The work of the poet is the work of comparing these relative truths so as to be able again, in the now, to recognize the eternal verities as they were recognized by the poets of old. Euripides, a master who perhaps first recognized the Delphic truth, serves as model for H.D. By lending her creative energy to the translation of the play, she receives the return in her own writing, to be projected and crystallized in her poetry. This is the process by which "the circle of the Zodiac is reduced to the size of a clock-dial" ("H.D. by Delia Alton" 187) and the picture falls into place.

H.D. wrote to Bryher about the process of translating *Ion*, of how it allowed her to find these patterns that had been set up in visionary experiences on a trip to Corfu years earlier: "I feel this Ion is a sort of fancy-dress edition of my phallic phantasy—evidently is. Also all the sun-god stuff and the Delphic, hitches on to us in Corfu. One can not explain it 'away' and I don't want to—but it is good to get the pattern" (*AF* 528). H.D. seemed to realize that she was training herself for something that would be quite real to her later on. As Eileen Gregory puts it, *Ion* is not only a beginning, but an exercise "to comprehend repetitive patterns—but without the immediate engagement with actual events and memories" (*H.D. and Hellenism* 206). Gregory cites an unpublished letter in which H.D. cannily tells Bryher that "the attitude one takes at this time ... is all-important for the rest of ones [sic] life" (206). Just as the poet must, in order to grasp these patterns, be able to weave the eternal into the specific, she must also discern the ways in which events—dreams, visions, experiences of all kind—in her life form a matrix, outside the regular time-line of a chronology. It is for these reasons that she returns to the visions she experienced in and around "Corfu," weaving, weaving.

In *Majic Ring* the scene abruptly changes again, moving from the mountains and the boy to the deck of the *Borodino*,[7] from which H.D. had a visionary experience that haunted her for decades. She is discussing, with a phantom whom she believes to be Peter van Eck, a dolphin that never was as it leaps from the water, and she is in a sense this dolphin, this Delphic entity. She is out-of-time at this point, and like the rogue dolphin, she finds herself "out of time in my human development, ahead in some way, undeveloped or arrested in development, in other ways" (128). Looking out from the boat into the timeless realm (she believes she has a glimpse of the islands of the blessed, or of Atlantis, just as Kaspar does, by way of Mary Magdalene, during his vision at the end of *Trilogy*) is at first a terrifying, humiliating experience for the young H.D. Over the years she works, by writing, to reclaim these paranormal experiences, to put them in their proper place, away from the shame and social awkwardness that come from trying to match up her story with those who were not privy to the visionary experience.

In her notes to Euripides, H.D. envisions the lines of his poetry as "portals, as windows, as portholes I am tempted to say that look out from our ship our world [sic], our restricted lives, on to a sea that moves and changes and bears us up, and is friendly and vicious in turn. These words are to me portals, gates"

(278). Niké A-pteros guards the gates to the temple; though the temple at the opening of *Trilogy* is in ruins, a mere shell, H.D. will, beginning with shell-fish consciousness, re-build the eternal temple for the present, re-manifest the eternal truths in the now. This entire process is encapsulated in the work of translation that she has done, as a study for her own original work. The work of translation is a craft, but H.D. is making the transition from craftswoman to initiate, from making art to The Art. If translation were merely a craft, there would be no need to bring the lines back: there are spiritual truths that can be renewed through the act, and that is what H.D. is interested in:

> I know that we need scholars to decipher and interpret the Greek, but we also need: poets and mystics and children to re-discover this Hellenic world, to see *through* the words; the word being but the outline, the architectural structure of that door or window, through which we are all free, scholar and unlettered alike, to pass. We emerge from our restricted minds (with all due reverence to them, of course) into a free, large, clear, vibrant, limitless realm. (278)

This realm, like the eternal characters, is neither Greece nor Egypt nor Asia Minor, but all of them at different times, the eternal vision. The vessel itself could be the body, or perhaps the mind, or the body-mind of ordinary existence.[8] This is a vision that resonates with Blake, to be sure, with the same attention to dream-logic and detail as in "The Marriage of Heaven and Hell." If the work of translation is for H.D. a study, it is also a model of the writing process—for what purpose would there be to writing, if it were merely a craft? Other crafts are useful, but one cannot use words, unless they be portals, doorways. Whatever H.D. saw in

Euripides's Delphi, it can be seen through the window or portal or H.D. television screen of her translation; but that energy can also be used for turning a camera on to H.D.'s own secret, her mystery, the heart of the quest forgotten even by her, the jewel or jewels in the net hang there, reflecting one another or itself, just back of the page.

Works Cited

Chisholm, Diane. "H.D.'s Autoheterography." *Tulsa Studies in Women's Literature* 9:1 Women Writing Autobiography (Spring, 1990). 79-106. Print.

Duncan, Robert. *The H.D. Book*. Frontier Press, 1984. Print.

Gregory, Eileen. *H.D. and Hellenism: Classic Lines*. Cambridge: Cambridge U.P., 1997. Print.

H.D. *H.D. by Delia Alton* [Notes on Recent Writing]. *Iowa Review* 16.3 (Fall 1986): 174-221. Print.

———. *Hippolytus Temporizes and Ion: Adaptations of Two Plays by Euripides*. New York: New Directions, 2003. Print.

———. *Majic Ring*. NP. Yale University Rare Book and Manuscript Library, Yale Collection of American Literature, H.D. Papers, YCAL MSS 24. Print.

———. *Notes on Thought and Vision & The Wise Sappho*. San Francisco: City Lights, 1982. Print.

———. *Trilogy*. New York: New Directions, 1973. Print.

Surette, Leon. *The Birth of Modernism*. Montreal: McGill-Queen's UP, 1993. Print.

Sword, Helen. "H.D.'s *Majic Ring*." *Tulsa Studies in Women's Literature* Vol. 14 no. 2 (Autumn, 1995). 347-362. Print.

Notes

1 It was written between 1943 and 1944; she revised it in 1954.
2 Records of all that has ever happened, accessed via a region of the invisible astral plains, which are most easily accessed through vision or astral "travel."
3 *Trilogy* 152. The jewel is part of a circlet seen in a vision—the flaw helps the vision give way to the next layer.
4 See quotation from *Majic Ring*, above. Here are some more words of great significance to H.D. *The Gift*, written in between *Ion* and *Majic Ring*, explains H.D.'s supernatural gift in the context of a personal family mystical history involving the dialogue between Moravian and Native American mystery traditions.
5 Cf. Leon Surette's *The Birth of Modernism* for a detailed discussion of occult historiography.
6 H.D. refers to the "band of initiates" in *Trilogy*, all of them poets and she one of them, as the "companions of the flame."
7 In February 1920 H.D., Bryher, and Havelock Ellis set off to Greece and Corfu aboard the *Borodino*, which belonged to Bryher's father. H.D. had several visions and otherworldly experiences during this trip, all of which affected her profoundly, and all of which are frequently mentioned in her writing over the decades. The incident with "Peter van Eck" (Pieter Rodeck) aboard the *Borodino*, in which she believed to watch dophins leaping out of the water with islands in the distance accompanied by a physically-altered Rodeck, is recounted in *TF*, *MR*, and *TSWOTS*, among other writings.
8 See *Notes on Thought and Vision* for an early exploration of the various "bodies" coexisting with the physical body and their roles.

The Road from Delphi: Henry Miller and Greece

Ian S. MacNiven

For almost five years Lawrence Durrell had been urging Henry Miller to come to Greece, and in this he had a strong ally in Betty Ryan, the lovely young American artist who lived downstairs from Miller at 18 Villa Seurat. In Henry's words, "she seduced me with her faithful, ravishing descriptions of Greece" ("First Impressions" 85). And his Paris artist friend and neighbor Mayo, *nom de peinture* of Antoine Malliarakis, urged him further, "Miller, you will like Greece" (*Colossus of Maroussi* 14). In October 1938 Henry got as far as Marseilles, but in a war-induced panic he considered hopping the next ship for America instead, then returned to Paris. Finally, in May 1939, he stored his manuscripts and books and headed south again. This time he made it, and stayed for five months.

Henry Miller would never be the same again.

Greece is a dangerous land for a seeker, a visionary. Miller arrived primed for a revelation, for an epiphany. Not, to be sure, one that had anything to do with Christianity: Delphi, he considered, was the pre-Christian Navel of the World. His approach to it was indirect. He began with Eleusis, site of the Eleusinian Mysteries, traveling "along the Sacred Way, from Daphni to the sea." It was definitely "not a Christian highway," he said, "no suffering, no martyrdom, no flagellation .... Everything speaks now, as it did centuries ago, of illumination, of blinding, joyous illumination." He convinced himself that he was gripped by holy ecstasy, like a Corybant: "I was on the point of madness several times ... running up the hillside only to stop midway, terror-stricken, wondering what had taken possession of me" (*Colossus* 44). The book that emerged from his sojourn in Greece, *The Colossus of Maroussi*, while supposedly a portrait of his new friend George Katsimbalis, is more importantly an account of his own possession by the spirit of Greece. It was a Greece in which the ancient land he intuited blended almost seamlessly with the Greece he experienced. Indeed, his main diatribes were against those who wished to change Greece in their own image–Greeks returned from America who sang to him the wonders of Chicago over the "backwardness" of Greece, and the resident English: "An evening with these buttery-mouthed jakes always left me in a suicidal mood," he raged (*Colossus* 108).

By the time he arrived in Greece, Miller had an underground reputation as a controversial author largely unread because his books could not be published in the English-speaking world. Readers of contraband copies of the two *Tropics*, such as George Orwell or Durrell, considered him a ground-breaking leader in free expression, one who had advanced honesty of expression beyond the also-banned *Lady Chatterley's Lover*. Others, including George Bernard Shaw, branded him a pornographer, one who used "verbatim reports of bad language" (Shaw to Durrell). Increasingly, however, Miller thought of himself as a visionary, a mystic, a holy man bent on purging the dross from existence. Looking back over his life from the vantage point of his eighty-fifth year, Miller would write, "It is strange that the countries I most wanted to visit I have never seen– India, Tibet, China, Japan, Iceland. But I have lived with them in my mind" ("Mother" 187). Miller, after seeing Delphi, could better imagine India, China, Tibet, and *Devachan*, that mythic locus that he would rhapsodize over for most of his life. Earlier he had written, "When I go to Delphi I shall consult my own oracles" ("First Impressions" 88). These oracles, internalized, guided the course of his life and writing.

Within days after landing at Piraeus, Henry traveled by boat to Corfu and a rendezvous with Larry and Nancy Durrell. They headed north to wild Kalami below Mount Pantokrator, where they "baptized ourselves anew in the raw" at the isolated shrine of Agios Arsenios, and Henry found himself adopting an easy amalgam of Christian and pagan Greek attitudes (*Colossus* 16). He was fascinated by the arduous life of the Corfiot peasants, and wanted to join the women carrying water from the springs so that he could, like them, *feel* the ache of muscles, the throb and pulse of stressed arteries. Larry sternly dissuaded him: he would lose face with the natives. Then the Greek army was mobilized, and Miller and the Durrells moved back and forth between Corfu and Athens. In Athens, Durrell's great doctor friend Theodore Stephanides took Larry and Henry to the observatory to view the Pleiades: "Rosicrucian!" exclaimed Larry, another visionary.

Of course, the basic text for the impact of Greece on Miller is *The Colossus*. But there is also "First Impressions of Greece," drafted earlier. Miller had come to Greece with the fantasy that he could give himself a year's vacation after twenty years of continuous writing and scrambling to get by in Paris, yet writing had become perhaps even more necessary to him than discovery, food, and drink as stimulative to companionship and visions. In fact, it was tied up with all of these. At the home of the painter Niko Ghika, with George and Aspasia Katsimbalis and the future Nobel laureate George Seferis, Henry noted: "Ripe, fecundating atmosphere–for conversation, dream, work, leisure, indolence, friendship and everything. Everywhere the ancestral spirit. The whiskey excellent, especially favorable for discussions about Blavatsky and Tibet." He opened a fresh notebook and wrote:

>Island of Hydra – 11/5/39
>
>The birthplace of the immaculate conception. An island built by a race of artists. Everything miraculously produced out of nothingness. Each house related to the other, as though by an unseen architect. Everything white as snow yet colorful. The whole town is like a dream creation: a dream born out of a rock. ("First Impressions" 58-59)

It was to be a dream trip, yet one grounded in reality. Henry gave the notebook to Seferis, inscribed "For his most sensitive majesty, King George Seferis of Smyrna!"

Part of this reality, merging repeatedly into dream, is the voice of Katsimbalis, talking, "a living organ, a voice pealing heavy sonorous notes." Listening to his evocations, not only of Greece but also of Paris, of Shanghai (which Katsimbalis had never visited), Henry remarked prophetically in "First Impressions," "I feel as though I may suddenly bifurcate and no longer tell my own story but his." They were linked together as brothers, Henry claimed, "handcuffed for eternity" (*Colossus* 65). Together they visited many of the stupendous places of classical antiquity. Henry tried to see everything in human terms: "Epidaurus is merely a place symbol: the real place is in the heart" (*Colossus* 80). His was a human-centered universe; humankind's antagonists lie within each person: "the enemy of man is not germs, but man himself, his pride, his prejudices, his stupidity, his arrogance" (*Colossus* 82). In fact, "every war is a defeat to the human spirit" (*Colossus* 83). They explored Agamemnon's Mycenae, where Henry refused to descend with Katsimbalis down the "slippery staircase" to Erebus, the claustrophobic descent into the deep cistern that kept Mycenae alive during sieges (*Colossus* 91). Miller had flinched, and Part I of *Colossus* ends at Mycenae.

In Part II Henry flies alone to Crete with the purpose of seeing Knossos. His experience of Crete seems oddly disembodied: it might as well have been entitled Forty Days in the Wilderness. It is a digression on the path to Delphi. There are no revelations. The eponymous Colossus is absent. So is, for Henry, that vivid spirit which he found everywhere in mainland Greece and its close-lying islands.

Life seemed to begin again when Miller returned to Athens, and in Part III the spirit of the first part is reborn. Katsimbalis met him every day for an enthralling lunch that blended into dinner. Finally, Pericles Byzantis, Ghika's friend, offered accommodation at a new government pavilion for foreign students at Delphi. "It was decided," Henry wrote impersonally, as if he had surrendered all personal initiative, that Ghika and Byzantis would take him to Delphi (*Colossus* 188). Katsimbalis would meet them there.

Henry recorded the trip faithfully. They rode in a "beautiful" Packard; stopped at the Thebes museum; as the plain of Thebes rolled past, Ghika, facing rearward over the front seat, recounted at length the dream of death and transfiguration that he had experienced the night before; they paused for lunch at Levadia; Ghika got out to vomit at Arachova (perhaps seeing Greece in receding frames while facing backwards had unsettled his stomach). "From Arachova to the outer precincts of Delphi the earth presents one continuously sublime, dramatic spectacle. Imagine a bubbling cauldron into which a fearless band of men descend to spread a magic carpet. Imagine this carpet to be composed of the most ingenious patterns and the most variegated hues. Imagine that men have been at this task for several thousand years...." Miller spent half a page creating a fantastic picture of color and subtlety. "Finally, in a state of dazed, drunken, battered stupefaction you come upon Delphi." Through the "twilight mist" Delphi appeared "even more sublime and awe-inspiring than I had imagined it to be" (*Colossus* 192). They found Katsimbalis, had a "scanty meal," generously supplemented with wine and cognac, that Henry enjoyed "immensely," being "in the mood to talk"–he confided this as though it were an unusual state for him. With Delphi outside the windows, what did he discourse on? Kansas! And how empty and monotonous it was. His companions were astounded, but for Henry this was a mere subliminal image, the equivalent of an artist applying a turpentine-diluted wash to a canvas before attempting a masterpiece.

After a night of fierce rains, "It was now time to inspect the ruins, extract the last oracular juices from the extinct navel ... the splintered treasuries of the gods, the ruined temples, the fallen columns ... Suddenly, as we stood there silently and reverently, Katsimbalis strode to the center of the bowl and holding his arms aloft delivered the closing lines of the last oracle" (*Colossus* 194). Miller does not say which "last oracle" this might be, but surely he had in mind the response, by tradition the last response ever vouchsafed by the Pythia, given to Julian the Apostate, the fourth-century Roman emperor attempting to revive classical Greek culture:

> Tell to the king that the carven hall is fallen in decay;
> Apollo has no chapel left, no prophesying bay,
> No talking spring. The stream is dry that had so much to say.

Apollo was dead. The time to revive Greek culture had passed. Henry tried to thrust this deadly conclusion away: "For a second, so it seemed, the curtain had been lifted on a world which had never really perished but which had rolled away like a cloud and was preserving itself intact, inviolate, until the day when, restored to his senses, man would summon it back to life again." Miller applied this oracular voice to his own predicament, as a drifter in the immense tragedy sweeping a world at war. Henry's optimism was incurable, however. "I recalled other oracular utterances I had heard in Paris, in which the present war, horrible as it is, was represented as but an item in the long catalogue of impending disasters and reversals, and I remembered the sceptical way in which these utterances were received." Henry preferred a longer view. "Victory and defeat are meaningless in the light of the wheel which relentlessly revolves. We are moving into a new latitude of the soul, and a thousand years hence men will wonder at our blindness, our torpor, our supine acquiescence to an order which was doomed" (*Colossus* 195).

Miller, Ghika, and Katsimbalis drank from the sacred Castellian Spring, and Henry saw his presence at Delphi as part of a fated Plan, a continuum that had led him from 1923 to this moment. His friend Nick at the Orpheum Dance Palace on Broadway had been born near Delphi, and through his "terpsichorean instrumentations" Henry had met June, who became his wife; without her goading and inspiration he would never have become a writer, nor left America, nor met Betty Ryan or Durrell, who propelled him to Greece and into the company of Seferis, Ghika, and Katsimbalis–and so on to Delphi (*Colossus* 195).

Now a world at war threatened to disrupt his writing career. Very well, he would turn his back on that world, a world that had refused to heed him: some years earlier Henry had held on to a fantasy that if he could spend an hour talking to Hitler, make him laugh, the then-approaching conflict could be avoided. Miller had stayed at the Villa Seurat, talking, and never pressed for his audience with Der Führer. While at Delphi, Miller, his passport stamped "Invalidated" a few days earlier, was awaiting passage on the next boat to leave Piraeus for New York.

Henry and his party visited the museum: the colossal Theban *kouros* statues, "which have never ceased to haunt me," and especially significant for Henry, the beautiful youth Antinous, "last of the gods," evocative of "the eternal duality of man." He continued, "Nothing could better convey the transition from light to darkness, from the pagan to the Christian conception of life, than this enigmatic figure of the last god on earth who flung himself into the Nile. By emphasizing the soulful quality of man Christianity succeeded only in disembodying man; as angel the sexes fuse into the sublime spiritual being which man essentially is. The Greeks, on the other hand, gave body to everything, thereby incarnating the spirit and eternalizing it" (*Colossus* 196).

Then, suddenly, impulsively, as if in panic, Henry wanted to return to Athens. He had been in Delphi only two nights and one full day, and was expected to stay several days in all. After Katsimbalis and Ghika returned with him to Athens, Henry decided that it was a premonition of the arrival of funds, and the presence of a ship that would take him to America in ten days, that had led to his desire to return, but these were quite clearly just excuses made up to cover his "imperious desire" to leave Delphi, and his rudeness to Byzantis. No, he did not wish to give time for disillusionment to set in. Delphi must be perfect *in his imagination*. Then he could preserve its idealized image intact.

Like the final situation of the travelers in E.M. Forster's masterful short story, "The Road from Colonus"– the aged protagonist is dragged away from the caravansary, disappointed, missing the revelation that he is sure would have been vouchsafed him had he stayed– everything that happened to Henry in Greece after Delphi partook of anticlimax. He made a final brief circuit with the Durrells, this time getting half-way down to the Mycenean cistern before panic sent him once again back to the surface. He might have been called the Orpheus of Brooklyn, but Henry was no Orpheus: the Underworld was not for him. He was a man of light. He and the Durrells spent a miserable Christmas in Sparta: "To me at least," Henry wrote, "it was really beginning to look like Christmas–that is to say, sour, moth-eaten, bilious, crapulous, worm-eaten, mildewed, imbecilic, pusillanimous and completely gaga" (*Colossus* 220-21). Unlike Forster's protagonist, however, Henry came away rich in experience and realization.

"The Greek earth opens before me like the Book of Revelation," Miller would write in the concluding

paragraph of *Colossus*:
> I never knew that the earth contains so much; I had walked blindfolded, with faltering, hesitant steps; I was proud and arrogant, content to live the false, restricted life of the city man. The light of Greece opened my eyes, penetrated my pores, expanded my whole being. I came home to the world, having found the true center and the real meaning of revolution.... .
> I refuse categorically to become anything less than the citizen of the world which I silently declared myself to be when I stood in Agamemnon's tomb. From that day forth my life was dedicated to the recovery of the divinity of man. Peace to all men, I say, and life more abundant! (*Colossus* 241)

Miller left Greece for America on 28 December. With the world crashing into war, he drafted *The Colossus of Maroussi*, a paean to cross-national, multi-lingual friendship, to Greece, to peace. An idealized yet real portrait of Greece and the Greek character. Restlessly, still professing to believe that the war had nothing to do with him, Miller set out on his year-long tour of the United States with the avowed intention of writing a parallel panegyric to his native land. He was appalled at what he saw, and he set down his thoughts with blazing honesty. *The Air-Conditioned Nightmare* is a book so vitriolic toward American civilization that Miller withdrew it from publication, even though it was contracted for by New Directions. He did not wish to–or dare to–so criticize his country in the midst of a desperate war. He would write a sequel, *Remember to Remember*, two years later.

Long before *The Air-Conditioned Nightmare* finally appeared, Miller had found refuge on Partington Ridge in Big Sur, south of San Francisco, overlooking the Pacific Ocean. The man who had lived most of his life in cities, in Brooklyn and in the Fourteenth Arondissement in Paris, the confirmed urban dweller who liked to claim that the soul thrived on garbage cans, now found himself in wild isolation, living in an abandoned convict's cabin, without a heating system, without running water, without close neighbors. It was Greece that enabled him to make this transition. Like the Greek women carrying water up the goat trails from the springs, Miller now had to carry or drag all his supplies up a sand-and-stone trail from the Pacific coastal highway. In hot weather he stripped bare to a thong to do this, like some ancient Hellenic athlete. Daily from the thin walls of the cabin came the clatter of Miller's typewriter. Perhaps recalling Durrell's cry of "Rosicrucian!" on seeing the Pleiades through the powerful telescope in Athens, he launched into his long-promised vast trilogy, *The Rosy Crucifixion*: the *Sexus*, *Plexus*, and *Nexus* volumes. Literary criticism may not have dealt favorably with the trilogy–even Miller's great friend Durrell urged him to withdraw and revise *Sexus*–yet in it Miller finally finished writing the June saga of his life inspired by her. If she had indeed pointed him in the direction of Delphi and the Rosicrucians, that direction turned out to be nearly the whole of his creative life: after *The Rosy Crucifixion*, he had neither the energy nor the inspiration for further revelations. And his trip to Greece, climaxing at Delphi, inspired Henry's greatest non-fiction, *The Colossus of Maroussi*.

Works Cited

Miller, Henry. *The Colossus of Maroussi*. New York: New Directions, 1945. Print.

―――. "First Impressions of Greece." *Sextet*. Santa Barbara: Capra, 1977. Print.

―――. "Mother, China and the World Beyond." *Sextet*. Print.

Shaw, G. B. "To Lawrence Durrell." 9 Sept. 1937. Quoted in Ian S. MacNiven. *Lawrence Durrell: A Biography*. London: Faber, 1998. 170. Print.

The Omphalos and the Pythia in Lawrence Durrell

Paul H. Lorenz

Lawrence Durrell did not accompany Henry Miller, George Katsimbalis, Pericles Byzantis, and Niko Ghika on their 1939 trip to Delphi (Miller 188), but during a 1974 lecture at the California Institute of Technology, Durrell presented photographic evidence that he had visited Delphi as a young poet on holiday before the war. The image shows the young Durrell, "so pleased with himself," leaning against the omphalos in a pose less dignified than that of Orestes when he is discovered at the omphalos by the Pythia at the beginning of Aeschylus's *Eumenides*. Durrell reveals his impiousness when he comments, "I could have taken it home in the car if I could have lifted it" (*Blue* 30-31). There is little evidence that this early visit to Delphi had much formative effect on Durrell's early work, but by 1974, Durrell was more respectful of the power of Delphi, of the danger involved in his "innocently sitting astride the *omphalos* ... like an idiot fiddling with the safety catch of the universe" (*Blue* 33). By 1974, he was aware of the danger of his casual unconcern next to shrine of the Pythia, "where the goddess of all poetic inspiration officiates" (*Blue* 30). After all, Durrell warned his audience, had the goddess not been on vacation that weekend, she would have crushed him "like a bedbug" for his impudence (*Blue* 30).

Durrell's changed perception of Delphi seems to be the result of his trip to Delphi in 1963 to visit with his wife Claude who was recuperating after surgery for a fibroid condition (MacNiven 533-34). This visit was quickly followed by two publications, a poem and an essay, both simply entitled "Delphi." The poem deals with divination, prophecy, and memory in a timeless universe. The poem indicates that Durrell had found a way to site Delphi in his own personal "Heraldic Universe," a universe in which, as Durrell told Henry Miller in 1936, he was, "SLOWLY BUT VERY CAREFULLY AND WITHOUT ANY CONSCIOUS THOUGHT DESTROYING TIME" (*Letters* 18, emphasis his). Past and present merge in the poem as Durrell turns his attention to the oracle:

> Once upon the python spoke,
> Now he lacks interpreters,
> Withering in his laureled fires
> All the bitter rock inters,
> From within those jewelled eyes
> Tells you only what you know,
> Know, but dare not realise. (ll. 14-20)

Later in this essay I will show that more than time is destroyed in Durrell's "Heraldic Universe." The individual identity of both persons and places are similarly only illusions, and Delphi, its Oracle, and the Corycian cave do not exist only in Greece; they are equally at home and equally real wherever we find them, in Egypt, in Cambodia, and even in the south of France.

The essay on Delphi is an attempt by Durrell to understand what Delphi was all about. He has read the *Description of Greece* by Pausanius, the *Deipnosophistai* of Athenaeus (both works of the second century CE), and consulted the *Dictionary of Classical Mythology*. He finds that modern scholars advance theories, but offer no certainties. "It is as if nothing were provable anymore, everything has become shadowy, provisional" laments Durrell in his first paragraph (273). Is Delphi located where it is because the eagles of Zeus determined Delphi to be the center of the world (Howatson 175) or because, as the Homeric *Hymn to Pythian Apollo* has it, Apollo was tricked into choosing this location by the spring Telphousa? What does it mean to say that Apollo slew the dragon and out of the rotting of that dread beast grew the oracular power of the Pytho? Archeological evidence indicates that Delphi was sacred to an earth goddess long before it became sacred to Apollo (Howatson 175) and dragons, such as the two dragons that Athena assigned to guard Erichthonius in the play *Ion* by Euripides, frequently guarded people and places sacred to the goddess. The Priestess of Apollo in the *Eumenides* of Aeschylus begins the play by tracing the genealogy of the oracle beginning with the Earth goddess followed by Themis and Phoebe, making Apollo the fourth god to speak through the Oracle. Durrell's Villa Seurat friend, Buffy Johnson, argues that the omphalos, too, is a symbol of the fertility of the Earth Mother and that the omphalos at Delphi was sacred to the goddess Themis or Gaia before the advent of Apollo (30).

In the essay, Durrell asks what rotting has to do with oracular power ["Pytho" means to rot]. The answer he got from George Seferis was that "In such fertilizing compost the power of the god of harmony, light, and prophecy took root and sprouted. Perhaps the myth means that the dark powers are the light's yeast; and that the stronger they are, the more intense the light when they are overcome" (276). But Durrell's interest in Shakespeare leads him down another path. With reference to *King Lear*'s "Ripeness is all" and *As You Like It*'s assertion that "ripe" is very close to "rot," Durrell suggests another interpretation of the myth. He argues that, in ancient Greece, fruit that had dropped from the trees was more highly prized than fruit that was picked. His source is Athenaeus, in Durrell's words:

> the Athenians when they placed a ritual meal for the Dioscuri (the twins) made sure that it consisted of cheese, barley cake and *fallen* olives and pears, in remembrance of their ancient mode of life. The gods preferred the perfect maturity of the *fallen* fruit. Even today the oil of the *fallen* olive is reserved for the use of the Church. And as for the twins ... did they represent perhaps (notice the perhaps) the dichotomy which resides at the heart of man's psychology and which is reflected in his language? The truth-telling oracle of Delphi never lost sight of the double-axe of man's mind, and the double nature of his consciousness, the double sex of his psyche ... (276)

From the perfect ripeness of matured thought the oracle spoke. In plays such as the *Ion* of Euripides and the *Eumenides* of Aeschylus, it is clear that the wisdom of the goddesses of Delphi was as evident as the healing powers of Apollo in the pronouncements of the oracle.

Yet, the meaning of Delphi and its oracle remains a challenge to us, because, in Durrell's words:

> it is built on two enigmas and neither of them is easily decipherable – the omphalos and the oracle. In an age looking for both physical and intellectual points of reference these two symbols stand for something important, even momentous.... Perhaps this is the moment – perhaps *today* the oracle is due to make its re-entry into the world. If it did, if from the heart of

the rock we heard one of those terrific and yet ordinary judgements upon the world of affairs, would we be ready to receive it, act upon it? (275)

While Durrell ends his essay by suggesting that those who seek to drink of the Castilian spring, of the sacred water of inspiration, should seek out Greek poets such as Dionysios Solomos, Kostis Palamas, Angelos Sikelianos, Constantine Cavafy, George Seferis, and Odysseus Elytis, Durrell's contemplation of the meaning of Delphi did not end in the 1960s; it became one of the focal points of his last series of novels, *The Avignon Quintet*.

The five volumes of *The Avignon Quintet*, [*Monsieur, Livia, Constance, Sebastian,* and *Quinx*] were published between 1975 and 1985. The novels are set in the same time period as Durrell's earlier and more famous *Alexandria Quartet* and the characters and settings of the *Quartet* are interwoven into the fabric of the "riper," more mature, *Quintet*. I do not have time in this short essay to do more than outline the Delphic influences in the *Avignon Quintet*, but I think, even in outline, you will be able to get an idea of how Durrell's experience of Delphi helped shape both the structure and themes of the *Quintet*. In the *Quartet*, Durrell had attempted to investigate the nature of modern love by manipulating the subject-object relationship according to the principles of Einstein's relativity principle (*Balthazar* 5). The approach in the *Quintet* is quite different. Early in the first novel, *Monsieur*, one of the characters, Sabine, makes a comment that basically summarizes Darley's attitude toward relationships in the *Quartet* when she says that she cannot "envisage a love without jealousy and exclusiveness" because men are just figments of themselves, animals whose deterministic behavior does not need decoding; but this attitude is not allowed to go unchallenged. Piers, who gets the final word, argues that Sabine is not correct. Love in the *Quintet is* "Like a cipher or a riddle to which the answer is always ambiguous in a Delphic way" (101). This passage announces another way of investigating modern love that goes beyond the simple observation of physical qualities and human behavior, the mechanical manipulations of Einstein's relativity theory, to look for deeper underlying principles that also govern the universe. In the science of the *Quintet*, this leads Durrell to abandon Einstein, who, at the core, "is no more profound than Agatha Christie" ("Arabesques" 203) in order to experiment with the science of India, its Western near-twin, quantum mechanics, and Heisenberg's Uncertainty Principle in his novels. In the relationships of the *Quintet*, more emphasis is placed on a serious consideration of the double nature of consciousness and the double sex of the psyche. For Durrell, just as it is in the court of Athena in the *Eumenides* where Athena, in the temple of the oracle, shapes the future through her love, "It is not men who create the future; it is women who are the powerful ones" ("Arabesques" 209), and every attempt to deprive women of the right to shape the future has the same effect as depriving an artist of the right to self-expression ("Arabesques" 209). It is a turn back to Delphi's origin as an oracle of the Goddess.

 There is also an ongoing series of references to Greek drama, especially to what is most probably the best known of the ancient Greek plays dealing with the Delphic oracle, *Oedipus Rex*, sometimes familiarly referred to in the *Quintet* as "Adipose Rex" (*Livia* 195). Unlike Freud, Durrell focuses on the blind egos of

Oedipus and Jocasta, the hubris that makes them believe that they have the power of the gods to change fate (*Constance* 356). He would like to encourage the Oedipuses of today to accept the truth that "the Big Boss, whose shrine is at Delphi, neither hides nor reveals, but simply signifies or hints!" (*Quinx* 28). More interesting is Durrell's focus on Tiresias, the blind seer whose dual nature allowed him to see the whole truth of the human condition. Blanford, an avatar of Durrell, claims to sometimes have the insight of Tiresias, the knowledge that "the whole of humanity seems simultaneously present in every breath" (*Livia* 194), while an unknown power leads him around "like a dog" (*Quinx* 135). The character Constance even describes her newfound ideal of love-making in Tiresian terms:

> The male and female commerce centres around sperm and milk – they trade these elements in their love-making. The female's breasts first gave him life and marked him with his ineradicable thirst for creating – Tiresius! The breasts are prophecy, are vision! Her milk has made him build cities and dream up empires in order to celebrate her! (*Constance* 284)

In an interview with Robert MacDonald, Durell explained that the vision of Tiresias "is a purely Gnostic vision which has nothing to do with the physical or biological side of man. It is his intuition, his affectivity which is the visionary part of him." The present age, Durrell contends, makes the mistake of imagining that bisexuality is physical. For Durrell, "love-making on the physical plane is even more psychic than physical" (157).

In terms of narrative structure, the Delphic influence on the *Quintet* is fairly easy to see if we are willing to collapse space and time in order to view the events of the novel from an eternal perspective. In the second chapter of *Monsieur*, Durrell invents a Gnostic Mystery Religion, which is loosely based on his experience of Delphi though the positions of Delphi and Eleusis are transposed on the Sacred Way. It begins with a small group of pilgrims leaving Alexandria through its Canopic Gate seeking enlightenment or something to believe in at a desert oasis called Macabru. In a village not far from Alexandria, their guide introduces them to a madman, "in a state of perfect bliss" whom "people came to visit as if he were an oracle" (87). The modern pilgrims are disgusted by the spectacle and do not consult the "oracle," but continue their long and arduous journey to Macabru. There, they are introduced to a Mystery Religion, which teaches that the god who rules today is in fact the "Prince of Darkness" who has secretly overthrown the "Virgin of Light" so that he can wreck havoc on the world (107, 109). Then, after eating *mummia* (mummy flesh, reminiscent of the desiccated flesh of the Delphic dragon killed by Apollo) and consuming a cup of drugged wine as at Eleusis, the initiates are asked to look into the glittering eyes of an unusually large serpent whose spirit possesses them to show them a vision of the true state of their souls (112-114). In this curious melding of Egyptian, Eleusian, and Delphic rites, the pilgrims see what the Oracle of Delphi saw, a vision of truth emanating from rottenness: the wisdom of the Goddess.

The omphalos of the *Quintet* is not the stone Durrell leaned upon in the late 1930s; instead it is the omphalos of Angkor Wat. The Bayon at Angkor Wat is constructed in the form of a temple-mountain meant to represent the center of the universe. Its decoration contains an elaborate depiction of the Hindu myth of the

Churning of the Sea of Milk, which brought about our world. The scholar Paul Mus sees the serpents that the giants are using to churn the milk not only as the tools of creation, but also as rainbows connecting the world of the gods with the world of humans (Dagens 111). When Durrell's characters visit this omphalos, they are impressed by two things: "the troubling stench of rotting bat manure," and the image of "a smiling Buddha shaded by a nine-headed naga like a big palm fan" watching over a world at war (*Monsieur* 240-241). Durrell's characters understand the message as an oracular prophecy: "This is the world, the real world, munching itself to death. Your world and mine" (*Monsieur* 241).

The pilgrims at Macabru, very early in the *Quintet*, do not take the opportunity to consult the oracle because they are not ripe enough to take oracular pronouncements seriously. By the end of the *Quintet* in *Quinx*, however, Durrell's characters are ready to seek out the wisdom of an oracle. Instead of going to Delphi, where the oracle has been silent since the time of the emperor Julian [360-363 CE] (Howatson 176), they go to a Gypsy festival at Les Saintes Maries de la Mer in the Camargue to have their futures told by the queen mother of the Gypsies, whose enigmatic pronouncements, delivered in almost unintelligible language in a state of high intoxication, are transmitted to the supplicants through an intermediary (85-88). Some of the pronouncements tell the supplicants what they already know but dare not realise. Blanford, the novelist, is told, "you are worried about a building, something like a house which you wish to make beautiful. But it takes much writing" (86-87). Other pronouncements of the Gypsy oracle are as enigmatic as the pronouncements at Delphi. Lord Galen, who has been looking for the mythical treasure of the Templars (who are identified in the *Quintet* with a gnostic belief similar to that taught at Macabru), is told "The treasure is real and a very great one, but it is locked in a mountain and guarded by dragons who are really men. Great dangers attend the search" (88). However, she does not say that Lord Galen will be the one who finds the treasure for that is beyond the limitations of her vision (185). Indeed, while the treasure may be real, there is no guarantee that the treasure is actual gold. Galen's principle investigator, Quatrefages, is convinced that Phillippe Le Bel had already spent the Templar gold and that his search concerned "another sort of treasure" (*Livia* 163).

Lord Galen is encouraged. The treasure, gold bars and coins, Lord Galen is told by paid sources, was found by Austrian "dragons" (actually dragoons) constructing a German munitions dump in a cave under the Pont du Gard. The cave, however, turns out to be a sort of Corycian cave sacred not to Pan, but to the Gypsy's Saint Sara. When the Persians came to sack Delphi in 480 BCE, after the oracle told the Delphinians not to worry about holy property belonging to the oracle, they took refuge with their goods in the Corycian cave on Parnassus. (The oracle's advice is a Greek analog of the Taoist concept of *wu-wei* or "non-doing," a concept that explains much of the motivation of Durrell's characters in the *Quintet*.) At this point miracles began to happen. The sacred weapons that no human could touch stirred of themselves. As the Persians approached the temple of Athena Pronaia, they were struck by thunderbolts and two large chunks of Parnassus itself crashed onto the invading army. At this point the Delphinians descended from the Corycian cave and drove off the remaining Persians, keeping the power and the efficacy of the oracle intact (Herodotus 8.36-38). The last sentence of the *Quintet* is often quoted, but it needs to be interpreted in light of this Corycian symmetry. Just as the treasure seekers, the Gypsies, and the curious begin to enter the cave in search of the real treasure of the gnostic Templars, the thought comes to Blanford that "'It was at this precise moment that reality prime rushed to the aid of fiction and the totally unpredictable began to take place'" (201). Nothing needs to be done; the gods can take care of themselves.

In a final note, the Delphic connection also explains the presence of the Bacchic extravagances that appear in the *Quintet*. The *Ion* of Euripides speaks of the Delphic orgies associated with the feast of Bacchus in the same matter of fact ordinariness that Durrell uses to describe the orgy Prince Hassad throws for his friends at the base of the Pont du Gard just before he leaves France at the beginning of World War II (*Livia* 250-263).

Delphi, with its omphalos and Pythia, clearly forms one of the anchors around which Lawrence Durrell developed his ripest and most challenging work of fiction, *The Avignon Quintet*. The "Heraldic Universe" of Durrell's fiction attempts to view the world through the eyes of Tiresias or the Pythia, through eyes unencumbered by the illusory nature of time and matter. Delphi, indeed, the living spirit of ancient Greece itself, gave an understanding of the world freed from the confines of the logical positivism that permeated the intellectual life of the 1930s in Europe. As the character Livia tells a young and foolish Blanford, long before Freud and the development of modern psychology, "Long before those barren Jewish evaluations of the human psyche, the Ancient Greeks evolved their own, more fruitful, more poetical and just as reasonable." (*Livia* 110). Throughout the *Quintet*, Durrell asks his readers the same questions that Livia then poses to Blanford: "Which world do you prefer? Which seems the more fruitful?" (*Livia* 110).

Works Cited

Aeschylus. *Eumenides*. Tr. George Thomson. In *An Anthology of Greek Drama, Second Series*. Ed. C. A. Robinson. New York: Holt, Rinehart, Winston, 1954. 69-100. Print.

Dagans, Bruno. *Angkor: Heart of an Empire*. Tr. Ruth Sharman. New York: Abrams, 1995. Print.

Durrell, Lawrence. *Balthazar*. New York: Dutton, 1960. Print.

———. "Delphi." (1965). In *The Ikons and Other Poems*. (1966). Redding Ridge, Connecticut: Black Swan, 1981. Print.

———. "Delphi." (1965). In *Spirit of Place: Letters and Essays on Travel*. Ed. Alan G. Thomas. New York: Dutton, 1969. 273-277. Print.

———. *Blue Thirst*. Santa Barbara, California: Capra, 1975. Print.

———. *Monsieur*. New York: Viking, 1975. Print.

———. *Livia, or Buried Alive*. New York: Viking, 1978. Print.

———. *Constance, or Solitary Practices*. New York: Viking, 1982. Print.

———. *Sebastian, or Ruling Passions*. New York: Viking, 1984. Print.

———. *Quinx, or The Ripper's Tale*. New York: Viking, 1985. Print.

———. "Jumping About Like Quanta." Interview with Robert MacDonald. In *Lawrence Durrell: Conver-*

sations. Ed. Earl Ingersoll. Madison, New Jersey: Fairleigh Dickinson University Press, 1998. 149-162. Print.

———. "Lawrence of the Arabesques: The Durrellian Galaxy." Interview with Jean-Pierre Graf and Bernard Claude Gauthier. In *Lawrence Durrell: Conversations*. Ed. Earl Ingersoll. Madison, New Jersey: Fairleigh Dickinson University Press, 1998. 201-212. Print.

Euripides. *Ion*. In *Orestes and Other Plays*. Tr. Robin Waterfield. Oxford World's Classics. Oxford: Oxford University Press, 2001. 1-47. Print.

Herodotus. *The History*. Tr. David Grene. Chicago: University of Chicago Press, 1987. Print.

———. "To Pythian Apollo." In *The Works of Hesiod and the Homeric Hymns*. Tr. Daryl Hine. Chicago, University of Chicago Press, 2005. Print.

Howatson, M.C. *The Oxford Companion to Classical Literature*. Corrected 2nd ed. New York: Oxford, 1989. Print.

Johnson, Buffie. *Lady of the Beasts: The Goddess and Her Sacred Animals*. Rochester, Vermont: Inner Traditions International, 1994. Print.

MacNiven, Ian. Ed. *The Durrell-Miller Letters, 1935-1980*. New York: New Directions, 1988. Print.

MacNiven, Ian. *Lawrence Durrell: A Biography*. London: Faber, 1998. Print.

Miller, Henry. *The Colossus of Maroussi*. New York: New Directions, 1941. Print.

Sophocles. *Oedipus the King*. Tr. David Grene. In *An Anthology of Greek Drama, First Series*. Ed. C. A. Robinson. New York: Holt, Rinehart, Winston, 1949. 51-100. Print.

Contributors

Stephanie Allen is assistant to the director of the New Jersey Culture and History Center. Her current projects include editing a collection of New Jersey poetry and compiling a bibliography of South Jersey poetry. *Atlantic City: It's Early and Modern History*, for which she wrote the introduction, has been recently published.

Linda Ben-Zvi, Professor emerita, English, Colorado State University and Theatre Studies, Tel Aviv University, has been a John N. Stern Distinguished Professor, Colorado, Fellow at Bogliasco Foundation, Liguria; the Library of Congress, Washington, D.C.; the National Endowment for the Humanities; the Newberry Library, Chicago; and Lady Davis Professor at Hebrew University. She has also been a Visiting Professor at the University of Michigan; New York University; Hunter College, CUNY; Universidad Autonoma, Madrid; Venice International University; University of Trento, Italy; and Waseda and Aoyama Gakuin universities, Tokyo. Among her 12 authored and edited books are four on the American playwright and novelist Susan Glaspell: *Susan Glaspell: Her Life and Times* (Oxford University Press), awarded the George Freedley Special Jury Prize, of the American Theatre Library Association, 2004; *The Complete Plays of Susan Glaspell*, co-edited with J. Ellen Gainor (McFarland); *Susan Glaspell: Essays on her Theater and Fiction* (University of Michigan Press); and *The Road to the Temple by Susan Glaspell* (McFarland). In addition, she has published four books on the works of Samuel Beckett.

Martha C. Carpentier is a Professor of English at Seton Hall University in New Jersey, specializing in British and American modernism. Her books include *Ritual, Myth, and the Modernist Text: The Influence of Jane Ellen Harrison on Joyce, Eliot, and Woolf* (Gordon and Breach, 1998) and *Susan Glaspell's Major Novels* (University Press of Florida, 2001). She is the editor of *Susan Glaspell: New Directions in Critical Inquiry* (2006), and co-editor of *Disclosing Intertextualites: The Stories, Plays, and Novels of Susan Glaspell* (2006). Most recently she co-edited *Her America: "A Jury of Her Peers" and Other Stories by Susan Glaspell* (University of Iowa Press, 2010). Martha is the co-founder, president, and webmaster of the International Susan Glaspell Society and she participates in panel presentations and staged readings of Glaspell's work at major conferences annually, such as the Eugene O'Neill International Conference and the American Literature Association Conference. Her most recent paper, presented at ALA 2013, is " 'The Gesture' of Protest: Susan Glaspell and American Idealism in 1917."

Victoria Conover works in the office of Arts and Humanities at Stockton College. She has recently co-published articles on the American poet H. D. ("Introduction: Two Unpublished Stories by H.D.: 'Hesperia' and 'Aegina.' " *Paideuma* 39 (2012): 3-15; " 'Jubilee': An Unpublished Story by H.D." *Resources for American Literary Study* 35 (2012).)

Noelia Hernando-Real is Assistant Professor of English and American Literature at the Universidad Complutense de Madrid (Spain). Recent publications include *Self and Space in the Theater of Susan Glaspell* (McFarland, 2011) and the co-edition of *Performing Gender Violence: Plays by Contemporary American Women Dramatists* with Barbara Ozieblo (Palgrave, Macmillan, 2012). Noelia Hernando-Real is Vice President of the International Susan Glaspell Society.

Artemis Leontis is Associate Professor and Coordinator of Modern Greek at the University of Michigan. She completed her BA at Oberlin College, did postgraduate work at Aristotle University of Thessaloniki, and received her PhD in Comparative Studies at Ohio State University. Her first book, *Topographies of Hellenism: Mapping the Homeland* (1995, Greek translation in 1998) was listed as an outstanding academic book of 1992-1997 by Choice magazine. *Greece: A Travelers' Literary Companion* (1997) is an anthology of 24 stories by Greek writers introducing readers to the landscapes of Greece through Greek perspectives. With Lauren Talalay and Keith Taylor, she co-edited *"What these Ithakas mean..." Readings in Cavafy* (2002), a companion to the exhibit, "Cavafy's World," which she curated at the Kelsey Museum of Archaeology. The TLS chose it as a "Book of the Year" for 2002. Her *Culture and Customs of Greece* (2009) presents an overview of contemporary Greece for a general readership. She is completing a cultural biography of Eva Palmer Sikelianos, for which she was awarded a Michigan University Fellowship at the Institute for the Humanities in 2011-12.

Paul H. Lorenz is a professor of English and chair of the Department of English, Theatre and Mass Communication at the University of Arkansas at Pine Bluff.

Ian MacNiven has written the authorized biography of that self-proclaimed Hellenophile Lawrence Durrell, and has completed a soon-to-be-published biography of James Laughlin, American poet, publisher, and appreciator of all things Classical. "Greece has marked me indelibly," MacNiven says, "as the land and her people do to all who approach with open heart: Henry Miller, Patrick Leigh Fermor, Edmund Keeley, among countless others. And Delphi embodies for me an unequaled holy place where ancient and modern Greece meet."

Barbara Ozieblo is Professor of American Literature at the University of Malaga, Spain; she specializes in women's writing and theater. She has taught American Drama in the USA and in South Korea. She is the author of *Susan Glaspell: A Critical Biography* (2000) and co-author of the Routledge volume in the Modern and Contemporary dramatists Series *Susan Glaspell and Sophie Treadwell* (2008). She is co-founder of the International Susan Glaspell Society, and was its President until 2009. She has organized a number of conferences on American Drama in Spain, published volumes of collected essays on American Drama, and is International Secretary for ATDS. Apart from publications on Glaspell, Ozieblo has published on other American dramatists, such as Lynn Nottage, Suzan-Lori Parks, and Gina Gionfrido. Most recently, she is co-editor of *Performing Gender Violence* (Palgrave, 2012). She is currently working on the cognitive approach to theater audiences.

Contributors

Tom Papademetriou is the Constantine and Georgeian Georgiou Endowed Professor of Greek History, and Executive Director of the Interdisciplinary Center for Hellenic Studies at The Richard Stockton College of New Jersey. His research focuses on the history of non-Muslims under Ottoman rule with emphasis on the Greek Orthodox Churches of Anatolia. He is actively engaged in building a strong Hellenic Studies program in which he teaches courses on the history of the Tourkokratia, Modern Greece, the Balkans, and the Middle East.

Matte Robinson is an Assistant Professor at St. Thomas University in Fredericton, Canada, where he teaches American Literature and Modernism. His current interest is in H.D.'s later works, particularly her occult source material. He is currently co-editing a scholarly edition of H.D.'s Hirslanden Notebooks with Demetres Tryphonopoulos for ELS Editions.

David Roessel is the Peter and Stella Yiannos Professor of Greek Language and Literature at The Richard Stockton College of New Jersey and the author of *In Byron's Shadow: Modern Greece in the English and American Imagination*.

Mike Solomonson is Chair of the Fine and Performing Arts Department at Northland Pioneer College, located in northeastern Arizona. His primary research interest is twentieth-century American theater history. His essay on playwright Rebecca Gilman was recently published in *Violence in American Drama: Essays on Its Staging, Meaning and Effects*. He also is co-author of a full-length play *Intimations from the Brook*, which is adapted from the Susan Glaspell novel *Brook Evans*.

Demetres P. Tryphonopoulos teaches and researches in twentieth-century American poetry. He is the author, editor, or co-editor of ten books, including *The Celestial Tradition: A Study of Ezra Pound's "The Cantos"* (WLUP, 1992), *The Ezra Pound Encyclopedia* (Greenwood Press, 2005), and *H.D.'s Majic Ring* (University Press of Florida, 2009). Current projects include Ezra Pound's Radical Politics in the Later Cantos and translations into English of Andreas Empeirikos's surrealist collection Υψικάμινος (*Blast Furnace*), Odysseas Elytis's Τό Ἄξιον Εστὶ (*Worthy It Is*), and Iakovos Kambanellis's play Ἡ αὐλή τῶν θαυμάτων (*The Courtyard of Miracles*).

Gonda Van Steen earned a BA and MA degree in Classics in her native Belgium and a PhD degree in Classics and Hellenic Studies from Princeton University. As the Cassas Chair in Greek Studies at the University of Florida, she teaches courses in ancient and modern Greek language and literature. Her research interests include classical drama, French travelers to Greece and the Ottoman Empire, nineteenth and twentieth-century receptions of the classics, and modern Greek intellectual history. Van Steen's first book, *Venom in Verse: Aristophanes in Modern Greece*, was published by Princeton University Press in 2000 and was awarded the John D. Criticos Prize from the London Hellenic Society. In her book *Liberating Hellenism from the Ottoman Empire* (2010), revolutionary uses of Aeschylus's *Persians* (1820s) and the Venus de Milo take center stage. Van Steen recently published another book titled *Theatre of the Condemned: Classical Tragedy on Greek Prison Islands*

(Oxford University Press, 2011), which discusses the ancient tragedies that were produced by the political prisoners of the Greek Civil War (late 1940s through 1950s). She is currently working on a book manuscript that analyzes theater life, performance, and censorship under the Greek military dictatorship of 1967-1974. She has also published articles on ancient Greek and late antique literature and on postwar Greek feminism.

Steven R. Wertzberger teaches English at Mainland Regional High School in Linwood, New Jersey. He is co-author with David Roessel of " 'Stepchild of the Sun': An Unpublished Story by Susan Glaspell," which will appear in the 2013 issue of *Resources for American Literary Study*.

Michael Winetsky is an intellectual historian, cultural critic, and a playwright. His paper "A Playwright of Pragmatism: Susan Glaspell's Unity of Science and Religion," published in *Ecumenica Journal of Theatre and Performance*, was recognized with the 2011 Prize for Best Published Article from the International Susan Glaspell Society. He is an adjunct assistant professor in the City University of New York, appointed in English at the Borough of Manhattan Community College and in Interdisciplinary Studies at the College of Staten Island.

Index

Alden, John, 219-220, 221-225, 227
    and George Cram Cook, 225-226, 227-228
The Athenian Women, 103-105
The Avignon Quintet, 297-304

Barney, Natalie Clifford, 4, 6, 8, 11-14, 17, 21-25, 40-43
Boissy, Gabriel, 70-71
Boyce, Neith, 235
    on the Provincetown Players, 239-241

The Colossus of Maroussi, 282, 285, 290
The Comic Artist, 193-194
Cook, George Cram, 89, 210-211
    death in Greece, 108-110
    and Hellenism, 90-91, 220-221
    influence of Haeckel, 98-99
    influence on others, 145
    on moving to Greece, 106-107
    theatrical philosophy, 145-146

Dell, Floyd, 96-97
Delphic Festival
    criticism of, 83, 88
    and the Greek Army, 66-68
    "S.," anonymous critic, 53-56, 60
Doolittle, Hilda (H.D.), 27-28
    aboard the *Borodino*, 243-244, 248-249, 258
    on her experience in Greece, 246, 259-260

on translating *Ion*, 275
Duncan, Isadora, 18, 30, 97, 99
Duncan, Penelope Sikelianos, 3
Durrell, Lawrence
    essay on Delphi, 294-297
    in Delphi, 293

Fitzgerald, F. Scott, 120-121
Freud, Sigmund, 244-245, 254-255
Fugitive's Return, 119-120, 123-125, 128, 129-134, 135-136, 167-168, 171-173
Glaspell, Susan, 91
    and Aristotle's *Poetics*, 183-186, 194-196, 197-198
    arrival in Greece, 165-166
    and classicism, 212-213
    and Cook's death, 232-234
    on Cook's legacy in Delphi, 231-232
    diminished reputation, 121-122
    and Greek Drama, 182-183
    influences on, 125-128, 129
    and Jane Ellen Harrison, 160, 167, 170-171, 175-177
    and Neith Boyce, 235
    and primitivism, 201-203, 208-209, 215-216
    relationsip with Greece, 157-158, 181-182, 207-208
The Glory of the Conquered, 213-214
The Great Gatsby, 122-123, 134, 137-138

Hapgood, Hutchins, 232-236
Harrison, Jane Ellen, 159-162, 163-165, 168-170
    Prolegomena, 162-163
"H.D. by Delia Alton," 265-267, 273

Inheritors, 186-189, 205-207, 211-212
Ion, 267-278

Index

Kazantzakis, Nikos, 26

Lazarus Laughed, 150-153

Marco Millions, 149-150
Majic Ring, 246-247, 250-253, 256-257, 266, 276
Metaxas, Ioannis, 58-59
Miller, Henry
    in Greece, 283-284, 285-290
    on travelling to Greece, 281-282

Nazi Germany, 56-57, 84-85, 87-88
Nietzsche, Friedrich
    and Greek Drama, 51, 82-83
    influence on Angelos Sikelianos, 63-64
    influence on Eva Sikelianos, 64-65
    influence on George Cram Cook, 97

O'Neill, Eugene
    and George Cram Cook, 153-155

Pratsika, Koula, 2, 40
Prometheus Bound, 1-2, 23, 31-32
Provincetown Players, 89
    in Greenwich Village, 102
    origins of, 101-102
    unraveling of, 105-106

Sikelianos, Angelos, 3, 25
    Delphic Vision, 25-28, 48-49
    speech to Greek Army 68-69
Sikelianos, Eva Palmer
    and amateur performers, 19-21

    at Bryn Mawr, 5-6
    and the Delphic Festivals, 52-53, 60-61
    on the end of the Delphic Festival, 73
    directing Swinburne, 15-19
    and George Cram Cook, 29-30, 49, 110-112
    and Greek music, 18-19, 23,
    on moving to Greece, 2
    and music, 10
    performance as Sappho, 4-9
    studying Wagner, 9-12
The Spring, 146-148
The Sword Went Out to Sea, 266-267, 271

Trilogy, 265, 269

The Verge, 189-193, 196-197, 214-215

SELECTED BOOKS FROM SOMERSET HALL PRESS

Christian Faith and Cultural Heritage: Essays from a Greek Orthodox Perspective, by Demetrios J. Constantelos.

Church and Society: Orthodox Christian Perspectives, Past Experiences, And Modern Challenges: Studies in Honor of Rev. Dr. Demetrios J. Constantelos, edited by George P. Liacopulos

Dante and Byzantium, by E.M. Karampetsos. An analysis of Byzantine art and theology on Dante's thought and writings.

Fate and Ambiguity in Oedipus the King, by Stelios Ramfos, translated by Norman Russell. A literary and philosophical reflection on the world-famous play, with a Foreword by renowned actor Olympia Dukakis.

Myth and the Existential Quest, by Vassilis Vitsaxis, translated by Deborah Brown Kazazis and Vassilis Vitsaxis.

Pomegranate Seeds: An Anthology of Greek-American Poetry, edited by Dean Kostos.

Thought and Faith: Comparative Philosophical and Religious Concepts in Ancient Greece, India, and Christianity, by Vassilis Vitsaxis, translated by Deborah Brown Kazazis and Vassilis Vitsaxis.

Two Traditions, One Space: Orthodox Christians and Muslims in Dialogue, edited by George C. Papademetriou.

Women of Fire and Blood, by Lili Bita. A collection of poetry reimagining twelve ancient Greek goddesses and heroines from a feminist perspective.

Somerset Hall Press specializes in scholarly and literary books, including history, theology, philosophy, poetry, and Greek studies. For more information, please visit **www.somersethallpress.com**.